The Hawai'i Pet Book

Keeping your dog and cat
healthy, happy and housed
in the tropics

by Toni Polancy

photos by
Deborah Booker
courtesy of *The Honolulu Advertiser*

Barefoot Publishing, Inc.
Practical books about Paradise

Why?

No other state in the union has its own pet book. So why Hawai`i?

Because we are a unique state in which to own a pet: unique in climate, history, culture and attitude, and especially unique in the way we live and interact with our pets.

No other state quarantines its dogs and cats (and no other state is rabies free). No other state has 9-inch long centipedes, stumpy-tailed felines, hallucinogenic toads, aggressive mongooses, biting ants, bacteria-laden geckos, angry boars—at least not all at once, all in the same garden.

And though many states have dangerous plants, Hawai`i has them in proliferation and our warm weather means we are out among plant life, hiking and playing with our animals perhaps more than pet owners anywhere in the world.

And speaking of weather, our tropical climate lets fleas hatch all year long, prompts cats to produce extra litters, and plays dangerous tricks with bacteria and germs.

Like much of life here, living with a pet in these islands—whether it's an *ʻīlio* (dog) or a *pōpoki* (cat)—is an exciting adventure, an adventure for which this book will help you prepare. - *Toni Polancy*

No gratuity was accepted from any of the sources listed in this book. If you would like your pet-related business considered for future printings of this book, please email information to tpolancy@cs.com.

The Hawai'i Pet Book
*Keeping your dog and cat
healthy, happy and housed
in the tropics*

Copyright 2003 by Antoinette Polancy
Published by Barefoot Publishing, Inc.
32 U`ilani Road
Kihei, Hawai`i 96753

ISBN 0-9666253-1-5

Includes index

A portion of the profits from this book
is shared with humane societies
throughout the Hawaiian Islands.

Cover photo of Rocky, a pitbull, courtesy of
Claire Sheehan, Maui Humane Society.

Printed in the United States of America

Design by Ann Rose Graphic Design, ann@annrosedesign.com
Cover by Mike Sidney, mike@inkrgb.com, www.inkrgb.com

Table of Contents

This book is dedicated to

caretakers of animals and humans

in these islands and everywhere.

Deborah Booker photo courtesy of *The Honolulu Advertiser*

Poi dogs,
stumpy-tailed cats,
borrowed pets, and
an accidental tourist
who finds the
meaning of aloha.

*An inspector for
a termite company
follows a specially
trained beagle as
it sniffs for termites
on the main
staircase in
Honolulu's Iolani
Palace, our nation's
only royal palace.*

Blessings for our animals...

Rev. James Roessler of Christ Lutheran Church in Mililani prays over "Max," a mixed springer spaniel, while his owner holds him. No one seems sure which of our immigrant cultures brought the Mediterranean custom of blessing animals to Hawai`i; perhaps it was the Portugese. But attendance doubles at the annual special Sunday service which includes as many as 70 dogs, cats, birds, rabbits, horses, and cattle.

Deborah Booker photo courtesy of *The Honolulu Advertiser*

And fires that burn the heart

Aimee Anderson's first night on emergency call as an animal control officer occurred 14 years ago, but she still can smell cane burning, still can see smoke rise bright against a starless sky.

At one in the morning, she was called to a cane fire near Ma'alaea on Maui. Sugar industry workers routinely set cane fields on fire as part of the harvesting process. They set the fire at night and they set it in a circle, all around the perimeter of the field so that it burns inward and doesn't get out of control.

Anything inside that ring of fire is doomed to a fiery death. As the fire burns, red flames and sparks snap at the sky. And sometimes you can see dark objects hurtling out of the flames: rats running for their lives. But this first night on the job, Anderson was called because a cat had crawled out of the inferno.

"It was an orange male," Anderson remembers. "The fire had melted off its ears, the pads on its paws and its testicles. His hair was singed off."

The cat was tame, probably a lost or forsaken pet, but it was in excruciating pain, burned much too badly to survive. It was Anderson's job to euthanize the cat; her hand shook as she administered the injection that would end the cat's suffering and his life.

"It was so lonely," she remembers, "just him and me. And the sad thing is that he was so happy to be reunited with a human that this cat purred the entire time as I was putting it to sleep."

Sometimes we abuse our pets by oblique methods, in stupid ways.

"It happens all the time," says Anderson. "People want to get rid of their dog or cat so they dump it in a cane field where the animal will die of starvation or be injured by a vehicle. We have cats killed by feral dogs, too. And people don't stop to think about the cane fires, what that will do to their pet."

For the 14 years that Anderson has been with the Maui Humane Society, she's been hearing the same statement from curious, well-meaning people: "I could never do your job."

As Animal Control Supervisor and Chief Cruelty Investigator, she

> 'It was so lonely. Just him and me... and he was so happy to be reunited with a human that this cat purred the entire time I was putting him to sleep.'

plays cop, attorney, nurse, guardian angel and Dr. Doolittle to hundreds of abused animals each year. It's her job to investigate reports of cruelty to animals, decide whether to save or euthanize the animals, and see that owners who abuse their animals are prosecuted. The stories can break your heart.

Like the dog that neighbors watched grow skinny and weak and finally collapse. Animal control officers confiscated the dead animal, which was being cared for by a teenage boy. Tests showed the dog died of flea and tick anemia. The parasites had literally sucked the red blood cells from the dog. "People don't realize parasites can kill a dog," Anderson says.

> An animal control officer may risk her life saving an animal. And a few weeks later, participate in its death.

Like the horses left to starve in a field. Like the mother dog and her litter of puppies found shot to death by an owner who didn't want them. Like owners terrified by the intentional poisonings of their pets.

Some people ask, "How do you cope?"

And Anderson responds, "There is death and dying day after day. It's like being in a war. It's like being a nurse in a trauma ward. You deal with it because you have to. We're all egotists. You think no one else can do it and no one else can care as much as you do. So you learn to compartmentalize it, to put it away.

"Then when you're not there, when you go on vacation, it all comes flooding back and you can't sleep and you can't stop thinking about the animals, maybe about one particular animal or another."

The most difficult thing about her job, says Anderson, is that it pulls you two ways; it tears you in half.

"We are animal control; our job is to protect people from animals. But we work for the Humane Society and, in that respect, we are supposed to protect animals from people."

For example, one of the Society's six animal control officers may risk her own life capturing a dog wandering the middle of a busy highway. She saved the animal's life. And the officer feels good about that. She brings the dog to the animal shelter where it is put up for adoption. But the dog hangs around the shelter for several weeks and no one adopts it. Eventually, the control officer participates in euthanizing the animal she rescued.

Two or three people participate in euthanization. One person holds the animal and caresses it while another administers the injection that will "put the pet to sleep" painlessly. A third person may also help hold and caress a large dog. In Maui, about half of the 3,583 dogs brought to the shelter in a recent year were adopted, and only about 20 percent of the 6,464 cats were adopted. In addition, 1,558 other "pets" such as chickens, rabbits and guinea pigs were brought in. Both Anderson and Kelly are often asked why the Humane Society "puts animals to sleep." Shouldn't an organization that calls itself "humane" be a no-kill shelter? That, Anderson says, is a luxury every humane society works toward: the luxury to let all animals live.

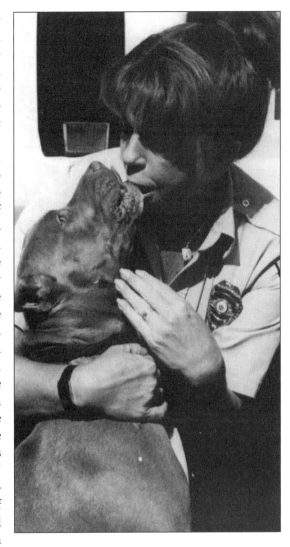

Aimee Anderson and a friend.

fetch
more information
For a complete list of your island Humane Society's services, see the Humane Society area of the Resource section at the back of this book. pages 307 to 308.

"The no-kill philosophy?" she muses. "What that means to me is that you have the ability to deny or accept a pet into your shelter. We don't have that luxury. We have to accept every pet that comes in."

She glances around the small facility. "And where would we put the 11,500 animals that came through here last year?"

We have *poi* dogs, of course...

In Hawai`i, we call our mutts *"poi* dogs." Where does the *poi* come in?

In very early Hawai`i, dog meat was a delicacy for humans. Dogs were fed poi, the beaten root of the taro plant, to fatten them up for feasts at which they were part of the main course.

Some *kama`aina* (longtime Hawai`i residents) say a true poi dog must not carry the characteristics of any one breed, but be very mixed. Others insist a poi should have some of the characteristics of his Polynesian ancestors. Early Hawaiian dogs were descended from canines who came with the first Polynesian settlers. They were small, short-haired and short-legged, with distinctive pointy ears and slightly up-curled tails. Not aggressive barkers, they fit in well with Hawai`i's laid-back lifestyle.

POI: a very mixed-breed dog

photo courtesy ARCHawaii

"Perhaps *poi* dogs are beloved here because we islanders are so ethnically diverse," muses Pamela Burns, Hawaiian Humane Society executive director in a newsletter. "Or maybe it's their convenient and cuddly size, just big enough to scare a burglar but still small enough to fit on your lap or lie next to you on the *pune'e* for a nap.

"Since they are a blend, *poi* dogs tend to have personalities that blur the distinction commonly attributed to particular breeds and no one characteristic stands out—neither too mellow nor too active, not too independent nor too territorial, not too loud nor totally silent.

"Whateverthe reason, *poi* dogs make great pets and recent research shows that the people of Hawai`i continue to choose them as companions far more than any other breed," Burns concludes.

And stumpy-tailed cats

Put animals on an isolated island in the middle of the ocean, far from the rest of the world, and strange things occur. They breed among themselves and whatever traits they bring to the genetic pool multiply, forming unique designer animals. Poi dogs with large ears and short legs. Cats with crooked

tails unknown anywhere else in the world. "We think they came in through Japan and then evolved into a cat with a unique tail," says Jocelyn Bouchard, Maui Humane Society director of development . The

tail is crooked, but it is not a rumpy tail, she explains. A rumpy-tailed cat, such as the Manx, has no bone at all extending from the cat's posterior, or rump. Instead, stumpy tails include one or two bones. A true crooked-tail cat is born with an appendage that is of the stumpy variety, short, that juts out at a jaunty angle. If you own a crooked-tail cat, count yourself lucky. The cats, some people say, bring good fortune.

Stumpy-tailed cats are seen often on Maui; six-toed cats are also common in Hawai'i.

Borrowed dogs, and...

It happens often here in the land of *aloha*. We pet owners walk our dogs at a local park or beach and soon tourists gather. The visitors drop to their knees on grass or sand, grinning as our dogs cover their faces with sloppy kisses. "Oh, I miss my dog back home," they say, tears in their eyes. We listen courteously as they describe the best dog in Dallas or the smartest cat in Kalamazoo.

"Thanks for the doggy fix," they sigh, still smiling down at our pets as they reluctantly go on their way.

So grocery store owner Chris Borges has hit upon what may be the ultimate act of sharing. Every day, she loans her 13 dogs to tourists. Her Maui Grown Market in Haiku is a last stop on the long, winding road to Hana, a popular tourist adventure. The dogs climb into cars of smiling strangers and spend the day swimming, hiking and riding—soothing the souls of tourists who miss their own pets back home.

> "I know people when they're on vacation must miss their dogs, so I let them use my dogs."

"I know people when they're on vacation must miss their dogs, so I let them use my dogs," Borges told the *New York Times*. She adopted the dogs, all unwanted pets, over several years and hopes to someday open an animal sanctuary. For now, she lends the dogs without charge to visitors. Both parties benefit: the tourists enjoy the dogs and the dogs enjoy their exercise.

Borges began lending dogs several years ago with a yellow Labrador named Mahi Mahi who would beg tourists to take her in their cars. Visitors fell in love with Mahi Mahi, Borges said, and some still send her postcards.

Dogs are loaned on a first-come, first-served basis because Borges does not want the dogs disappointed, waiting for a driver who doesn't show up. The dogs decide whether or not they will go along when rides are offered, either accepting or declining the enticement of an open car door. Borges says she has never lost a dog and, as far as she knows, the dogs have never had a bad experience.

She does not charge for the canine loans.

"I'm not trying to make money from my animals. I'm trying to share them with people," she says.

It's an ultimate act of *aloha*, giving new meaning to "pet-friendly."

A million cats,
compromised by progress

It's 8 p.m. A full moon hangs too low in the sky to give much light. The woods are dark and full of shadows. The ocean whispers ominously.

"Take that jug of water; follow me," Laurie Woodward says. Clutching several pans of cat food and wielding a flashlight, the petite woman in a backward baseball cap burrows into the kiawe brush. I follow her flashlight beam into the darkness, try to match her quick and sure strides dodging fallen trees, ducking under hanging branches and shaking off sharp thorns sticking to our boots.

Fifty feet into the brush we come to a clearing of sorts.

"Here kitty, kitty. Where are my kitties tonight?" Woodward calls softly.

"They are usually right here," she whispers. "Something must have scared them."

She points to a large truck buried back even deeper in the kiawe.

"Homeless people are staying there and they have dogs. Sometimes that scares the cats away."

Iolanda Marquardt photo courtesy of Maui Humane Society

We walk a few steps deeper into the darkness and two orange cats appear, watching me furtively; the larger rubs himself lovingly against Woodward's big army boots.

"There you are, Jasper!" she coos.

Suddenly a large calico is sitting on a rock. A tabby crawls out from under a bush. Two more cats, patchy black and white, appear. Another orange cat hops from a tree branch and two grays, hardly more than kittens, creep from behind a sand dune. Woodward lifts bushes and branches, finds plastic lids she uses for feeding dishes and fills them with dry cat food, chanting to the cats as she works. "Here's Waddles. Waddles eats much too much. Where's Bernie? Where's Dickens? There's Tiger. Tiger! Be nice to the other cats. Wally! How's your injury? Almost gone? Good cat!"

> As fast-track Hawai'i develops, the cats' hiding places vanish. They are confined to ever-shrinking bits of land...

Five more furry apparitions materialize. Most cats attack the food eagerly, but one comes over and mews up at me curiously, craving affection more than sustenance.

"They like you," Woodward says. "You must be a cat person."

Yes. I'm a cat person. But my affection pales in comparison to Woodward and her cat caretaking cohorts. Dedicated caretakers throughout the islands plunge nightly into parks, cane fields, gulches, parking lots and kiawe patches to feed and administer to a fraction of the state's hundreds of thousands of hungry and homeless cats. For the past eight years, Woodward has spent four hours every night caring for four cat colonies in the center of Kihei, Maui; hundreds of invisible, mysterious balls of fur lurking in ditches and woods, near parks and shopping centers in one of the fastest growing towns in the nation. As fast-track Hawai`i develops, the cats' hiding places vanish and they are confined to ever-shrinking bits of land or locations higher in the mountains.

Many of the cats were once pets, abandoned by owners who left the islands or left the town. Others are offspring of former pets, born wild in a warm climate that lets felines produce three litters a year instead of the usual two; born hungry and just able to eke out a survival eating birds, lizards, chickens, bird eggs, bugs and humans' trash.

Caretakers usually work at night because cats are nocturnal and because the caretakers prefer privacy. Woodward asks me not to disclose the locations of her cat colonies. Too many people don't like cats and

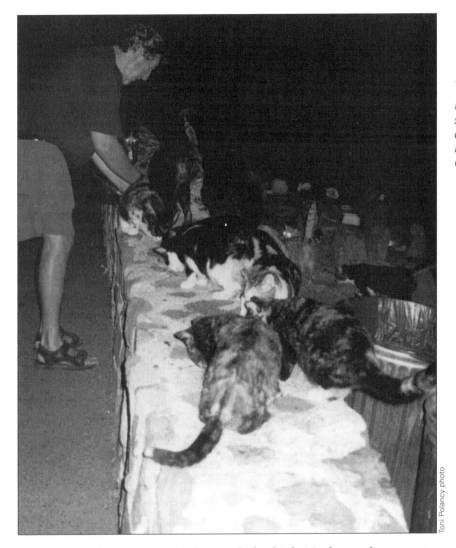

*It's
suppertime
on Diamond
Head Road,
O`ahu.*

Toni Polancy photo

might try to harm them. And some kids think it's fun to harass cats, setting string traps that can lead to maiming or a slow, excruciating death. Hawai`i's feral cats come under increasing criticism for killing Hawai`i's birds, too, including endangered birds, and programs are underway in some preserves to trap and kill cats.

The state Department of Health classifies felines as a public health risk. They can carry diseases such as toxoplasmosis, which can endanger the fetus of pregnant women. Cats also may suffer from worms, parasites, respiratory infections, leukemia and feline AIDS.

Done feeding, Woodward counts heads: 17 felines. Everyone is here. "Sometimes I'm afraid to come," she says as we traipse back to the car. "I don't know what I'll find. Maybe an injured cat, hit by a car. Maybe a body. Every week I lose one or two cats, but one or two more always appear."

Woodward's cats are healthy-looking; none seem skinny, mangy or flea-ridden. Most of her cats have a small clip on their left ear indicating they have been neutered. Caretakers on all islands feed and care for the cats, keeping them mange- and flea-free with antibiotics and flea control products. They also capture the cats and take them to humane societies or veterinarians to be tattooed or microchipped for identification, neutered or spayed and returned to streets and woods.

Since neutered and spayed cats no longer can reproduce, it is hoped that within a few years the number of feral cats will drop drastically, eliminating or at least lessening the islands' feral cat problem. O`ahu already reports a dramatic decline in the number of feral cats brought into the shelter. In addition to the dog and cats sterilized in its adoption program, the O`ahu shelter provides nearly 3,000 feral cat sterilizations a year.

There's an added benefit to sterilization: male cats become more mellow, less inclined to fight over the attentions of females. Most cats curtail the vicious fighting that can lead to cysts and infections.

It's dinnertime behind a Hanalei, Kaua`i, restaurant.

Two more blocks down the road, at a shopping center, we hear caterwauling; a furious cat fight is underway. Woodward shakes her head.

"Oh, oh, The Terminator's here," she says. The Terminator, she explains as she parks the car for the third of four colonies she feeds each night, is a huge "intact" (unneutered) male who has recently invaded the colony, fighting and terrorizing the other cats. Woodward heads for the brush behind a dumpster to break up the fight. "Hey! Cut that out. Stop it!"

The fighting subsides and cats begin to appear. Patches is a big black and white who'd rather be petted than fed, although she looks like she's eaten plenty. Marlene is petite, shapely. Black and white, she appears to wear a tuxedo like the actress Marlene Dietrich in the movie *Blue Angel*. Despite her small size, Marlene is the matriarch and leader of the colony, Woodward explains. Sort of tough, like the real Marlene Dietrich.

> Every cat stops his eating and tenses, watching as The Terminator swaggers across the parking lot.

Woodward spreads food around and while the animals eat, she cleans the area, picking up fast food restaurant bags. "People throw this stuff around and the cats try to eat it, paper and all, and I'm afraid they'll choke," she explains. This parking lot is a dangerous and unhealthy place for the cats, she says. They become too accustomed to cars and aren't careful. And some cats run across the road to get here. "It's easy to park here so sometimes cars stop and I've seen men just get out and urinate here. One time I had to clean it out of one of the cat's water dishes. So now I try to hide the water, further back in the …"

Suddenly, a huge black cat appears. The Terminator is back and he's worthy of his name, huge and scarred and mean-looking. Every cat stops his eating and tenses, watching as The Terminator swaggers across the parking lot, glaring, his muscles moving. One by one, the cats slink away as he approaches. One large gray cat stays, defiant, and The Terminator snarls. That cat, too, steals away.

Then Marlene, pretty Marlene Dietrich, walks gracefully, boldly, up to The Terminator. Half his size, she mews something and The Terminator's shoulders drop. He turns, rather humbly, and walks away.

"It's like that musical," I say. "*Cats*. They all have personalities."

"Yes," Woodward agrees, slamming down her car trunk. "And the drama plays out every night."

We have trackers and grabbers...

There's another kind of dog owner in Hawai'i, one who considers his pet both a companion and a tool: The feral pig or wild boar hunter. Wild boar hunting has a traditional history in Hawai`i and is experiencing a resurgence in popularity.

Believed to be descendants of pigs brought to the islands by the first Polynesians as a food source, today's wild boars forage through our wooded mountains and valleys, threatening the islands' ecosystems by destroying essential plant life. The big pigs with tusks commonly weigh in at 300 to 400 pounds, are vicious when cornered, and have been known to attack animals and people.

Attitudes toward boar hunting vary on the islands...

Hawai`i's boar hunting dog can be of any hunting dog breed or a mix of several, including pit bull or Rottweiler, and on the job he is classified either as a "tracker" or a "grabber." Wearing high, thick canvas collars to protect their jugular veins, the dogs hunt in packs of two or more, fanning out in search of boar. A tracker sniffs out the pig and her barking signals to other dogs that the quarry is near. Grabbers corner the boar and hold it for the hunter by barking and sinking their teeth into the boar, who may fight ferociously. It's a loud and lively encounter and one the dogs, trained from birth, relish. Unfortunately, some hunters physically abuse their dogs to promote aggressive behavior. They may avoid neutering the dogs, believing intact dogs to be more aggressive.

Dogs are often injured during the hunt, having been gored by the pig's tusks, and may have numerous scars to show for their work. Some dogs die of their injuries.

It's not unusual to see packs of large dogs in the back of a pickup truck, headed for a mountain pig hunt. Boar hunts are legal in Hawai`i, providing recreation for hunters and their dogs and food for island luau. Hunting dogs are excused from Hawai`i's stringent leash laws, provided they are under the control of their owners at all times. "Control" means returning immediately to the owner when called. But hunting dogs sometimes lose their hunters and are left to wander through the mountains, forming packs, reverting to a feral state or ending up at humane societies. Mangy, flea-ridden and bone-thin from weeks or months in the mountains, they are often too aggressive to be re-adopted.

Attitudes toward boar hunting vary on the islands, but for those who participate the hunt is a valued tradition.

And whispers of giant cats on deserted islands...

"You should put the giant cats of Kaho`olawe in your book," a woman told me, her voice a whisper, her eyes wide. She had heard stories, she said, about giant cats living on Kaho`olawe, a barren, deserted Hawaiian island.

"Yes, it's true," my elderly neighbor verified. "For 30 years or more I've heard the story. The cats over there have inbred for generations," he said, pointing to the reddish lump of land rising sullenly off Maui's southern shore. "And life there is so hard the cats had to grow to a really huge size to survive."

As a former journalist I jumped at the chance to uncover this amazing story. For pet lovers like myself, this would be akin to an anthropologist finding an unknown colony of pygmies in the African jungle. And the story made sense. A cat colony would have to be pretty tough to survive on dry, barren Kaho`olawe, where not many plants or other animals live.

"The cats have inbred for generations."

Kaho`olawe has long been used and abused. First, for many years, cattle ranchers grazed all the foliage from the island, then winds blew off its topsoil. Next, the U.S. military used it for bombing practice during and after World War II. Now the government is spending millions of dollars to clean it up.

I called Paul Higashino, restoration manager of the Kaho`olawe Island Reserve Commission. Yes, there are feral cats on Kaho`olawe, he said. He has seen glimpses of the very shy felines—flashes of black fleeing at the sight of humans. But none of the cats seemed particularly large, he said. Most likely the cats had been on the island for generations, he commented. (After all a cat "generation" takes less than six months.) And probably, they were brought to the island by ranchers or the military.

What Higashino did know for sure is that every few years Kaho`olawe has a "mouse explosion" and is inundated with a rash of rodents. In 1996, the military base there was overrun with mice and 15,000 of them were caught in one crackdown.

So, if any ancestors of those mice remain, and they probably do, it's safe to guess the cats are well fed. Higashino has also seen half-eaten centipedes, bird tracks on the beach, and large crab holes. Any of those creatures would make a meal for a cat. Not for your average pet, maybe--but for a giant cat of Kaho`olawe.

A dog who entertains, silently...

Anthony Phillip Tarvers III thanks heaven for his dog Sasha—and well he should. By snoozing happily while wearing a lei and sunglasses, the Shar Pei supports Tony. For about two hours, from 8 to 10 each evening, Tony and Sasha perform in Waikiki on the busy avenue of Kalakaua. Sasha snoozes, or at least tries to, with her live pet mouse Mickey atop her head, kind of busily doing nothing, to the delight of passing tourists. Sasha, though silent and still, discreetly clutches a dollar bill under her paw. Thousands of people from around the world have taken her photo, many of them also taking the hint and adding to the money under her paw. The fund goes to sustain Sasha and support Tony's humble

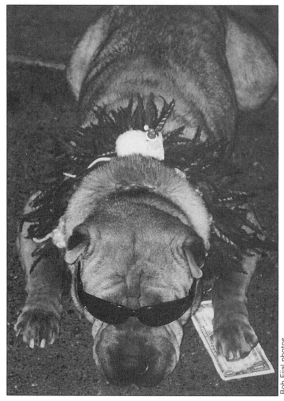

Bob Fijal photos

Hawaiian lifestyle. He, Sasha and Mickey live in an old van not far away. Sasha is a bit of a celebrity, having appeared as a news item in some publications and on Japanese television.

Tony says he first met Sasha in 1995 when she was 2 years old. Malnourished, she was still the size of a puppy and covered with fleas. He took her home to his Waikiki apartment where pets were not allowed and soon he was asked to move. So Tony took Sasha with him to his job as cook in a restaurant, tying her outside the back door, and eventually he lost his job. By now, Tony loved Sasha, but she seemed to be bringing him bad luck.

One day, as Tony, jobless, played on the beach with friends, a tourist placed a flower lei around Sasha's neck. With her Shar Pei wrinkles, sad face, and saucy tiptoed, hip-swaying strut, Sasha attracted a lot of attention. Laughing, Tony added a pair of sunglasses. People began to take pictures. Some of the charmed tourists wanted to tip Sasha. That seemed like a good idea, seeing as how she had lost Tony his apartment and his job. Adding a little white mouse he had trained to play happily on Sasha's head, Tony began visiting Waikiki's main strip each night, sitting silently in a favorite spot and letting things happen.

Sasha and her Tony.

Waikiki's main drag is filled with street performers, religious naysayers and hucksters of numerous varieties, including prostitutes, who draw the ire of police, politicians and especially hotels and businesses trying to sterilize the area. Although he falls into none of those categories, over the years Tony has been cited and arrested more than 20 times for soliciting without a license.

Nevertheless, Tony gets teary-eyed when he talks about Sasha, whom he credits with giving him a purpose in life and helping him break a drug habit. Sasha brings out the best in people, Tony says. He cites the laughter and smiles Sasha brings to the faces of thousands of tourists, many of whom don't speak English, but happily connect with the universal love and appeal of a wrinkly dog and her pet mouse.

Sitting an hour with Tony, hunched on a curb near a Waikiki alley, it's easy to agree. People quickly gather, cameras in hand. A man and woman, tourists from Japan, run toward us.

"There he is! There is Sasha!" the man squeals. "Smile, dog!" he orders as his video camera blinks.

Sasha, mouse on head, dollar under paw, doesn't move a wrinkle.

And a ghost town that forgot its pets

For more than ten years, from about 1830, sugar and pineapple fields covered much of these islands like soft, comforting blankets. The plantations sent their sweet product throughout the world and employed thousands of immigrant workers. Many of those workers lived in small, dusty villages or "camps," mini-communities that included wooden cottages with front porches and shade trees. There, neighbors enjoyed their well-earned rest after a long day's work and children played games of hide and seek among the wide kiawe trees.

Ah, but Hawai'i grew up, and on, and the world changed. By the latter half of the 1900s, sugar became more economical to harvest elsewhere. Hawai`i's labor cost too much and its land was too valuable. Anyway, the *malihini* (newcomers) needed room for more resorts, more houses, more growth.

Plantations, one by one, closed down. Families who had lived in plantation camps for generations moved away. Bulldozers leveled the houses, knocked down the trees. Winds whipped the red earth into dust clouds that danced across the fields. Nothing much remained. Except the pets.

Of hundreds of camps hiding in fields across the islands, Waine'e Village camp in western Maui was one of the last to close. In 1994 Amfac/JMB Hawaii Inc. announced that it would, in phases over several years, shut down the tiny village which dated back to 1916. By the autumn of 1998, all residents of the camp's 75 houses had left. Except the pets.

Over several days the Maui Humane Society officers and volunteers rescued nearly 100 animals, including 80 cats, 12 dogs, a rooster, a chicken and two pigeons, according to the *Maui News.*

Most of the animals were tick-infested, suffering from heartworm, and starving. They had to be destroyed. Only three of the 12 dogs were saved and made available for adoption.

Sadly, about 80 more cats and at least five more dogs were believed to be wandering in and around the camp, hungry, ill, wondering why their families had abandoned them. What had happened to the children who once threw balls for them to chase, who hiked the West Maui Mountains with them? Where were the people who had loved them, the people they had loved and trusted?

*An old boot
and a crumbling
shack, reminders
of a once-bustling
plantation camp.*

Toni Polancy photo

We host innocent victims of war

Our world looks large on a map, but it is really such a small place. Tyrannies and troubles, thousands of miles and oceans away, affect all of us—eventually even the least significant of creatures. The war in Iraq touched the lives of Hawai`i animals. Deployment to the Middle East placed some military personnel in the unfortunate position of having to relinquish their pets because they could not find anyone to care for the animals on short notice. O`ahu's Hawaiian Humane Society found permanent homes for some of the pets and recruited foster parents for others. Volunteers agreed to care for the pets for a period of six months or longer until soldiers returned to these islands.

It was one less worry for departing soldiers and one more joyful reason to return home safely.

Photo courtesy of The Hawaiian Humane Society

And a stranded visitor who finds ALOHA

Imagine being a 2-year-old dog, hardly more than a puppy, really. You're part terrier. and weigh just over 20 pounds. You have lived much of your life with the men on a Taiwanese tanker traversing the Pacific Ocean. One night a fire badly damages the tanker, named Insiko 1906. You smell the smoke and feel the heat. You see much excitement as the men put out the fire. You absorb a sense of fear you cannot comprehend, as the men live on deck for days and days, praying for rescue.

Eventually a cruise liner spots the burned-out tanker 200 miles south of Hawai'i and comes to its rescue, a metal giant, lurching closer and closer. The crew and your owner, Captain Chung Chin-po, climb aboard the liner, but somehow in the confusion—so many languages, so much excitement—you are left on the tanker. The men who raised you abandon ship and pretty much abandon you too, leaving you with some food and water, but leaving you, nevertheless, alone to die a painful death, starving or drowning. You wonder why they are leaving you; you bark, hoping they will remember you, but the cruise ship pulls away and becomes a speck in the ocean, your last contact with humans, with life.

Your name is Hokget—which means happiness, good fortune, blessing—except you don't feel very blessed right now, alone on a burned out tanker in the middle of an ocean, water churning all around you.

Ah, but, little girl, you can't imagine what is happening in Hawai'i, when people learn a dog has been left drifting at sea. First, the Hawaiian Humane Society pledges funds for a rescue operation. The newspapers write stories and donations pour in, all to save you, little Hokget. Among your benefactors is a real Hawaiian princess, Regina Kawananakoa, who charters a jet to search for you. You, of course, are just a dog and can't

Hokget at the Kaua'i Humane Society.

Photo courtesy Kauai Humane Society

suspect that so many people care. You are just a little dog alone on an abandoned tanker, wondering why you've been left, sleeping steamy nightmare-filled days and awakening long nights to shivers. The days turn into weeks; the food runs out. And the rescue efforts fail. Your tanker has drifted so far the team can't find you. By now, much of the world knows of your plight, even the fishermen plying the Pacific. Poor Hokget, people say. Poor little dog. What a way to die.

Then, three weeks after your tanker was abandoned, a Samoan fishing boat spots it. The fishing boat is short of fuel, so other fishermen pick up the search. The first of the Hawai`i fleet, the 70-foot *Kawika*, breaks off a journey to the fishing grounds and searches the area for six days. With squalls and sea swells hampering the effort, with dwindling fuel, the *Kawika* hands off the search to the 50-foot *Pacific Fin*. Finally, the Fin closes in on your tanker after a Coast Guard helicopter spots it from the air. A crew member boards the *Insiko* to search for you, but the past 24 days adrift have had a dream-like quality; nothing seems real and you are afraid of the stranger. It takes the man an hour to find you, hiding in a pile of tires. He feeds you carefully, just a little at first, until your tummy is accustomed to food again. In all, fishermen have lost about $100,000 worth of catch, searching for you. Meanwhile, the Coast Guard steps in and tows the boat to Hawai i to avoid spilling the 60,000 gallons of diesel fuel on board and causing an environmental tragedy.

Well, little Hokget, 22-pound dog that has caused a million pounds of concern, you know the rest of the story. At Honolulu Harbor, hundreds of humans wave at you. Cameras flash and blink. Someone puts a circle of flowers around your neck. You don't know that a *lei* means welcome, but the humans are smiling and that's good. The tanker and those weeks at sea seem a nightmare from which you have suddenly awakened. Kaua`i Humane Society director Rebecca Rhoades takes you on a plane to that island where you, even you, must fulfill a 120-day state quarantine. Rhoades puts you in the very first kennel with lots of windows so people can wave at you, where she visits you several times a day. You are a show-off, wagging your tail in joy. It is so good to have friends again, to have people around you!

Finally, little Hokget, your quarantine over, you go to the island of O`ahu to live with a family of your very own. There you will experience even more the meaning of aloha. *Love.*

Finding Love

2

You can
buy a pet
or save one.
Or you
can just
let a pet
happen.

*Ninja, a dachshund,
shows his affection
for owner Jane
Brown at the
Hawaiian Humane
Society's annual
PetWalk.*

Meet Slasher, a too-gentle giant

He's a tough old dog. A purebred pit bull with muscles rolling across his back. He weighs over 100 pounds and he has a tattoo on his left leg. It's his name, SLASHER, in big bold letters.

The day I visit, Slasher is on his last leg at the Hawai`i Island Humane Society at Kea`au on the Big Island. It's his third go-round here and, despite his size and his brutish looks, he's here not because he's a bad dog, but because he's a good one. Slasher's first owner, the one who had him tattooed, went to jail for crimes unknown to Slash. So Slasher got a second owner at the shelter. This one was a guy who figured that a 100-pound pit bull named Slasher would make a great watchdog. But the guy soon learned that Slash, instead of attacking a burglar, was likely to saunter up and greet him with a big sloppy kiss. He might knock the burglar over, but it would be from clumsiness, not clout. And feeding 100 pounds of smoochy pooch was not what the guy had bargained for.

So Slasher finds himself at the shelter a third time. Pit bull is a popular breed in Hawai`i, but this time nobody's taking Slasher. He is in a cage for animals who have been up for adoption for over a week, dogs on a deadline, you might say.

I feel sorry for Slasher. I consider putting him on a plane and taking him back to Maui with me. But how? He is almost twice the size of the largest pet crate. And Archie, my male dog, is a wuss. He'd be traumatized simply by Slasher's size.

I go home and try to forget about Slasher, but he keeps lunging into my thoughts. So two months later I telephone the shelter. Surely someone has adopted this purebred pit bull.

"We really liked Slash," Duane Mendoza, Kea`au shelter manager, says. "But we only have so many kennels, and other dogs are waiting for a chance. We hoped Slasher would find the right match, but it didn't work out that way."

The Humane Society tried, Mendoza explains. The county only reimburses the society for 48 hours of care, but they kept Slasher five weeks anyway, at their own expense, hoping he'd be adopted. Slasher was twice featured as "pet of the week" in the local newspaper.

But finally Slasher, the gentle giant, was euthanized.

You might say Slasher was a victim of his size and his breed's reputation. People expect bit pulls to be tough, mean. Somehow, Slasher wasn't. He had the body of a bull and the heart of a lap dog.

To put it more simply, Slasher was adopted by the wrong people for the wrong reasons. After all, enduring love and lasting matches happen when you choose a dog, or a friend, for his heart, not his looks.

Obtaining a pet in the islands

When a friend offered O`ahu resident Bill a full-blooded Labrador retriever pup, he eagerly accepted. The cute little female was supposed to turn into a loving 40-pound dog. She's loving all right, and at 70 pounds, she's almost twice as much love as Bill bargained for, and a lot more dog than his landlord agreed to.

Sue bought her 80-year-old mom a Jack Russell mix puppy because her mom is a fan of a television show that features a Jack Russell. Sue's mom loves the dog, which she named Frazier, but when he grew into a sturdy 25-pound guy with the strong personality characteristic of his breed, he was just too much for her to handle. Frazier was hard to housebreak, too. Now he's Sue's dog and only visits "grandma" occasionally.

How do you pick a pet who will grow up to be what you expect, who will be compatible with you, your family, your neighbors and your landlord? First of all, you need to do much more research on cat and dog breeds than you will find in this Hawai`i-specific book. Go to your nearest public library and peruse the shelves for books dealing with breed characteristics. You have access to your statewide system via library computers; your library can order any book you want. Find some of the books recommended in the research section of this book.

It's not easy. Our tough quarantine laws won't let you bring Uncle Charley's yellow Lab's newborn puppy in from the mainland.

Don't decide on the spur of the moment that you want a pet because it's cute or because your children are lobbying for one. Weigh the pros and cons of having a pet carefully. If you've decided you do want one, visit several sources and give yourself at least a month to find the right type of pet. You may already have a preference for a cat or a dog. Here are some Hawai`i-specific considerations:

Cat or dog?

- **Cats.** To make ends meet in our expensive state, many people hold more than one job, often as many as three or four part-time jobs. If your work keeps you away from home for many hours each day, a cat is a much better choice than a dog. Cats tend to be more solitary animals and don't mind being alone as much as dogs do. Cats are

Who says you have to choose between owning a cat or a dog? Certainly not Casey and Whiskers, who peacefully share a Makawao, Maui, home.

clean (so are most dogs, by the way) and will use an indoor litter box; you won't have to rush home from work to walk your cat.

A cat will welcome you at whatever hour you come home, rub herself lovingly against your legs as you fix supper, snuggle close by as you watch television and stalk the house while you are asleep, hunting mice and geckos, an added benefit in our often critter-ridden homes. Most cats are nocturnal creatures. If she is like my cat Skat, your cat will awaken you occasionally by gently touching your cheek with a butterfly kiss.

- **Dogs.** If you want more intense interaction and/or protection, and have a few hours a day to spend with a pet, choose a dog. Dogs are friendly, needy creatures; they must have your company and, preferably, also the company of other dogs. A lonesome dog may defecate or urinate in your home to let you know he's unhappy, as has happened to several pet owners I've known. The solution is to get a second dog, sort of a pet for your pet. Having a dog or two means never having to say, "I'm not busy." Dogs vary much in breed, temperament and size, so go back to the library and/or your computer and study.

What should you look for?

Personality is a pet's most important trait. After all, you will be living with this creature for a long time, perhaps ten or fifteen years. You needn't spend quite as much time choosing it as you spend choosing a spouse, but given divorce statistics these days you may actually live longer with your pet than with a husband or wife.

In a following story, Grayson Hashida, past director of the Big Island's Hawai`i Humane Society, tells how to choose a pet. A dog, puppy, kitten or cat should acknowledge you, not ignore you. And that holds true whether you choose the pet at the pound, at a pet store, at a breeder's kennel or at your neighbor's home.

Forget about picking the cutest puppy or kitten. Instead, get down on the floor with the litter. See which baby is curious, comes up to you and wants to play. Puppies or kittens that have been socialized in their first few weeks are more outgoing, curious, eager, and eventually seem more intelligent. Three traits go a long way to making a great pet: intelligence, the inclination to bond with a human, and the ability to focus; that is, to pay attention and concentrate on your commands.

Which cat?

How do you see your cat spending its days and nights? Indoors? Outdoors? Or a little of each? If your cat will spend all of its time indoors, choose either a kitten or an adult cat that is now spending all of its time indoors. You can easily train a kitten to stay indoors all the time and it will probably not even miss life outdoors, but changing the habits of an adult cat can be difficult.

If you let an intelligent cat choose between living indoors or out, she'll probably choose both as our cat,

Toni Polancy photo

Finding an apartment that welcomes pets was so difficult that Evan Porter Hoku stood at an entrance to O'ahu's Kahala Mall, seeking a new owner for his much-loved cat.

Skat, has. Skat adopted us while she was very pregnant, setting up house in a planter by my front door. We welcomed her into the house. After the kittens were born, she was spayed and Skat's been with us for four years now. Very determined and demanding, she spends days sleeping in a living room rocking chair, ignoring my three dogs, and nights with her feral cat friends outdoors. It's an ideal arrangement from her point of view: good food, soft bed, flea control, and affectionate humans.

But if you choose to let your cat go outdoors, you should know that your cat will probably have a shorter life than she would if she remained indoors. Hawai'i has few roads and many cars; even neighborhood streets are busy at certain times of the day; many cats are killed or injured by cars. And the great outdoors has other dangers like accidental or intentional poisonings and infections from other cats.

Another question: what do you want your cat to do for you? Chase rodents (and occasionally bring them back as gifts)? Then let her out. Or just hang around and be loving? Then, keep her in.

Dogs: which breed?

First, decide why you want a pet. Protection? Company? A running mate? Hunting? Status symbol? A pal for the kids? Or just someone to care for and love? Those are all sound reasons to obtain a pet. But each of those reasons demands a dog with a different temperament.

You'll also need to consider the size of the dog. Large dogs require space and room to run or/and you should have time to take the pet on walks at least twice daily. If you rent your apartment or home, or intend to purchase a condominium, you will find that few Hawai'i apartment complexes welcome pets, especially on "neighbor islands." Ideally, longhaired dogs should be given at least a half hour of daily grooming. They can also be expensive to have clipped. Some small breeds tend to bark a lot, but so may an untrained large dog.

Good dog! (for apartments)

So many Hawai'i residents live in apartments and condominiums! According to an article in DOGFANCY magazine, these breeds—small and easy to train—are wise choices for elderly people living in apartment:

- Bichon Frise
- Boston Terrier
- Cairn Terrier
- Cavalier King Charles Spaniel
- Dachshund
- Miniature Poodle
- Miniature Schnauzer
- Papillon
- Pug
- Yorkshire Terrier

From "Size up the ideal apartment dog" by Arden Moore, DOGFANCY, July 2002.

Our top breeds

These are the ten most popular breeds of dogs in the islands, in order of preference.

- Poi (very mixed breed)
- Labrador retriever
- Golden retriever
- American pit bull
- German shepherd
- Rottweiler
- Doberman pinscher
- Poodle
- Chihuahua
- Dachshund

Protection?

There's nothing like a big, barking dog to protect your home and many, many *kama`aina* (longtime residents), including those who live in apartments, have large dogs. It's surprising to note the huge dogs people keep in Waikiki apartments, to see 80-pound Rottweilers and Labrador Retrievers running their owners along Ala Wai Canal. But your dog's instinct to guard you, a member of its pack, is so great that even a relatively small dog can appear surprisingly ferocious when you are in danger. His barking will alert you to unwelcome visitors and may discourage burglars, who will simply move on to less challenging locations.

My dogs, Archie (45 pounds) and Betty (19 pounds), are loving and friendly to everyone. However, a recent incident showed how protective smallish mutts can be. My kitchen was being renovated and I tripped on

Deborah Booker photo courtesy The Honolulu Advertiser

Winning Golden Retrievers proudly display their ribbons during a Golden Retriever Club of Hawai`i show at Thomas Square in Honolulu. Breeders and clubs are listed in the Resources section at the back of this book.

an electrical cord. Landing on the tiled floor, I let out a cry of anguish. Betty and Archie came running from another room just as two men who were working on the kitchen reached down to help me up. The dogs saw me on the floor, in distress, two strangers bending over me. In the dogs' minds, an attack was in progress. Baring their teeth and snarling, the dogs hurled themselves at the workers. When the men backed off, the dogs surrounded me, keeping the men at bay by snarling and growling. I patted the dogs, praising them for their good intentions, until they calmed down.

Chances are, your dog will be protective, whatever its size.

From where?

Where will you get your pet? In Hawai`i, your choices are somewhat limited. You can buy a cat or dog from a pet store, from a pet "warehouse," from a breeder, from a rescue league, or from your local humane society. Our state's tough quarantine laws (see the Quarantine chapter of this book) won't let you bring Uncle Charley's yellow Lab's newborn puppy in from the mainland. Nor can you travel a few states over to purchase that rare Schipperke.

If you can't find what you want in Hawai`i, you may have to search the Internet for a breeder. Australia, New Zealand and Great Britain have no rabies; therefore animals brought into Hawai`i from those countries can avoid quarantine. But if you go the Internet route, you take your chances on whether the breeder sends a healthy pet well representing its breed. (See the related story, this chapter.) You may want to travel to those countries to pick a pet yourself, as some Hawai`i pet owners do.

It may not be the smartest way to get a pet, but on these islands, you may be able to just let a pet happen. All neighbor islands have an excess of feral cats and homeless dogs and, if you wait long enough, one is likely to turn up at your door. You can feel good about giving a stray animal a home, but you are also stuck with whatever you get. Eliminating the "let it happen" route, here are some of your choices in Hawai`i.

- **A large supplier**

  Pets Central, the state's largest dog supplier, off Nimitz Highway in Honolulu, gets all of the approximately 100 puppies sold each month from Australia.

  Prices for puppies start at about $1,000 and may go as high as $4,000, says an assistant manager. Puppies come in to the warehouse at 8 or 9 weeks of age and are current on all vaccinations (for parvo, distemper, hepatitis, kennel cough) as well as being wormed and microchipped.

The dogs are sold with a seven-day guarantee and a 90-day health warranty. The warranty will cover up to $1,000 for any disease-related illness, a company spokesperson says.

Pets Discount Warehouse, a pet supply store affiliated with Pets Central, sometimes offers cats and kittens for adoption. They are obtained from island cat rescue societies, a Pets Central manager says.

- **Local breeders**

Pets Unlimited, an O`ahu pet store, occasionally sells pets from breeders or from individual families. Prices, at the time of publication, start at about $300 for a mixed breed puppy, a store manager said. However, he very honestly recommends that you don't buy from his store—that you purchase your pet directly from a breeder, perhaps one you've located through newspaper classified ads.

"You should go to the breeder's home (or kennel) and see where the puppy came from so you know what you are getting," he said. "See the parents and especially the size of the parents because dogs can vary by size and temperament within a breed."

Puppies should be with their mother and their litter mates and be interacting closely with humans for the first two or three months of life. This is a crucial time when puppies become socialized, learning to

photo courtesy of Faye Yamamoto

As a judge, left, stands by, Faye Yamamoto shows her prize-winning Rhodesian Ridgeback, Bronto, at an American Kennel Club competition. Professional breeders and owners show their dogs at functions throughout Maui, the Big Island and O`ahu.

Tips for breeders, from breeders

Several breeders indicated that they are careful about who they sell to and occasionally exercise their "right of refusal," rejecting a buyer. Their advice:

Know where the dog or cat you bred is going. Make sure the animal will have proper care. If you are uncomfortable about a buyer, you have a right to gently reject the sale.

How do you assess a buyer?

Keep quiet, let the potential buyers do the talking. And don't let them hurry you.

"I get to know the buyer," says a longtime Honolulu breeder. "I decide if they will take proper care of the pet or whether this is just a lark for them. It usually takes six months (to have puppies available), during that time we keep in touch. I make sure they really want the dog. I listen to see if they ask questions that show they will take care of it."

Be careful when selling to people who don't own their own home, says another breeder who will not sell to renters.·

"People move too often and it's hard to find a place that will let you have a pet. I don't want to see my dogs at the humane society some day.

She says she occasionally relents and sells to renters, if they seem determined to have (her breed). She requests a phone call or letter from the landlord verifying that the potential buyers are long-term renters and the dog will have a stable home.

Get the new owner's address and make an appointment to stop buy and visit. Does the family seemed settled and organized enough to give proper care to a pet?

Keep in touch with the new owners.

Your job doesn't stop with the sale of an animal. You should be able to provide breed information and advice to the new owners. Be sure to get their phone number as well as their address and don't wait for them to call you. Call in occasionally to check on the animal, at least during its first year.

Hard to believe all these beautiful pups came from one mom. Kai-Ridge kennel's "Flashy April" managed to nurse all of them by taking turns.

Michael Johnson photo courtesy of Faye Yamamoto

interact with other dogs and with people.

Puppies bred at "puppy mills," mass-produced at kennels where they have little opportunity to interact with people or chance to play with mother and siblings, may never catch up and relate well to humans or other dogs. We've all come across dogs who cling to their owners and refuse to interact with other people or pets. Chances are good such dogs were not socialized as pups.

- **Animal rescue leagues**
No-kill animal shelters are always seeking kind people to take in cats and dogs and other animals they've either rescued or simply accepted into their shelters because they are no longer wanted by their owners.

So many miniatures:
Here's a smart idea. Combine your search for the ideal small dog with a visit to Kaua'i and stop at the Kaua'i Humane Society which often has an excess of small and miniature dogs, both purebred and/or mixed breed, available for adoption. A long-haired miniature Dachshund, a Papillon-looking puppy, a King Charles mix, and a Yorkshire Terrier mom and pup were all staring wistfully from kennels the last time I visited. Humane Society executive director Rebecca Rhoades isn't sure why that island has so many lost and abandoned small dogs, but says dogs and puppies are often found wandering rural roads. The Kaua'i facility sends several small dogs to O'ahu's humane society each week, where they are quickly adopted.

For example, in Hawai'i it is very difficult to find pet-friendly apartment and home rentals and frustrated tenants sometimes must part with their pets. Also, Hawai'i is a transient place; residents leaving the state sometimes decide not to take pets along.

Most private shelters keep a low profile in the islands, a groomer says, because they can be inundated with unwanted pets dropped off by owners.

"I know a woman who rescues cats, and people will literally throw their cats over her fence, into her yard to be rescued," the groomer said.

That's very true, confirms Patti Blasko, who with her husband has operated the K-9 Rescue League for several years. She offers a post office box and phone number, but prefers her Wai'anae address be kept confidential.

"People just drop pets off, tie dogs to my fence," she said.

When we spoke, the League was not accepting animals because its kennel was full, a condition in which no-kill shelters often find themselves. The Blaskos live in a residential area and a county ordinance says they can have only ten dogs.

The K-9 League advertises in O'ahu newspapers to find homes for five or six pets a month. Most are strays or throw-a-ways, found wandering island roads, Blasko says. They are brought to her home to be cleaned up, put on heartworm medication and socialized. They are sterilized and a veterinarian checks their health. If deemed adoptable, they are given to good homes. Special foster homes are found for aggressive or chronically ill pets, Blasko says.

To obtain an animal from K-9 Rescue you must own your own home or have proof that your landlord approves. (See the Resource section of this book for a list of other shelters that offer adoptable dogs and cats.)

- **Humane societies**
Here's a chance to save a life as well as gain a pet. On neighbor islands, you'll usually have a wide variety of cats and dogs to choose from. On O'ahu, you may have to visit the Hawaiian Humane Society several times before you find the right pet. If you don't see a pet that appeals to you on the first visit, try again in a few days. The cost to adopt a dog or cat, including shots, neutering and microchip, is approximately $50 at all island humane societies.

Why is that dog or cat at the humane society?

When an owner turns a pet into a humane society, he answers a few questions that will give you a clue to the pet's personality. Sometimes a pet is given away for simple reasons:

- We can't afford to feed and care for it.
- We are going to the mainland and can't take him along.
- We're moving to a new apartment where he's not allowed.
- I got married and my spouse doesn't like animals.
- We have a baby now and don't have time for a dog.
- The cat scratches the couch.
- The dog's just too big and eats too much.
- The dog barks and the neighbors complain.

Read the reasons carefully and see if they are concerns you can deal with, maybe with a little help from a training class. Here's your chance to save a life.

fetch
more information
For complete lists of pet shops and breeders, see the Resource section at the back of this book.

Deborah Booker photo courtesy The Honolulu Advertiser

It's a match at O`ahu's Hawaiian Humane Society. The dog and his future pal are sure. Now if they can only convince mom.

Choosing a pet

Here's the best way to pick a pet
at an island humane society or anywhere.

Approach the kennel and look for a pet that walks up to the front of his cage to meet you, says Grayson Hashida, past executive director of the Hawai`i Island Humane Society. A friendly dog will get up to greet you, make eye contact and sometimes say "hello" with a bark or a whine of greeting. A socialized cat may not get up to greet you, but she will usually offer a mew or a purr and expect a petting from you in return.

For best results, consider a mature pet, Hashida says. "In older pets (a year or more of age), personality is easier to judge. Training and handling has a great deal to do with your pet's behavior, but personality and demeanor are inborn."

Don't fall in love with a pet just because it's cute, Hashida warns. Take time to consider :

1. your home,
2. your work habits,
3. the amount of time you have for a pet.

Do you have hours to spend each day? Or just minutes? A small dog needs much less walking and exercise than a large one. And a cat requires even less interaction. Don't choose a furry cat if you won't enjoy brushing

Choosing a cat

A veteran pet owner uses this method for choosing cats who are good mousers (a real benefit in Hawai`i with its many rodents). He runs his finger along the outside of the cage. The cats that show interest and try to bat his finger, indicating an eagerness to play or hunt, are potential adoptees. He says he's never been disappointed with his choice.

it occasionally; don't choose a long-haired dog if you can't afford to have it professionally groomed ($40 and up per visit) every six weeks or so.

Once you spot a pet you'd like, take advantage of humane society "greeting rooms": quiet cubicles or fenced areas where you and your prospective pet can be alone together and become acquainted. Plan to spend a minimum of half an hour petting and playing with the animal; then decide. Is this the pet you want to live with for the next ten years or longer?

Don't be shy about "interviewing" various pets. It may take several visits to find the perfect pet for you and your family.

Think big, please

"It's so unfair. Puppies and small dogs always get adopted first," says a humane society volunteer. "I feel so sorry for the big dogs...the bigger they are, the less chance they'll get adopted. And sometimes these are the pets that are best behaved. They aren't as nervous as little toy dogs and most of them don't bark as much. They can be great guard dogs. But no, everybody wants a toy dog."

Ask to see a report

Most humane societies keep records on the canine and feline clients, listing information such as how the pet was obtained, where it was

Read these before you choose a pet

A breeder recommends these books for future dog owners. Your public library has many more books geared to help you choose the right pet for your circumstances.

- **The Perfect Match: a dog buyer's guide**
  by Chris Walkowicz,
  Howell Book House, New York

- **The Puppy Report, how to select a healthy, happy dog**
  by Larry Shook
  Ballantine books, New York

found, why it was turned in, any suspected health problems, what humane society aides have discovered about the animal's temperament, and how it gets along with others of its species. Ask to see any reports or documentation the society may have.

In these islands, pets happen

JoAnn Allencastre photo

You never know where pets will come from. JoAnn Allencastre was walking by a dumpster in Wailuku, Maui, when she heard a mew. She discovered six kittens sealed inside a plastic bag. JoAnn found homes for four kittens who survived; two others died. A friend, Jacquelyn Riegel, pictured here, helped care for the litter.

Lee Stack, right, met Thumper in a Big Island orchard. A few days later Petey showed up. It's not unusual to find small breeds lost or abandoned on Kaua`i and the Big Island.

Patty Page, of the Big Island, found these pups abandoned and dying in an alley in Hawi.

Photo courtesy ARCHawaii, the Big Island

Toni Polancy photo

A checklist: before you choose your pet

❑ **Consult with a specialist, first.**

Before you begin searching for your pet, talk to people who know about the type or breed you are considering. Call and discuss the breed you are considering. Ask for advice and recommendations.

- Breeders. Many top breeds are available right in Hawai'i, and most breeders are happy to share information with you. Breeders are concerned with quality and some even go to the extent of importing sperm so their pups will of the highest quality. If they do not have puppies available, they can help you find a quality out-of-state breeder whom you can trust.

- Breed clubs. See the resource section again. Is there a club for the breed of pet you are considering? Call and find out as much as you can about that breed and any special island considerations. For example, does the breed do well in Hawai'i's heat?

- Hawai'i's all-breed clubs. Most islands have all-breed clubs that welcome a variety of pets. Many members are anxious to share their knowledge and experiences.

- A veterinarian. You should choose a veterinarian even before you choose a pet. Ask the vet if he knows a reliable breeder or source for the type of pet you seek.

❑ **Healthy?**

Wherever you get your pet—from a private home, a breeder, a pet store or the humane society—look for these signs of good health and care:

- The animal's coat should be clean and free of matted fur or parasites. If you are buying from a breeder, expect the pet's coat to be glossy and trimmed, if the pet is old enough to be trimmed. At the humane society, the coat of long-haired adult pets may appear sun-burned or faded. (Like your hair gets when you are in the sun too long.) Check the undercoat for new hair growth. Does it appear shiny and healthy?

- The eyes should be clear and clean with no signs of running or mucus build-up.

- The ears should be clean, free of both wax build-up and mites.

- A puppy or kitten should appear eager and friendly; avoid animals that seem listless or disinterested in your advances.

❏ **Ask questions. Get it in writing.**

- Who is the current veterinarian? What is the pet's health history and which shots has it had?

- For how long will the seller guarantee the pet's health? Three months is a reasonable time for infectious diseases such as leptospirosis and parvo. If your pet is pedigreed, you may want a year's contract to guarantee against hereditary problems and genetic imperfections. Study your breed.

❏ **Pedigreed?**

- Ask for pedigree papers, including at least three generations if you expect to show the pet. Ask for written records.

- If you are told your dog is eligible for American Kennel Club registration, get it in writing.

- Have the seller sign and date pedigree papers. Don't pay for the pet and accept it based on the breeder sending papers later.

❏ **How old?**

- Puppies and kittens should be at least 2 months old and ideally, 3 months old, before they leave home. They should be weaned and able to eat pet food.

❏ **Housetrained?**

- Expect kittens to be litter-box trained before they come to your home. You will probably have to train your puppy yourself over several days or weeks.

How to pick a good dog or two

Sitting quietly in a kennel at the Maui Humane Society, the hairy dog captured people's attention. Archie was odd looking; probably part Airedale with haphazard wisps of blonde fur between waves of auburn. Passersby pointed and chuckled, but the dog hardly reacted. He didn't seem to have much personality. Still, I noticed how focused he was on one of the attendants. As she moved about, administering to other dogs, his eyes never left her. I like calm dogs that pay attention, so I took him into a humane society play yard where prospective owners can interact with dogs they might adopt. He ignored me and I feared he might not make the transition to a new owner well, so I left him.

Still looking for a pet, I returned to the Humane Society ten days later. The funny-looking dog was still there. This time there was a big sign on his cage, written by the attendant who had moved to the mainland U.S.A.

Somebody please adopt this dog.
He's the best dog here
and he doesn't have much more time.

I brought the dog home. I named him Archie. I fed him regularly, took him everywhere with me, and within days Archie had transferred that focus, that bonding, to me. But, there was a slight problem. When I took Archie to the park to exercise, he hardly moved. He was only 3 years old, but he acted so elderly. I figured he needed a friend, someone to play with, sort of a dog of his own to perk up his life.

The Maui Humane Society lets you bring your current pet along to help choose a new one. I picked a handsome full-blooded Pekingese from the kennels and he and Archie and I went into a play yard to get to know each other better. The result was instant hate. The Pekingese jumped up on my lap, snuggled down and growled when Archie approached as if to say, "Go away. This is my human now."

Archie and I came back to the shelter a second time. This time, I chose a playful looking mutt almost as big as Archie. Inside the play yard, Archie and the mutt rubbed noses and sniffed each other briefly, then ignored each other. Another rejection.

The third attempt would be the last, I vowed. As soon as I got to the Humane Society I spotted a small golden terrier/Chihuahua and gasped. The dog had recently nursed a litter of pups and her breasts were engorged, swollen and hanging almost to the ground.

"It looks so awful," I told an attendant. "Will she ever be normal again?"

The attendant gave it some thought. "She was brought in with an adult puppy she was still nursing. The puppy was adopted a couple of days ago, but mommy here obviously has a problem. Her breasts will dry up some, but will probably always hang quite a bit."

The little dog looked into my eyes and whined hopefully. I'm a sucker for a sad story so I took her into the yard with Archie and me. Despite the swollen breasts, she ran joyously to Archie and gave him a big lick. She sloshed over to me, jumped up on my lap and kissed me bountifully. Then she jumped down again, gave Archie a second kiss, and they began to chase and play. Archie was delighted. And I was the owner of a second dog. I named her Betty, like the blonde girl in that Archie comic strip.

This story has a very happy ending. Betty's breasts were soon fine. Five years later she and Archie are the best of buddies, romping daily at the park, playing like puppies. And I am hopelessly in love with both of them.

My dogs were chosen for their personalities, not their looks. That's absolutely the best way to choose a pet or, come to think of it, a spouse.—Toni Polancy

Betty and Archie, buddies forever.

But what if you can't find the perfect pet in Hawai'i?

Have your heart set on a special breed of dog or cat? A purebred who's especially classy or just plain cute? With over 175 kennel and pet clubs in the state, you may be able to find what you want on these islands. See the Resource guide at the end of this book for a list of kennels and breeders, and check out Honolulu newspapers too. Classified sections usually contain a full column or two of Pets For Sale. Those should be the first places you turn to if you are looking for a particular breed of dog or cat.

> 'Think about it. If you were going to send (a dog) away to a far-off country, would you send your best? Not likely.'
> —Hawai'i breeder

But what if you still can't find the pet of your dreams? Easy, you might say. I'll just go to the Internet and locate a breeder in England, New Zealand or Australia. Those countries have strict rabies laws and imported pets don't have to endure Hawai'i's strict quarantine.

But, don't do that. Do not go to the Internet and mail order a pet from some foreign country, advises a kennel club president. The problem with out of country sources, she maintains, is that "they sometimes unload their junk on us. Think about it. If you were going to send (a dog) away to a far-off country, would you send your best? Not likely."

Buyers have experienced problems with dogs purchased sight unseen, parents unknown, from foreign countries.

"There have been lawsuits over hip problems in large dogs. Down under and in some countries they are just not as concerned about some health issues as we are here," she says.

Buying from mainland breeders is a bit safer, but Hawai'i's quarantine law presents unique problems. The process of qualifying for quarantine takes several months. By the time a dog or cat can enter Hawai'i he is nearly a year old. "So you've got this (pet) on your hands you've never met before and he's already almost grown and if there are problems, it's too late to do much about it," the breeder points out.

Her suggestion: Find a breeder in *Dog Fancy* or *Cat Fancy* magazine, or go on the Internet if you want to. But before you buy, travel to the country where the pet is located and see what you are buying. And have the pet checked by a veterinarian before you purchase it.

fetch
more information
Naming your new pet? See page 327 of the Resource section for suggestions.

Care and Feeding

3

Deborah Booker photo courtesy of *The Honolulu Advertiser*

Washing, brushing, feeding and spoiling your poi dog and cat.

Sultan, a "labradoodle" guide dog, "nose" what he wants as he takes owner Patricia Blum shopping at the Manoa Safeway. Guide dogs are exempted from state laws that forbid dogs in restaurants, markets and other places where food is sold.

Your pet's plate lunch

We pet lovers get a lot of conflicting information about feeding our pets: advertisements, magazines, books, materials from pet organizations. For every article that says it is important to feed expensive pet foods, there is an article that says all pet foods have to meet certain standards and so all are safe and healthy to feed. But, it's not that easy.

> **Half of Hawai`i's dogs are overweight,** estimates one O'ahu veterinarian. And nothing shortens your dog's life like being fat.
>
> "Keep your dog as lean as possible," he advises. "I like to (see) older dogs almost skinny. A thin dog should live a longer life and is less likely to suffer diabetes and arthritis."

Your pet's dietary needs are based on how much exercise he or she gets, so they will depend on whether your pet lives primarily indoors or outdoors. Obviously, a pet confined in one of Honolulu's high-rises should eat less food than a similar sized pet that lives, for example, on a ranch in Kaua`i and has the run of the land.

What kind of food? What's "fixed formula"?

Job Michael Evans in *The Evans Guide for Civilized City Canines* comments:

"Canned foods are not a good sole ration for your dog… They are 50 to 78 percent water… You are paying meat prices for water. The greasiness of some canned foods makes them the equivalent of a laxative for dogs. These foods are loaded with sodium nitrite (salt)… High levels of sodium nitrite have been correlated with behavior problems, especially oral ones such as over-barking…"

He explains something we should all know: the difference between non-fixed formula dry foods (the less expensive major brands) and fixed formula dry or "specialty" (expensive) foods.

- **Non-fixed formula foods** are the brand names we are all familiar with in markets. They can be prepared from a variety of ingredients bought on the commodities market at the cheapest market price. The main ingredient of these, Evans says, "will be soy, wheat feed flour, wheamiddlins or corn gluten." These protein sources may provide inferior protein to your pet, he maintains, and to eat enough to get the amount of nourishment he needs, a dog would have to eat so much it

fetch
more information
For complete lists of Hawai'i's pet stores, see the Resource section, pages 310 to 313.

could make him overweight.

Non-fixed formula food can present a problem, Evans maintains. The dog must eat more, and therefore will defecate more often and have looser stools. That could be a real problem if you live in one of Hawai'i's many apartments.

- **Fixed formula** means the ingredients are always the same, no matter which commodities are cheaper. Evans recommends these more expensive dry fixed-formula brands which usually must be purchased from a pet store or a veterinarian. And he recommends feeding your pet twice a day, morning and early evening.

The University of California's Davis School of Veterinary Medicine seems to disagree. Its *Book of Dogs* says of the fixed formula debate: "Some dogs are exquisitely sensitive to variations between batches and may develop a mild stomach upset when fed a new batch. In such cases, choosing a fixed-formula brand is preferable. For the majority of dogs, however, minor variations in diet have relatively little impact."

How much food?

Throughout the nation, it is becoming increasingly common to hear of dogs and, to a lesser extent, cats, suffering from an illness that especially plagues people in

Tip
Keep ants out of your pets' food and water

Your pet needs water all day long, and in Hawai'i's warm weather, he needs plenty of it. Unfortunately, Hawai'i's millions of ants also require food and water, and they will invade your pet's dish, whether it's outdoors or in. Here is a very simple solution. Plantation workers used to put cans of water under table and bed legs to discourage creatures (like centipedes and scorpions) from climbing up. Apply that method to your pet's water and food dishes. Put a small or medium-sized pet dish inside a slightly larger bowl and fill the outer bowl half-full with water. Ants line up in neat little rows to drink water from the outer bowl but don't attempt to reach the inner bowl, leaving it clean for your pet. A variety of pet drinking fountains is also available through catalogs.

A customized treat for your pet

(and a great gift for pet-loving friends)

Food is expensive in Hawai'i, especially pet toys and treats. Whip up your own customized pet biscuits. This easy recipe from the Maui Humane Society makes a tin full of crunchy treats that are both healthful and economical.

You can shape the dough into bones or balls. Or roll the dough to about one-half inch thick and use a cookie cutter to make trees, bells, stars and other holiday shapes. Put some in a pretty container and wrap with a bow as thoughtful gifts for pet-loving friends.

And silly as it sounds, *you* can also eat these biscuits, slightly reminiscent of shredded wheat. What a hoot for your pooch to share his food with you instead of the other way around.

Be sure to cool these biscuits thoroughly before giving to your pet...and don't overfeed.

Be sure to refrigerate too; since no preservatives are used, these cookies don't keep as well as purchased treats.

Ingredients:
1 cup flour
3 cups uncooked oats (You may use the quick cook version, but uncooked oats make the biscuit crunchier and more satisfying).
1 cup chicken, beef or vegetable broth
1/4 cup vegetable or canola oil

Method: Mix oats and flour thoroughly. Using a fork or your fingers, knead in the broth and oil.

Shaping: Depending on your pet's size, you can use your hands to shape these into large or small balls, disks, or fancy figures like bones or people.

It's fun to shape these treats like bones or balls, but your pet will like them just as well cut in simple slices.

Baking: Bake the biscuits on cookie sheet in a 325-degree oven.
The size of your biscuit determines baking times. For flattened, teaspoonful-sized biscuits, about 25 minutes. Round balls, 35 minutes. Biscuits should be set and slightly brown around the edges. If you form balls, be sure they are baked through; partially cooked biscuits don't keep well.

Hawai'i: diabetes. Like people, animals can carry diabetes genetically, but many cases are the result of the pet being overweight and inactive.

Cats are independent creatures. If your cat goes outdoors, she will decide her own exercise pattern. If she is an adult indoor cat, you should pay attention to how much she plays and how much exercise she gets. If she is overweight and sedentary, you may feed her about 10 to 20 percent less than the amount of food recommended on pet food labels. But be sure to discuss this with your cat's veterinarian first.

"How much exercise?"

Few dogs in Hawai'i have the space to determine their own exercise pattern, so it is up you and your schedule to decide how much exercise your pet will receive. You should adjust its diet—less food for less exercise and vice-versa—so it doesn't become overweight. Most superior brands of dog food carry labels recommending the amount of food per pound of pet's weight. If there is a good reason why you can't exercise your dog for a few days (for example if you are ill or if you are gone), you can temporarily adjust the amount of food you give by as much as 10 percent less for a small dog and as much as 20 percent less for a large dog. (Again, discuss this with your vet first.)

Be sure not to cut back on exercise for an extended length of time; it's much healthier to exercise your dog and feed the recommended amount. Exercise is vital for even a small dog's bones, muscle tone and general well-being.

The older dog

As your pet grows older, she or he will probably become less active and require fewer calories. You can slowly cut his food intake over several months until he is getting about 70 percent of the amount he ate in his middle age. Or, if he enjoys eating and you don't want to cut the actual amount, consider low-fat pet foods designed for older pets.

The pet food "Catch 22"

Don't let your pet choose its food, a Hawai'i veterinarian advises. Your pet, like most pets, will probably choose the food that is loaded with fat and salt, "which makes them taste better, so the pet will choose them."

Aside from adding calories and salt to the pet's diet, such tasty food can become a "Catch 22."

"The pet likes the taste so much, he gobbles the food," explains the vet. "So you think 'Oh, he's really hungry!' and you feed him more fatty, salty food."

Compare labels, compare sodium and fat contents.

Cats versus dogs

Dietary needs vary greatly for dogs and cats; cats should not be fed a diet of strictly dog food and vice-versa. Cats require twice as much protein and B vitamins as dogs do, some specialists say. They also cannot digest some of the ingredients in dog foods. And dogs may grow fat on the richer cat food diets.

Cats are notoriously finicky eaters. In the *Cat Owner's Home Veterinary Handbook*, Delbert G. Carlson, D.V.M. and James M. Giffin, M.D. recommend introducing your cat to various kinds of prepared cat foods before she is 6 months old and then settling on two or three nutritionally complete rations and sticking with them. They warn against offering treats or meats because the cat will reject the nutritionally sound cat food for such tidbits.

Tip

With our warm weather and insect problems, it's best to give your pet his food at specific times of day and only in amounts that he will eat immediately. Don't ever leave wet or semi-moist food out for more than 15 minutes or so. It will spoil quickly in tropical weather. And even dry pet food attracts ants quickly indoors or out.

In *Ask The Vet*, author Dawn Curie Thomas, D.V.M. recommends feeding cats only high quality, balanced, all-natural cat foods, either canned, kibble or both, and also giving a food vitamin supplement.

So you're a vegetarian

If you are a vegetarian, as many people in Hawai`i are, you may find it unpleasant to serve meat or meat-based products to your pets. The consensus seems to be that your dog can get a well-balanced diet by eating legumes and protein-rich vegetables, the same foods you eat. However, cats require much more protein and calcium and you should not attempt to feed felines vegetarian diets. Again, discuss this with your veterinarian. Whatever your decision, if your cat goes outside she will probably supplement her diet with captured protein.

Home-prepared meals

Several of the more than 200 pet owners we interviewed for this book were feeding their pets well-balanced home prepared meals instead of commercially processed pet foods.

"There's no secret recipe," said one owner who has been home-preparing meals for her two dogs for several years.

"You prepare well-balanced meals for your family—meat or fish and vegetables and some high quality bread or grain and you cut up extra for the pets. If they won't eat the vegetables, you grind it all together or keep increasing the amount of vegetables until they are getting a good amount and a variety."

Several books on holistic healthcare and preparing your pet's food are available at book stores, Hawai`i libraries and via Amazon.com.

Wise feeding suggestions from a variety of sources:

- **Treats**, including table scraps and human snacks, should not exceed 10 percent of your pet's total daily food, even if you are reducing their food supply or increasing their activity to make up for the extra calories. The reason? Pets need certain nutrients the snacks may not provide.

- **Animals prefer their food served at room temperature**. If you are serving a refrigerated food, put it into the microwave for about 20 to 30 seconds (no more) before serving, then let it sit for five minutes after removing from the microwave. In Hawai`i, it isn't wise to let food sit out on a counter longer than that—ants may devour it and heat can quickly spoil it.

- **Meat and fish should never be served raw**. They can contain bacteria and other nasty things that spread disease.

- **Keep your pet from eating any food it finds in parks or on walks**. The food can be spoiled or poisoned. See paraquat poisonings in the Protecting Your Pet chapter of this book.

- **Put your pet's food dish in a quiet corner of the kitchen**, where the pet can eat in peace and is less likely to bolt down his food. Feeding a pet outdoors is not a good idea unless your pet devours the food and you remove the dish immediately. Food and dirty food dishes attract flies and ants.

- **Switching foods** on a finicky eater? Try this: decrease the old favorite food by 20 percent and mix with 20 percent new food. Increase the ratio of new food by 20 percent per day until the pet is eating only the new food.

A peanut butter cookie for your pet

Most dogs love peanuts, but they just don't have the teeth to grind them well and nuts can upset their stomachs. Here, from the *Community Clinic of Maui Cookbook*, is a very healthy snack your dog should really sink his teeth into. B.J. Ott, chief financial officer and deputy director of the clinic, says she uses a cookie cutter to create appropriate shapes and gives these as Christmas gifts to pet-loving friends. Notice the wholesome ingredients and lack of sugar.

PEANUT BUTTER DOG BISCUITS
4 cups whole wheat flour
1 cup rolled oats
1 cup unsalted peanut butter
1/2 cup unsweetened applesauce
1 egg
1 tsp. vanilla
1 ounce water

Preheat oven to 350 degrees.
Combine all ingredients.
Mix by hand until dough forms a ball. Roll to desired thickness (1/4 inch for small dogs; 1/2 inch for large dogs). Cut into squares or use cookie cutters for shapes. Bake for 45 minutes or until brown.
After testing this recipe, we recommend 30 minutes for the thinner shapes; 45 for the thicker. You may also want to add a little extra water to make the dough more pliable.

Tip: Small dogs may have trouble chewing or digesting crunchy peanut butter with large nut chunks. It's best to use smooth, non-chunky peanut butter for all dogs.

Mike Sidney Photo

What about pig ears?
and snouts... and things?

I don't know a dog who doesn't like pig ears, the crunchy brown treat that looks and smells so disgusting to humans. My dogs' eyes light up with excitement at the sight of the pig ear package; their tails start thumping. Several years ago, I used pig ears to train Archie, my part-Airedale mutt. He still drops to the "down" position as soon as I reach for the pig ear package, beating me to the command.

Pig ears are sort of the french fries of the dog world: crunchy and fatty. They are "loaded with fat and calories which can cause obesity, loose stools, heart disease and other health problems," says an advertisement for a commercial pig ear substitute. But a lot of other foods cause those problems too.

Meanwhile, "Keep your paws off your dog's chew treats," advises an item in *The Honolulu Advertiser* (February 11, 2002). "Those pigs' ears and cows' hooves can carry salmonella. Buy chews already packaged, not in bulk. At home, keep them away from food preparation areas. And be sure to wash your hands after touching them."

As if that weren't scary enough, some pig ear packages carry a warning to wash your hands after handling the package. Let me think about this. I'm suppose to wash my hands after handling a pig ear, but my dog can safely ingest it?

The veterinarian who treats my dogs is usually a very definite-type person, but she skirts the pig ear issue. She shakes her head and gazes fondly at Betty, my blonde mixed terrier. "Yes, pig ears are fattening," she says. "But... dogs sure love them."

Another vet suggests a substitute: a soft, odorless rawhide strip that looks something like a mocassin. My dogs took this with the enthusiasm of a kid who's been given a spinach-flavored lollipop.

> ## Tip
>
> Hawai`i's abundant ants love pig ears too. Once you've opened the pack, keep it in the refrigerator or in a tightly sealed container. And make sure your dog doesn't stash the ear away for later under the bed or in your laundry basket.

I solved the problem this way: I limit the pig ear treats to once every two or three weeks. On the day the dogs have pig ears, I let them run in the park an extra ten minutes; then I cut back their supper to about two-thirds of its usual portion. This satisfies all of us. I don't worry that the dogs will gain weight and they seem very happy to have less food if it means chewing on a crusty ear.

Dental care:
It's difficult, but important

Listen to this statistic: 80 percent of dogs and 70 percent of cats show signs of oral disease by the time they are 3 years old, according to the American Veterinary Medical Association. The AVMA, along with many humane societies, urge you to brush your pet's teeth regularly and seek dental care when necessary. Yet, many pet owners seem to draw the line at brushing their pets' teeth. It is just so difficult to do.

If you are not brushing your pet's teeth regularly now, or providing any kind of tooth care, at least do this. Gently pull back his gums and check the teeth near the back of his mouth. You may be shocked by what you find. Symptoms of oral disease in a pet include yellow and brown tartar on the teeth, with buildup along the gum line. You may have already noticed red, inflamed gums and/or persistent bad breath.

> Many pet owners draw the line at brushing their pets' teeth. It is just so difficult to do.

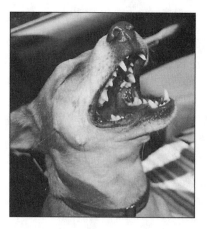

The bacteria that lurk in your pet's mouth can cause health concerns more serious than bad breath or even tooth loss, says an Hawaiian Humane Society article in *The Honolulu Advertiser*. An infection caused by periodontal disease may enter the bloodstream, with potential for infecting the heart, liver and kidneys.

"Caring for your pet's teeth is not silly or vain," Eric Ako, a veterinarian at The Pet Doctor in Honolulu, says in the article. "Neglected mouths harbor harmful bacteria that can eat away at gums and the jawbone, and shower infection on major organs such as the heart, liver and kidneys. As the caretaker of your animal, you are responsible for preventing this infection."

Treats and crunchy foods don't necessarily do the trick. Sue Sylvester-Palumbo, a veterinarian at Honolulu's The Cat Clinic, says in the same article. "Only brushing removes plaque at the gum line… It may take a while for (pets) to get used to brushing, but the results are worth the effort."

If you are going to brush your pet's teeth, begin as early as possible. It's easier to teach a young dog, or cat, new tricks. If you are teaching an older pet to accept brushing, stay with it, don't give up. Eventually your pet will appreciate the attention. At one of Honolulu's pet playgrounds, I met a woman who brushes her two cats' teeth regularly. She started when they were kittens and says the kittens seemed to think it was part of a game. Now, as adults, they don't balk at all when she brushes. Meanwhile, a pet owner who began brushing her collie's teeth when he was 4 years old offers this advice.

A good time to brush might be right after this dog consumes his birthday cake.

- Introduce your pet to his toothpaste first. Your veterinarian or pet store sells toothpaste that is safe to swallow, in flavors your pet will like, like chicken and peanut butter. Put a little of the paste on your finger and let the pet lick it off. Then put a dab on the brush and let him lick it from there.

- Introduce the paste-filled brush to the pet's mouth by very gently pulling back his lips and brushing just as much as he will tolerate. Let him lick the paste off his teeth.

- Attempt the tooth brushing every day, or even twice a day, for several days, and don't miss a day. You may not accomplish much real brushing in the first few attempts, but you should find yourself advancing a little each time. At some point, you will be encouraging your pet to open its jaw by pressing gently on the sides of the mouth near the jaw line. When you accomplish this, and the toothbrush isn't bitten in half, you're successful, the pet owner quips.

- Choose a relaxed part of your pet's day, perhaps after you've massaged or brushed him. And after your pet becomes accustomed to tooth brushing, make sure it is part of his routine, at the same time every day.

- If your pet balks at the sight of an actual toothbrush, try the more gentle fingertip type of "toothbrush" available at pet stores. A slightly nubby plastic fits over the tip of your finger.

Your veterinarian will also have helpful advice.

(Portions from Dental care vital to a healthier and happier life for your pets, *The Honolulu Advertiser*, February 10, 2002.)

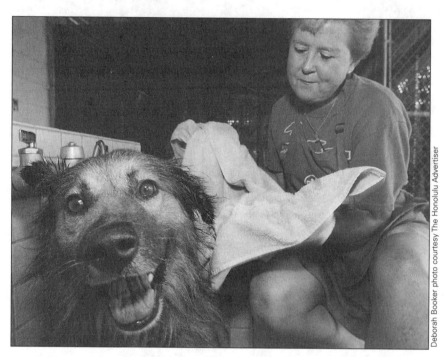

Jake, a Shepherd/Spitz mix, gets a towel rub down by volunteer Jean Fortner after a bath at O'ahu's Hawaiian Humane Society.

Deborah Booker photo courtesy The Honolulu Advertiser

Hair grows faster in warm weather, but how cool is a clipping?

Does pet hair grow faster in warm weather? Some studies say yes. But unless your pet has very long or thick fur, it may not be necessary to clip it at all. Long fur insulates your pet against heat as well as cold. Check with your vet before deciding on regular clipping. However, whether your pet is a dog or a cat, longhaired or short, he or she should be brushed daily. Daily brushing has many advantages. It cuts down on the amount of loose hair and hairballs floating around your home. It lets you familiarize yourself with your pet's body so you can ascertain if anything unusual is happening, and it also helps you bond with your pet.

Grooming tips for island pets

- Start regular grooming early, while your pet is young, so he or she becomes accustomed to grooming and learns to enjoy it. A young dog or cat will let you trim its nails; an older one who is unaccustomed to the function may balk.

- Make it fun. Keep your pet's brush and grooming accessories near your favorite chair, within easy reach when you are relaxing. Let the grooming provide a relaxing time for both of you.

- Groom your pet daily, using a brush with bristles stiff enough to reach through the fur. Your goal is to brush away loose hair, especially important for a cat, which ingests hair while grooming itself. At the same time, you'll be massaging your pet's skin and increasing blood circulation, especially important with indoor pets.

- As you groom, feel between your pet's toes, under its legs, and in the dense fur behind the ears, hidden places where ticks, so prevalent in Hawai'i, can lurk.

- Remember, you don't have to perform a complete grooming routine every day—just brush your pet for a few minutes if that's all you have time for. But you should thoroughly brush, clean and inspect your pet at least twice a week.

- Use a warm, damp cloth to clean your pet's ears and wipe around his eyes. Is there a heavy, stiff "tear" build-up? Could your pet have a head cold that you've failed to notice?

fetch
more information
For complete lists of groomers, see the Resource section, pages 307 to 310.

Tip

Go easy on the baths.
Skin irritation, itching and scratching can result from bathing your pet too often, eliminating his natural oils. Most cats keep themselves clean. And, depending on breed and activity, your dog may need to be bathed only once or twice a month. Check with your vet as to if and how often your pet needs a bath. If your dog swims in the ocean, rinse him afterwards in cool, clear water to remove ocean salt.

This pup, found on the Big Island, doesn't seem happy about his bath.

- Check your pet's anus. Use a warm damp cloth to clean. Watch for loose stools or any signs of worms. If your pet is especially furry, you may want to trim slightly around the anus to keep that area clean. Clip with a sharp thin scissors; don't attempt to shave.

- Wrap up the session with a relaxing massage. Work your fingers into the fur so that you are massaging your pet's skin. You can gently stimulate blood circulation throughout your pet's body this way. (Don't you wish someone would do this for you?)

- Nails also grow quickly in Hawai'i's warm, humid weather. Be sure to clip your pet's nails often or make a standing appointment with a groomer or veterinarian. Also, watch for special times when your local humane society or a pet store offers the service at special low rates.

- If you decide to clip your pet's hair regularly, consider learning to clip your pet yourself. Many helpful videos are available to show you how to clip and professional tools can be purchased from a pet store or catalog. Opt for cutting too little, rather than too much. And, if you are disappointed in your first attempts, be consoled in knowing that the pet's hair will quickly grow out.

- Shave? Some pet owners shave their dogs using electric pet grooming appliances. Check with your vet before doing this. And remember that exposed skin can get sunburned.

O'ahu's pampered pets can take a taxi, get a massage, eat surf-dog sushi, and even get married...

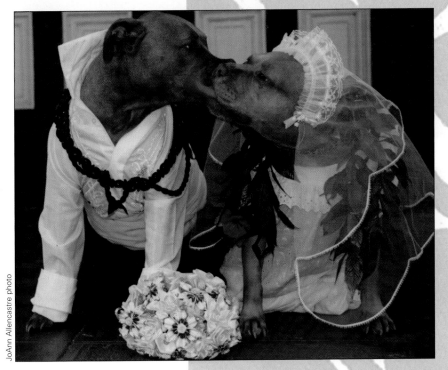

JoAnn Allencastre photo

Rocky and Simba are so fond of each other, their owners let them marry.

Tip

Want your pet to "kiss" for a photo? Spread a little jam or peanut butter on your cheek.

As our traditional family changes—more people opting to be childless, grandparents an ocean away from grandchildren—pets are increasingly important in our lives. Our canine and feline "children" are ever loyal and faithful, always loving, never bored or petulant. And they never "talk back" to their parents. They may sometimes be yippy, but they are never lippy.

More and more, we tend to coddle our pets, showering them with the luxuries we humans enjoy. Their country cousins on Hawai'i's neighbor islands may find luxuries limited, but O'ahu's pampered pets have plenty of extravagant pleasures right at their pawtips. And, being animals, they never feel guilty about their indulgences.

Our little darlings may not understand why we are transporting

Continued on page 60

Three friends enjoy a birthday party at Dino's Doggie Deli and Bakery at Pets Etc. in Kailua where a sign on the wall warns that the booth is for pets only.

them across the island for a puppy massage, but they enjoy the trip and the human contact. They may not quite understand the concept of a dog bakery, but the food tastes good anyway.

On Oʻahu, pets can dine on lavish treats like Surfdog Sushi at the Hawaiʻi Doggie Bakery, Peanut Butter Pooch Pie at Dino's Doggie Deli and Bakery or Corgi Cones at Purr-fect Paws.

Dog or cat, they can enjoy a perfumey full-body massage or a manicure at The Yuppie Puppy and wind up their day on the town with an aloha shirt from Waggin' Tail Pet Boutique or a *muʻu muʻu* from Purr-fect Paws.

If mummy or daddy has to leave precious kitty for a few days, a pet taxi will transport the little darling to Cozy Cat Lodge, where kitty has a choice between condo or suite with garden views and, just to keep tiny minds constructively occupied, in-room aquariums, sort of a kitty version of television.

"The pets that come here are children," says Jan Schmidt, who with her husband Bill turned their home into the Cozy Cat Lodge. "They're already pampered at home. They come here because they want the very best."

It's a tradition in Hawaiʻi to celebrate a child's first birthday with a big *luau*. Taryn Bundalian told *The Honolulu Advertiser* she honored her silky terrier, Kala, with a first-birthday bash at Thomas Square in downtown Honolulu. Festivities included a *piñata*, a birthday cake, and goodie bags for 13 doggie friends.

Lucille Niemitz hugs the community dog, Puna, a Lab-Samoyed, at Ponds at Punalu`u assisted living care center in windward O`ahu. Medical research cites the healthy effects of having pets. People with pets live longer and, we are sure, happier lives.
The O`ahu humane society's "Seniors for Seniors" program matches calm, housetrained senior dogs with senior people. Senior pet lovers can adopt one dog or one or two cats, age 6 or older, without charge. All adopted animals are sterilized, vaccinated, have a microchip ID and a health checkup.

Nowadays, pets can even marry or at least formally consumate their love. Rev. Kermit Rydell of Honolulu will perform a customized ceremony.

Take your dog to day care?

You went shopping Saturday and bought yourself a cute new puppy. It's Monday morning and reality sets in. You're due at work in an hour and you've got this little furry baby on your hands. It needs to be fed three times a day and urinates at least five times a day, and... so what do you do?

You take it to puppy day care, of course. Lilith Samson cares for puppies at Purr-fect Paws, her sister's Kailua pet boutique and bakery. Samson, already baking pet treats at the store, came up with the idea by necessity. When her boxer rejected one of nine pups in her litter, Samson had to feed and care for the unwanted pup. Her sister suggested she bring it to work—and a day care nursery was born.

Purr-fect Paws also holds two weekly events for dogs and their owners. Friday's Yappy Hour from 5 to 8 p.m. includes free treats for pets and complimentary coffee for the canine's companion. Saturday's LaPooche Parties focus on one breed at a time. A calendar sent to clients details dates for specific breeds.

Places to pamper pets

Cozy Cat Lodge
1532 Ulupi'i Street,
Olomana, O'ahu
(808) 261-1101
cozycatlodge@verizon.net

Dino's Doggie Deli and Bakery
26 Ho'olai Street
Kailua, O'ahu
(808) 263-2255

Hawai'i Doggie Bakery and Gift Shop
2038 S. King Street, Honolulu
(808) 949-DOGS

Purr-fect Paws
417 Ku'ulei Road
Kailua, O'ahu
(808) 262-4896

Waggin' Tail Pet Boutique
1365 Nu'uanu Avenue, Suite 3
Honolulu
(808) 585-8823.
waggintailhawaii@yahoo.com

The Yuppie Puppie Grooming Salon
Salt Lake Shopping Center
Salt Lake, O'ahu
(808) 839-1158

Ceremonial Services for Pets
Weddings, adoptions, birthdays, breeding, anniversaries, memorials, funerals.
Rev. Kermit Rydell
(808) 227-0150
WaikikiCentral.com

Also see Businesses in the Resources section at the back of this book.

Living with Your Pet

4

Our pets bring so much joy and peace to our lives. Here's how to make the relationship even better.

Honolulu resident Dick Jensen keeps a close eye on Galaxy, a West Highland Terrier. Jensen is carrying a Stool Tool, a device he designed to catch a dog's feces before it hits the ground, thereby keeping parks and playgrounds cleaner, he says.

Waikiki condo dog howls at sirens
What can his owner do?

As a kid growing up in Canada, Dave always owned several dogs. So when he bought a top floor apartment at Canal House, a Waikiki condominium building, he made sure large pets were allowed. He quickly acquired a beautiful male Dalmatian and named him Kimo.

However, Dave soon learned that he had acquired more than a companion; he had also bought himself a problem. Every time Kimo heard a siren test, he barked. And since sirens are as common in Waikiki as aloha shirts—police sirens, fire sirens, monthly tsunami sirens—Kimo had plenty of opportunity to vent his frustration.

Dave's neighbors were patient and never complained about Kimo, but Dave was apprehensive and concerned. Dave had his own fledgling business and it kept him away from the apartment long hours. Could Kimo be lonely? Was Kimo, a highly spirited dog, too confined in a Waikiki apartment?

And then there was the bark itself.

"It was more than a bark," Dave remembered. "It was almost a whine," as if the siren hurt Kimo's ears.

After much consternation, Dave gave Kimo to a friend on the rural windward side of O`ahu, where the dog had more room to run and full-time companionship from a family.

Although Dave's solution was a decent one, removing the dog from his home might have been avoided if he had tried some other methods to curb the barking.

Kimo was just communicating

First, dog behaviorists say, we need to realize and admit that barking is normal and healthy for all dogs. It's one of the prime ways dogs communicate, and it would be unkind to try to shut a dog up entirely. But what could Dave have done to discourage Kimo from barking every time he heard a siren?

Spend more time with him. Although Dave had to be absent much of each day, there might have been ways to keep Kimo with him. Since Dave had his own office, he might have trained Kimo to sit quietly as he worked or to accompany him on some of his around-town business jaunts. While a dog on the job may raise eyebrows on the mainland, in laid-back Hawai`i it hardly warrants a blink.

Try training classes. Professional dog training classes and plenty of practice with the dog might have taught him the manners he needed to be incorporated more successfully into Dave's life.

Behavior modification. Hawai`i dog "shrink" Kinee Hanson has other practical solutions. Hanson uses behavior modification methods on dogs to overcome canine problems such as biting, barking and bed-wetting.

"There are a lot of different routes this owner could go," she said.

- **Pennies in a can.** Put several pennies in a tin can and seal it. When the dog begins to bark, throw the can on the floor next to the dog. It will divert the dog's attention away from the improper behavior, says Hanson. "The dog doesn't like this and eventually it makes the connection. It says, 'Wait a minute. Every time I bark, this thing happens that I don't like.' So he stops."

- **The wet surprise.** Use water instead of pennies. Some pet behaviorists suggest filling clean cans half full of water and tossing the water at

"What? Me? Disobey? Never!" Archie says. "Well, not unless I spot a cat across the street."

your pet when it behaves inappropriately. If this seems extreme, not to mention damaging to carpets and furniture, use a squirt bottle. This method is particularly effective on cats since most of them dislike water. The key, of course, is to repeat these negative reinforcement methods every time your animal misbehaves.

Unfortunately, to be effective both the tin can technique and the water surprise require constant and consistent repetition. It requires you be home, ready to spring the surprise. That's difficult for busy people like Dave. There are more extreme means.

- **Bark collars.** Dog behaviorist Hanson also recommends bark collars. Like the "wet surprise," these dog collars are based on negative reinforcement. When the dog barks, a low, harmless dose of something unpleasant—sound, odor, or electric shock—is delivered via the collar.

  Electric shock. One kind of collar delivers a low-voltage electric shock, "not more than a vibration, really," Hanson says. Some collars automatically adjust to the dog's temperament, delivering a slightly stronger vibration each time until the dog learns to stop barking.

  Citronella. Some pet owners have had success with a dog collar that emits a harmless spray of citronella when a dog barks inappropriately. Citronella collars are available at the O'ahu's Hawaiian Humane Society supply shop, by mail order and at some pet shops.

A last resort: surgery. There are more radical, and definite, methods of controlling barking. Hanson describes a miniature poodle she adopted from a family who could not put up with the dog's nervous barking.

"She had already lost one home and I didn't want to give her up," so when her neighbors began to complain, Hanson contacted the University of California's Davis School of Veterinary Science and investigated having the poodle "surgically debarked." The simple operation is used on 50 percent of show dogs, Hanson says. Her poodle's loud bark was reduced to a quiet level that allowed her to keep the pet...and her apartment.

When a pet has a real problem, it's up to you to decide just how far to go to correct it.

The head collar

Training your dog to walk pleasantly on a leash without pulling can be an irksome chore. The head collar can make the job easier, say some Hawai`i pet owners and trainers.

The brand we tried, Gentle Leader, is one of several at island pet stores. It is marketed as "The 10 Minute Attitude Adjuster," and that pretty much sums up what it is designed to do: make your dog focus and pay attention to your commands.

Head collars look tortuous, like something between a muzzle and a choke chain, but the soft strap is more gentle than a metal chain. The head collar straps fit across the top of the dog's nose, under his jaw and rather tightly around his neck. The trainer (you) holds the leash firmly and walks with the dog in the heel position. If the dog lunges or pulls on his leash, the head collar gently pulls the dog's head toward the trainer. As soon as the dog stops pulling or lunging, the annoying tension is eased. You reward him with praise and/or a treat.

The head collar looks like a tool of torture, but it gently coerces a pet to pay attention and heel property.

In an unofficial test run, my dog Archie hated the collar. Rubbing his head against a tree, he succeeded in getting out of it. However, once we began walking, he quickly adjusted and did indeed walk without pulling. If walking your dogs is a chore, you may want to try a head collar.

My dog gets mad
when I leave for work;
then he gets even

Toby, a 2-year-old Lhasa Apso, became very anxious when his owner Tammy Kaku left their Manoa home. Even pepper sprinkled on the wall and wood-work didn't stop his clawing and chewing, so Toby occasionally gets a doggy anti-depressant to calm him.

Deborah Booker photo courtesy of *The Honolulu Advertiser*

You're off to work, leaving your dog Koa in your apartment, alone. He doesn't like it and he lets you know it by whining and barking at the door. Now, suddenly, he's up to a new trick. He goes to the wastebasket, pulls out a sticky napkin, takes it to your bed (where he's not supposed to be) and shreds it into wet little pieces. It's as if he's trying to tell you he's mad at you for leaving him, and is trying to get even.

You're right about his not wanting you to leave, but he's not being spiteful, says dog behaviorist Kinee Hanson.

"Dogs don't have the mentality for spite," she says. "Revenge can't even occur to them. Dogs aren't that complicated; they don't react emotionally. People react emotionally."

Here are some techniques, in thinking and acting, that you can try:

- **Think (or don't think) like a dog**

  Dogs simply exhibit stress, uncomfortable feelings when their routine is broken or when they are separated from their pack, which is you. If you want to break your dog of bad habits, Kinee Hanson suggests, "stop acting like a human being with your dog and use what I call *dogese*. That is, think and act like a dog. Think and act simply."

  That incident with the dog Koa actually happened to Hanson. How did she solve it? By trying simple solutions first. She put the wastebasket up out of his reach. She closed the door to her bedroom, hoping to break the destructive pattern before it became a habit.

  "Most destructiveness happens when the dog is feeling most stressed," she says, "in the first 30 minutes after the owner leaves. After that, the dog settles down and does what most dogs do all day: sleep."

- **The knuckle bone solution**

  The simple solution worked, but if it had not, Hanson would have gone on to another method she used with a different large dog. She kept a huge knuckle bone in the freezer. When she was leaving for work she made a big production of pulling the bone out of the freezer, showing it to the dog and leading him to a large crate/kennel, where the dog was allowed to chew and sleep all day.

  When she came home from work, while greeting the dog happily, Hanson took the bone away and returned it to the freezer.

  "He began to associate my leaving with something good: getting a treat. At that point, the dog could care less that I'm leaving."

  It's also smart to leave a radio on tuned to a news or talk station, so the dog will hear a human voice and feel less alone.

> **Tip**
>
> If you want to make your exits less stressful for your pet, keep your exits and returns as low key as possible. Say goodbye quietly and leave with no apologies or sorrowful goodbyes. When you return, say hello simply and softly to your pet. Keep the anxiety level low.

  "Give the dog something special to focus on," she suggests, and he'll react less to your leaving. Eventually it will become part of his pattern and he won't mind.

  "Does it take place overnight?" Hanson asks. "No. No behavior modification does. But the point is, it works."

Teach your pets to be good neighbors

A few words can make life happier and safer

On our small, crowded islands, most pet owners and their pets live either in condominiums (apartments with thin walls dividing us from our noisy neighbors) or in houses with small yards in which bedroom windows are just a whine away from our neighbors. It is very important that you teach your dog good manners, such as the appropriate time to bark, where to defecate, to walk on leash and to wait patiently for you. The better trained your pet is, the more the neighbors will appreciate him, the more he can accompany you and add to the joy of your life; and the safer he will be.

Your cat is safest kept inside your apartment or home. If she does go out, teach her to come when called and bring her in at night, when cats are usually noisiest and most active. Be sure your neighbors know your pet is neutered and nighttime caterwauling they may hear is not coming from your pet.

Reasonably priced training classes for your dog are available on most islands; your life and your dog's life will be more peaceful and happy if you both attend. You (and your spouse or housemate) are being trained as much as your dog. Once you learn the common dog commands and how to apply them to your pet, your job is to practice the commands with your dog over and over again, to reinforce them for the rest of the pet's life.

We won't discuss training techniques here because it is very important that you and your dog attend classes with a qualified trainer. The benefits will last a lifetime. Dog trainers say you can take your dog to classes as soon as it is fully vaccinated, at about 4 months of age. Puppy classes, good for socializing your pup to other dogs, can start when he is 8 weeks of age.

Fortunately, it is never too late to train your dog. Two of my dogs were adults, about 3 years of age, when I adopted them from the local humane society. They seemed to enjoy both the classes with other dogs and the extra personal attention from me as we practiced commands.

If professional classes are too expensive, borrow a book on training from a library, and rent or buy a video. Teach yourself the techniques and practice, practice, practice. Repeat. Repeat. Repeat, using simple commands and no extra words. Your life with your dog (and with your neighbors) will be much more pleasant if your dog responds to just these few simple commands:

- **Sit.** Your dog stops, sits and waits for you to tell him to get up. You'll need this command over and over again: on walks when you want to stop to talk to someone or wait for traffic, during mealtimes when he is anxious for the food you are preparing, and when he excitedly greets you or someone at the door.

- **Stay.** Your dog stops and remains in position until you tell him to get up. This command is both a convenienc—you want your dog to be polite and patient as you go about your business—and a safety precaution.

- **Come.** Nonchalantly. This is a simple statement, as in "Come on, we're leaving now," or "Come and eat, your food is ready."

- **Come, Archie!** With authority. It is absolutely essential that your dog know his name, or your signal, and respond immediately when called. You are not supposed to leave your dog off leash anywhere in Hawai'i except at Honolulu's two "bark parks." However, the truth is you will probably want to walk him on a beach or some undeveloped land. There are simply numerous times when you will need to call him, and he must know his name and respond to it.

- **No!** This all-inclusive command means "Don't do that!" and you'll automatically issue it (just as your dog has lifted its leg and is about to anoint your favorite stuffed chair; just as your cat is ready to pounce on your sleeping grandmother's twitching nose) with such resolve that your pet will obey. The ideal is to say this command in a

fetch
more information
For complete list of Hawai'i trainers visit the Resource section, pages 315 to 317.

Discourage cats *gently*

Is your cat bothering your neighbors? Try these solutions:
- **To discourage cats from digging in a garden,** bury a layer of small-gauge chicken wire under a light layer of dirt or mulch, or:
- **Plant a border** of marigolds, marjoram, rosemary or basil, scents cats don't appreciate, or:
- **Try mothballs** or a commercial pet deterent purchased at a pet or hardware store.
- **To keep cats off a lanai or fence,** scatter dry beans, macaroni or bird seed in metal pie tins and balance the tins on a lanai ledge or fence where they will easily tip. Cats dislike sudden and strange noises.

quiet, firm way that achieves the desired results.

- **Stop.** This is a command we did not learn in training class, but it's a very valuable one to teach your dog. Two of my three dogs respond immediately to "Stop!" issued in a tough tone of voice. It means "Halt right now." I use it when they are playing too roughly in the park, when they see a dog larger than themselves and want to run to it, when they are in any danger or when they are doing anything that might be dangerous to someone else. I don't use this often and I rarely speak in a rough or loud voice, so when I do holler "stop!" they know I mean business and they respond. Most of the time.

- **Ah! Ah!** Said loudly and without emotion, this means "don't," says Jocelyn Bouchard, who trained my dogs in classes at the Maui Humane Society. I relate this to dogs in a pack or a mother dog with puppies. All the mom (or leader) has to do is give the slightest warning growl to get the proper response from her litter. Pups will stop wrestling or back away from mom's food bowl or stop chewing her ear. When I use this command my dogs stop chasing the cat or withdraw from jumping on the couch. Usually.

After romping on a sandy beach, Miss Muffy doesn't appear as smart as she is. Since her owner spends time on both Maui and Kaua'i, Muffy wears dual dog tags.

Toni Polancy photo

- **Off.** "Off" means literally "Get off me, don't jump up." Or "Get off the couch. You aren't suppose to sit there." It is often confused with...

- **Down.** Ideally, it means a long stay in a prone, relaxed position. Tough to teach to people as well as their dogs, but handy if you want the dog to stay out of your way while you're busy. It's also useful if you want him to stop aggressive behavior or unwelcome behavior. A "long down" is the mark of a well-trained dog. Teach him a long down and your boss might let you bring the dog to the office occasionally.

- **Heel.** Heel is a much misunderstood command. It doesn't mean just "walk." It means walk exactly in pace with my left leg. It means, "No, you cannot sniff that utility pole. No, you cannot stop to talk to that other dog." It means your dog's total concentration is on walking, keeping pace with you and behaving the way you want him to. You'll train your dog to this by walking with him often (great fun in the islands where the walking weather is usually perfect) and using a short leash that keeps him in place as he walks.

  You may have to use a choke collar or a head collar that keeps the dogs head in position as he walks (see previous story) but just a short, taut leash usually works well. When he gets out of position, say "heel" and firmly but gently put him back into position. Walk with your pet daily and patiently repeat, repeat, repeat the "heel" procedure. Eventually you will be able to loosen your hold on the leash and the dog will remain in the heel position. A "well-heeled" dog will stop and sit when you stop walking.

Other "commands" your dog should know. Not necessary, but nice

Specialists who study such things say dogs are capable of learning the meaning to as many as 40 or so words, and even short phrases. My dogs don't know that many, but they do respond to a remarkable number of commands or, actually, suggestions.

- **Shi-shi.** To my dogs, this often-used local phrase for urinate means "It's time to go outdoors and eliminate." I utter those two words any time of day or night and my three dogs jump up, run out into the side yard and use a portion they have chosen as their bathroom area. I call them back in immediately, so shi-shi has come to mean "Go now, and come right back."

- **Clapping.** The light clapping of my hands is also a signal to the dogs to come into the house right now. At night a light clap is less disturbing to my neighbors than me bellowing the dogs' names.

- **Wait.** I like to think my dogs understand this command. For example, Betty just asked to go outdoors by whining softly at the door. I said, "Wait," meaning "Wait a few minutes until I finish this sentence and have time to let you out." Betty returned to her pillow resignedly. Truthfully, she may be interpreting this simply as "no."

- **"No"** followed by a word. My dogs seem to understand "No beach." They can be running from the park to the beach area and will stop and return at the "No beach" command. "No bark." They will stop barking when I say this, loudly. "No fight." My dogs tend to play in a wrestling, barking, snarling way that intimidates visitors. They will stop, reluctantly, at "No fight."

- **Park. Beach. Ride.** These are my dogs' three favorite words (probably because they do not know the words "steak", "hamburger" and "bones"). They associate "park," "beach" and "ride" with a good time and will run to the door leaping and dancing joyfully.

- **Stay home.** It may be the tone of my voice which says, "Sorry," but my dogs, who get excited when they see me don shoes or purse, understand they are not coming along. If I don't say "stay home" they bound happily for the door. If I say these two words, they hang back and sorrowfully, but silently, watch me leave.

- **Bad dog, good dog.** My pets hang their heads appropriately when I frown and growl "bad dog!" I sound upbeat and happy when I say "good dog!" and they like that. They wag their tails and, to my vivid imagination, seem to smile. It's a good idea to teach these two phrases before you attempt more complicated commands, so you'll have a way of showing praise or expressing displeasure.

- **Fetch or Go Get.** I've never been able to get my dogs, who don't seem to be particularly bright, to respond to either of these commands. However, my daughter's poodle/pomeranian mix proves the adage that poodles are smart. Miss Muffy will fetch whichever toy you ask for. "Go get doggy." "Go get ball." "Go get piggy."

Know thy neighbor

Half of my time is spent in an expensive haole (Caucasian) neighborhood on O'ahu, the other half in a middle income, culturally mixed neighborhood on Maui. In both locations, the situation is the same: houses literally stacked on top of each other. My neighbors' son's basketball throbs just a few feet from my door. I can hear their baby laugh, cry and even gurgle. They, in turn, listen to me calling my three dogs to go out. They hear the dogs bark briefly every time a strange dog passes the house.

It's a trade-off of the noises of life, and what makes it all bearable is that we know each other, at least a little. If I had a headache that required their son to cease the basketball bouncing, he would. I try to keep the dogs' barking to a minimum and remind my neighbors to let me know if the dogs bother them. Here are some methods for keeping peace in your neighborhood:

- **Knock on doors.** You may avoid a lot of problems, if you follow this tip from O'ahu's Hawaiian Humane Society: Take time to introduce yourself, and ask if the neighbors ever hear your dog barking. Your dog may be barking without your knowledge, when you leave or when he is lonely. Letting your neighbors know you are sensitive to their concerns will go a long way to making you and your pets welcome.

- **Complaints?** If you encounter any real animosity, back off, don't become angry or abusive. Make a sincere effort to correct problems, perhaps using some of the tactics in this book. If they don't work, talk to your veterinarian. He or she may recommend a trainer.

- **Compliments?** If you are a renter, jot down the date, name of neighbor (including phone number if you can get it), and document any praises your pet receives. This record may come in handy if you ever have a problem over your pet. At the least, when you are seeking another apartment or home, these compliments from neighbors are handy testimonials to your good pet care.

- **Try this.** I recently complained to tenants in the house next to mine that their late-night party kept me awake. The young women were polite and apologetic. The next day, they showed up at my door with a big bouquet of flowers. The gift had the required effect: impressing on me that they had the best intentions.

A few weeks later, I followed suit. Returning home from our evening walk, my two smaller dogs broke loose as I was unleashing them. A kind neighbor spent several hectic minutes helping me round them up. I took her an inexpensive present, with a note: "Mahalo for your kindness. I'll make sure the dogs don't get loose again."

Culturally mixed, packed too close, we *kama'aina* (longtime residents) know that being a peaceful pet owner in Hawai'i sometimes means an added dose of patience: a smile, a wave, a nod, a little *talk story*. Genuine caring. And lots of *aloha*.

The 'High-rise Syndrome' happens in low rises too

It's called the High-rise Syndrome, but on the neighbor island of Maui, the "syndrome" occurred not at a high-rise building, but a low-rise. His owner had put a leash on a puppy and secured the leash to a third-floor balcony rail. Then the owner left for work. The puppy wriggled between the rungs of the balcony, fell and died, hung by its own leash. Neighbors saw the incident and attempted to help, but the door to the apartment was locked and efforts to reach the pup were futile.

In large cities like Honolulu with hundreds of tall buildings, "high-rise" disasters are relatively common. A cat or dog can be injured falling, leaping or being thrown from a high window or *lanai*. And even

Toni Polancy photo

a fall from a second story apartment can be fatal.

An animal hurt in a fall from a balcony may suffer head or facial injuries and/or broken teeth, as well as fractured legs. If you live on the second floor or above, take these precautions:

• Keep tight screens on your windows so your dog or cat cannot fall.

• Screen the inside of your *lanai* or balcony. It's easy to buy soft screen on a 4-foot roll and tack it to the floor and/or ceiling of your *lanai*. Check with your building rules first: altering the exterior of your building may be forbidden.

• Never leave your pet tied and unattended on a *lanai* or balcony, no matter which floor you live on.

Keep your pet on the right side of the law

Pet ordinances are found in both state laws and county laws. About 70 percent of the state's population lives on O'ahu and, not surprisingly, that island has the most and tightest animal laws. O'ahu is the only island, or county, to require cats to be sterilized and wear identification if they are off their owners' properties. Maui animal control officers hope to have such an ordinance eventually.

The Hawaiian islands share certain animal laws, although penalties and interpretations vary slightly by island. So does enforcement.

Basically, ordinances on all islands call for registering your dog and prohibit:

- Dogs running free
- Dogs attacking people or other dogs
- Pets being off leash when they are off your property
- Pets defecating anywhere but on your own property unless you clean it up immediately
- Pets becoming a noise nuisance by barking, crowing or howling for long periods of time.

The animal nuisance law affects dogs, parrots, roosters, too.

Keep your pet quiet. Any animal that creates a nuisance–whether by crowing, screaming, barking or braying–for longer than ten minutes without stopping or for a half hour intermittently is in violation of the law, and a citation may be issued if a complaint is filed by those disturbed by the noise.

Photo courtesy Maui Humane Society

fetch
more information
for a list of laws regarding animals visit: www.hawaiianhumane.org/animallaws/index.html

It is illegal to:

- **Ride your dogs in the back of a truck unless** they are safely tethered so they cannot fall, jump or be tossed from the truck by a sudden stop;

- **Abandon your pet or be cruel to your pet.** Failing to feed, water or shelter your animal is considered cruelty. Dog fighting, for amusement or gain, is also considered cruelty. Hawai'i Revised Statutes provides that those convicted of cruelty to animals, including abandonment, can be fined up to $2,000 and receive sentences of up to 30 days in jail.

Smears

Readers write letters to the editors of our daily newspapers every day and often those letters deal with pets—specifically the problems living amid other people's animals. There are letters from neighbors about roosters crowing, about cats spraying gardens and leaving footprints on cars, about dogs barking. But one letter stands out in my mind, thanks to its graphic image. A woman wrote to *The Honolulu Advertiser* complaining about dogs in beaches and parks. She mentioned pet owners picking up after their dogs and "leaving smelly (or maybe the word was sticky) smears on the grass" where children play. She seemed to want to ban dogs from all parks and beaches.

I am constantly clipping items from the newspapers, filing them for future use. I didn't save that letter. There are so many complaints about dogs, after all, and, anyway, this pet book was nearly finished. Yet, over the next few weeks, that word—*smears*—often oozed through my mind. In the parks where my pets play, as I bent to pick up a sticky mess—a smear. As I watched other owners carry a shovel full of gunk, leaving, yes—smears.

I would be appalled to walk barefoot near a smear, to catch a ball that had bounced on a smear, to put a blanket down over a smear. At the same time, neither do I want to deny my dogs the joy of running free across a wide grassy stretch, of leaping playfully through a patch of *naupaka*, of bounding into the ocean.

Holly Lang photo

What's the solution? How do we eliminate smears? I suppose, eventually, we provide on all islands, enough strictly-pet, off-leash parks and beaches for our dogs and we prohibit or at least discourage people from playing in them. In the meantime, we recognize the need to be meticulous, to clean up as thoroughly as we can after our pets. From now on, when I go to the park, I will be carrying a spray bottle of water to erase, as best I can, my own pets' smears.

Stray dogs

If you find a stray dog, you must, by state law, notify a humane society or police and turn the dog over to an animal control officer. State law says unlicensed dogs become the property of the County and can be given away or disposed of after 48 hours confinement. Licensed dogs must be kept for nine days, during which time their owners can claim them. If an unclaimed animal is sold to a new owner, the original owner has up to 30 days in which to reclaim the pet, but the original owner must pay all costs of impounding and boarding.

Photo courtesy of Maui Humane Society

You know, of course, that you should never leave your pet unattended in a car in hot weather.
Well, triple that warning in our sunny state. Within as few as ten minutes, the temperature inside your car can reach 160 degrees. Leaving the windows open a crack doesn't help much. The few minutes you are away can stretch into several more before you know it, and your dog or cat can suffer heatstroke, organ failure or brain damage.

And don't assume that, just because the sky is overcast when you leave your house, the entire trip will be cool and comfortable. Weather conditions and temperatures can vary a great deal on any one island and may change within minutes. Unless you are planning to stay in the car throughout the drive, don't take your pet along.

Registration

Registering your dog and purchasing dog tags is required on all islands, although the cost varies by island (or county). Dogs must wear their tags at all times that they are off their property except when they are hunting.

- **Which dogs?** All dogs over 4 months of age must be licensed, including indoor dogs, dogs that are kenneled or fenced, and dogs that "never" leave your property. Dog licenses must be current, worn by your dog at all times and be clearly visible. Licenses are not transferable from one owner to the next, so if your dog changes owners, a new license is required.

- **The costs:** Licenses are good for two years. Costs vary by island and are subject to change. At the time this book is written, the costs are:

BIG ISLAND: Sterilized dogs, $2.10; unsterilized, $6.10

MAUI: Sterilized dogs, $6.25; unsterilized, $15.25

KAUA`I: Sterilized, $1.10; unsterilized; $3.10.

O`AHU: All pets, including cats, should wear identification at all times. Fees: $10 for a puppy 4 to 7 months of age or for a neutered adult dog. $28.50 for an unneutered dog over 8 months old. If the tag is lost, a replacement is free.

- **Where?** On O`ahu, get your dog license at any satellite city halls, the Hawaiian Humane Society and the Licensing Division of the Department of Finance. On neighbor islands, go to the Humane Society or the Licensing Division of any Department of Motor Vehicle office.

My pet's tatooed and wears ID. Why does he need a microchip?

The pet identification microchip is a computer chip, about the size of a grain of rice, inserted under the animal's skin. The procedure is painless and the animal is usually awake when it is performed. Once the chip is in place, a hand-held scanner is used to reveal the pet's identification number. That number is linked to a database containing the owner's name and phone number. The microchip cannot fade (like a tattoo) or be altered, and it cannot be lost (as identification tags or collars so often are).

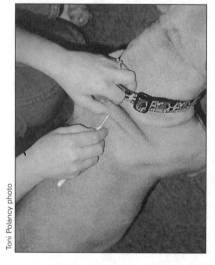

Implant of tiny microchip is simple and painless.

Toni Polancy photo

A microchip does NOT replace the need for identification tags and county dog licenses required by law, but the chip is an excellent way of ensuring your pet's safe return if it strays. When your lost pet is brought into the humane society, it is immediately scanned to see if it is implanted with a microchip. The goal is to return stray pets to their owners quickly and easily. If your pet does not have a microchip implant, talk to your veterinarian or ask your local humane society about obtaining one.

You can afford to "fix" your pet
Every island offers low-cost or free help

Each of our islands has an abundance of homeless cats—some estimates say there are as many as a million feral cats in Hawai`i. Our humane societies euthanize thousands of cats and dogs each year. To help reduce future pet populations, you should have your pet spayed (females) or neutered (males) or "fixed" (either gender).

In addition to ensuring that your pet won't add to the population, "fixing" your pet may also make it less aggressive and more focused on training—and you. Spayed females don't go into heat and that means male dogs won't be hanging around your property. Neutered males aren't as likely to go roaming, looking for females.

The surgery can be costly, but you can save a great deal of money by visiting your local humane society. All island societies offer some form of free or reduced-cost pet neutering and spaying.

KAUA`I: Spaying and neutering of dogs and cats is performed free by a Kaua'i Humane Society veterinarian. Call 632-0610.

O`AHU: Buy a "Neuter Now" certificate at the Hawaiian Humane Society, 2700 Wai'alae Avenue, or at any of several satellite city hall sites throughout the island; then make an appointment and take the certificate to a participating veterinarian. The certificates reduce the cost of neurtering. You can also download a form from the Web site (www.hawaiianhumane.org) to order a certificate by mail or fax. Or call 946-2187.

MAUI: Under the Spay and Neuter Assistance and Referral Program (SNARP), you will pay no more than you can afford. Get a Spay Neuter Incentive Program (SNIP) coupon from the Maui Humane Society or any public library including those on Lana'i and Moloka'i and in Hana. Or call the Helpline at 877-3616.

BIG ISLAND: The Hawai'i Island Humane Society sells coupons for discounted surgery at participating vets. Available at various times throughout the year, the coupons cost (at this writing) $25 for a male cat and $35 for a female cat, $50 for a male dog and $55 for a female dog. Call 329-1175.

**MOLOKA`I:** All male dogs and all cats are neutered at no charge. The charge for a female dog, at this time, is only $10. Dr. Antonio Rodrigues of the Moloka`i Veterinary Clinic visits Moloka`i weekly. Call 553-5355.

It's the law:
Tether your dogs in truck beds

Fortunately, few Hawai`i pet owners share the inhumane attitude of a truck-driving dog owner I met. I asked how he could be sure his two Rottweiler mixes would stay, untethered, in his truck bed.

"Oh easy," he said. "I train them."

"Really! How?"

"When they are about 6 months old, I put them in the truck and go. If they jump out they get hurt. They remember and never do it again."

"Oh my!" I exclaimed. "They could die!"

"Yeah. One did," he nodded. "But the next dog maybe won't be so dumb."

It's common to see dogs in the back of pickup trucks here. Many of them seem to be trained to stay without restraints and wait patiently while their owners attend to errands. But this method of pet transportation can be even more inhumane than keeping pets inside a hot car. Truck beds provide no protection at all from rain or Hawai`i's relentless sun. And even a slight fender-bender accident can send your pet hurtling out of the truck or into the hard side panels. Aside from being dangerous to your pet, riding with untethered dogs in the truck bed is against the law. Laws on most islands stipulate that you must have your animal securely and safely tied. O`ahu's law goes even further. It says you must have your dog secured with three ties inside the truck bed.

This dog's owner has come up with a truck bed contraption to protect her pet. The dog is in an anchored cage. She can enjoy the cooling breezes of an open ride or has the choice of ducking into a kennel to avoid rain or excessive sun. She also has water available at all times in an anchored bowl.

Toni Polancy Photo

Bob Fijal photo

O'ahu's feline law may be a concern for human's, but cats don't stay awake worrying about it.

O'ahu's cat protection law

O'ahu is the only island to have a Cat Protection Law. If you let your cat outside, it must:

- Wear identification.
- Have up-to-date vaccinations.
- Be sterilized if it is more than 6 months old.
- Not annoy the neighbors.

O'ahu's Cat Protection Bill of 1995 requires owners to provide cats over 6 months of age with identification. It may be either a microchip, a collar or a tag and it should include at least the owner's name, address and phone number.

There's added incentive for providing your cat with identification. The law says that O'ahu's humane society must hold cats (or dogs) without valid identification only 48 hours before destroying them or finding them a new home. If the animal has identification, it must be kept for nine days.

Did you know?

- In Hawai'i, it is against state law to harbor or breed a mongoose unless you have a good reason and a permit to do so. The fine is $250 to $1,000 for each mongoose. You may, however, trap or kill mongooses.

- Rabbits must be housed up off the ground. The fine for failing to do so is $100 or up to six months in prison.

- You must have a pigeon ownership permit to raise pigeons. You may fly or exercise 25 pairs of carrier pigeons in a residential area or up to 200 pigeons in a non-residential area.

- The feeding of garbage to swine is prohibited unless you have a permit to process the garbage or the garbage has been processed under conditions and procedures established by the Department of Agriculture.

- On the Big Island, it is against the law to give away any animal as a prize. The penalty is $500, the same as for abandoning an animal.

It is also unlawful for a cat over six month of age to be:
- outside its owner's property unless it has been sterilized.
- on anyone else's property without the person's consent.
- on a public street, park, sidewalk or anywhere else unless it is under the control of its owner; in other words, on a leash or other restraint not longer than eight feet.

The law also says it is unlawful for anyone to remove identification from a cat unless they own it. In other words, no one but a Hawaiian Humane Society representative can legally capture your cat, remove its I.D. and claim it is a stray.

A booklet published by the Hawaiian Humane Society and the County of Honolulu says: "When an owner retrieves a lost cat from the humane society, he or she must provide the cat with I.D." In other words, if you want to bail your cat out of the shelter, it must be microchipped or wear a tag.

The owner will also receive a citation if the cat is not spayed or neutered. If the owner sterilizes the animal within 30 days, the citation will be waived. If the cat is not sterilized in that time, the owner may be fined as much as $100.

So far, O'ahu is the only island to have such a law regarding cats. But feral cats are a problem on all islands.

Lost your pet?
QUICK! Do this!

When you first notice your pet is gone:

- **Search inside your home.** Search your own home thoroughly. An injured or traumatized animal may not come when you call, so be sure to look in closets, in boxes, in your washer and dryer and closed cupboards. Cats like to crawl into out-of-the way places and have even been known to crawl up into televisions sets and behind the motors of household appliances. Also check on top of cupboards, shower stalls and other high places. Cats love to look down silently from atop perches and may not respond when you call.

- **Outdoors, check inside your car first.** Your animal may have jumped in when you exited the car and become trapped there. Also check on top of the wheels and inside the engine of your car where cats love to hide.

- **As you walk around the outside of your home, listen for any low mews or whines.** An injured pet may not bark to get your attention, but he may whine or mew in pain.

- **Check the exterior carefully.** Hawai`i's unique architecture provides hiding places for your pet. Cats are apt to hide out atop our low single-story houses. Likewise, houses built up off the ground on "stilts" provide dark hiding places for pets. You may have to crawl under the house to check for a pet that has become ill or trapped. Be careful of centipedes and scorpions.

Next, check your neighbors' homes, yards and cars

Call upon neighbors, friends. Organize a team of friends or relatives who recognize your pet and begin searching the neighborhood, knocking on doors within at least a half-mile radius and asking if homeowners or apartment owners have seen your pet.

- **Search empty lots, fields.** Tell your search team to pay particular attention to wooded areas where your pet may have become

Tip
Lost a pet? Found one?
Some Island newspapers offer free help.
The Honolulu Advertiser: Free found ads. Reduced rate on lost ads.
Star Bulletin: Free found ads.
Penny Saver: Giving away animals, free ads.
Midweek: Free found ads for 1 week. Lost ads: 7 days for $12.95. Pet still lost, free for another 7 days.
Maui News: Found ads are free. Lost ads are regular rate.
Garden Island (Kaua`i): Found and lost ads free for 1 week.
West Hawaii Today (Kona, Big Island): Found ads free first 3 days then regular rate. Lost ads regular rate.
Hawaii Tribune Herald (Hilo, Big Island): Found and lost ads same: first 3 days free with 8 word limit, then regular rate.

Living

entangled. Check sewage ditches, construction sites, parks and beaches. Ask people along the way if they have spotted the animal.

- **Dog? Alert the police.** Most dogs are easily visible from cars. Call the local police department with a short description of your dog as soon as you are sure it is gone. Ask the police to radio an alert to police cars in your area. If police cooperate, this can be one of the quickest ways to locate your dog.

- **Visit your pet's usual haunts.** If you frequent a dog park or beach, be sure to check there first. Your animal may have headed there. Ask other pet owners there to help search for your pet.

If first attempts fail:

- **Go to the humane society,** and keep going back every day. Take a photo of your pet or a copy of the flyer. Fill out any forms and answer any questions and leave a copy of your flyer. If your pet has an ID tag or tattoo, the humane society will easily recognize her. Check back in person every day or as often as you can for several weeks. Your pet may turn up, but after a few days on the road she may not look exactly like her photo.

STOP ABUSE: Reward $1,000

People who witness animal abuse are often afraid to report it for fear of retaliation. Now CrimeStoppers, Honolulu Inc. has a pilot program with O'ahu's Hawaiian Humane Society to receive anonymous calls about cruelty to animals. Callers remain anonymous; all calls are confidential and can net the caller as much as a $1,000 reward.

Animal CrimeStoppers may pay a reward for information leading to:
- The recovery of stolen animals,
- The discovery of physical abuse or neglect of any animal,
- The discovery of poisoning or killing of any animal without need, or
- The discovery of raising an animal for fighting and/or using an animal for fighting.

Abusing an animal is a criminal offense and island humane societies and police departments have the ability to investigate cases in which an animal is abused

If you suspect an animal is being abused or neglected, call the Hawaiian Humane Society 24 hours a day at 946-2187, extension 280. Or call the Honolulu Police Department at 911. For more information, visit www.crimestoppers-honolulu.org/animalcs/intro.htm

- **Make posters and flyers.** Take two recent photos of your pet—one showing your pet's head close up and the other showing his entire body—to a copy shop. Create a simple flyer showing your pet Put your name and phone number on the flyer in big letters. Give copies to your search team and ask them to knock on doors, showing the flyer to everyone in a half-mile radius. Animals may travel great distance in a short time. Post copies of the flyer on light poles, neighborhood bulletin boards. Ask stores to post the flyers.

- **Widen the hunt with more hunters.** Ask cab drivers, truck drivers and anyone who drives a great deal to keep an alert eye for your pet.

Take out your camera, NOW. Don't wait until your pet is lost.

You probably take photos of your pet often just because you love her. Keep it up, even after the thrill of having a new pet is over. An up-to-date photo of your cat or dog is your greatest visual aid if the pet is lost. A recent photo will be indispensable in helping find your pet quickly. In fact, you should keep a set of clear, sharp, photos of your pet on hand. Take close-ups of her face, some shots from a distance so that her whole body is visible and also close-ups of any identifiable markings, such as unusual spots, scars, etc.

- **Advertise.** Advertise in community newspapers and include a photo of your pet. Sometimes people unofficially adopt animals they believe are strays. Seeing the pet's photo in the paper or on a bulletin board will alert them that the animal belongs to someone. Offer a small reward for information leading to your pet's return.

- **Consider the worst.** As brutal as it sounds you must also consider that your pet may have been kidnapped for a couple of unsavory reasons, as a lure to train fighting dogs or, if your pet is a valuable breed, for ransom. Your pet may also have been kidnapped simply because it is beautiful, valuable or cute. This is a horrendous realization, but if you can offer a reward and get your message to the kidnapper promising "no questions asked," your pet may be returned. By the way, pet kidnapping rarely happens in Hawai'i.

- **Keep looking.** Repeat all the steps above.

Take your pet to work? Well...

You may feel that you work like a dog. Or that your job is going to the dogs. Or, conversely, you may feel that everything at your workplace is just about purr-fect. But wouldn't it be even better if you could take your pet to work with you?

Just as workplaces around the nation are slowly becoming more child-friendly, they are also becoming increasingly pet friendly. It's not at all unusual to see a well-trained dog snoozing under a desk in a Hawai`i office or a cat lounging happily in a Honolulu store. There's even "Take Your Dog to Work Day," celebrated in June and promoted by O'ahu's Hawaiian Humane Society.

But, honestly, it seems silly to limit your pet's visit to just one day a year. A well-behaved pet adds a relaxed atmosphere to any place of business. It perks up my day to pet the big black cat lounging on the counter at the Ki-Hana Plant Nursery near my Maui home, or to visit Nancy and Russ Kanady at Dolphin Realty and be met by their poodle, Lucy. On O`ahu, I look forward to being greeted by Corky, a large parrot who hangs out in a cage at the entrance to LaMariana Restaurant and Bar at Ke'ehi Lagoon.

Employees at VIP Tours in Honolulu say tiny Precious has an official job title: stress reliever. Precious occasionally dances across desks and often naps in a playpen in the office near the desk of owner Raymond Gould.

Don't stare at the computer all the time, pay attention to me, Latte seems to say.
Part Chocolate Siamese, Latte likes computers and loves being near his owner, Marty-Jean Bender, when she's working at home.

Marty-Jean Bender photo

At Agape Graphics on Maui, owner Janlisa says her Papillon, "Panda," is a big part of the business. "He keeps the clients happy and just looking at Panda makes me relax," Janlisa declares.

But why is it called "Take Your Dog to Work Day"? Who says kitty can't go on the job, too? Stroking a purring cat is a great way to relax during a coffee break.

You'll note that in most pet-friendly businesses we've mentioned, the pet owner also happens to be the boss.

Want to bring your pet to work? plan ahead; try these tips:

• **Be sure talk it over with the boss** and your co-workers first and get everyone's approval. Beyond "liking" or "disliking" pets, make sure no one is allergic to pet dander. An allergy can be very stressful for the sufferer.

• **Make sure your dog or cat is well trained** and well behaved before you even attempt to bring it to work. At a minimum, your dog should respond to "sit," "come," "down" and "stay." Your cat should be of a calm nature and like people.

• **Arrange a short visit first.** Come in for an hour or so on your day off to acquaint the pet with the office, your bosses and your co-workers. Or perhaps you can bring the pet with you in the morning and take it home at lunchtime. A cat will be a bigger challenge. It may hide at first, but should calm down and come out in a day or so.

fetch
more information
Companies that would like assistance in establishing a pets-at-work policy can call O'ahu's Hawaiian Humane Society at (808) 946-2187, extension 222.

• **Confine the pet to your own work area,** either on a leash or behind a door or a child's safety gate. A small dog will be safe and happy in a baby's playpen.

• **Make sure your pet doesn't annoy anyone.** Your dog may want to greet newcomers with hugs and licks, but some people don't welcome wet kisses. Judge the reaction of humans your pet comes in contact with and act accordingly. Keep the pet away from anyone who doesn't seem to want its attention or doesn't initiate interaction. If your dog is a "kisser," licking or forcing attention on folks who may not welcome it, keep him at home.

- **Offer to sign a release accepting all risk** and liability in bringing the pet to work. You know your dog would never bite and your cat scratch, but your boss may feel better if you sign a release. The release should also note that your company is not responsible for damage or injury to your pet.

Photo courtesy Marty-Jean Bender

- **Keep your pet safe.** Transport your feline to the workplace in a kitty crate. Keep the dog leashed until it is well inside the office or store. And be considerate while transporting your pet. Ask permission to enter elevators, for example. Don't let a dog off leash if your business involves a lot of human traffic going in and out; your pet could escape through an open door. Also watch for electric cords or other dangerous items.

- **Remember the pet's needs.** Walk a dog at least every four hours. Provide a litter box for the cat and empty it as soon as it is used to avoid odors. A new cat litter is available that can be flushed down a toilet.

*Couch covers,
removable for
cleaning, are a
smart choice.
My dog Betty
appreciates
plenty of pillows.*

He'd make your life, and his, easier

If your pet built your house...

About 62 percent of Americans own pets. "Right this minute," says a *Washington Post* story, "there are 68 million dogs and 73 million cats napping on couches, grooming themselves on window benches, sniffing kitchen floors for stray food tidbits and whining to be let out of homes across the country. That means Americans everywhere are well acquainted with hairballs, shedding fur, snagged fabric, scratched woodwork, stained carpets, muddy paw prints. And worse."

It's wise to decorate your home with your pet in mind wherever you live, and on our tropical islands, it's absolutely essential. We leave our doors and windows open. Trade and Kona winds whip up insidious red dirt and slap salty ocean air into our homes. That means light-colored carpeting is out. So is that white couch you so admire. In Hawai'i, for your own peace of mind, whether or not you have pets, you may eventually decide to simplify your life with stress-free, easy-clean decor. Many longtime residents skip drapes and curtains entirely. Here, from a variety of interior decorators and sources, are some suggestions:

Floors

- **Tile, marble, stone, cement.** Avoid carpeting, which absorbs spots and absorbs odors. Use ceramic tile or, if you desire a more elegant look, use marble, stone or granite. Keep seams and grout lines thin and tight so accidents don't permeate the grout and cause permanent odors.

- **Laminates.** Paws scratch shiny hardwood floors, which are also difficult to maintain, but laminates such as Pergo are easy to wipe up and they come in a wide variety of grains, including bamboo.

- **Sea grass**. Rugs absorb dirt and odors. Instead, some island residents use sea grass matting to add a tropical ambiance. Sea grass matting is inexpensive, easy to clean, and doesn't show dirt.

Walls
- **Satin paint**. Avoid wallpapers, especially textured, burlap, or grass clothe. Wallpapers absorb odors, attract dirt, and are difficult to replace. A good quality semi-gloss or satin paint (or even today's flat paint) is easy to wipe clean and replace.

- **Textured paint** hides smears and dirt. Popular today, textured effects are usually achieved by using a sponge, squashed paper or a special roller and painting one shade of a paint color over a lighter or darker shade. Do it yourself and be sure to save some of the leftover paints so you can repair scratches and tail swipes.

Furniture
Realistically, even if you train your pets to stay off furniture, they probably will jump on it when you are not home. Prepare for it.
- **Cover up.** Choose furniture with removable covers that can be easily washed or dry-cleaned. And if you like to lie around petting your pets, buy furniture with low arms; it's easier for you to reach your pets and for them to reach you.

- **Cushions.** Cats can scratch and dogs may chew the wicker and rattan furniture that is popular here. If you feel you can train your pet, go ahead and try this type of furniture. Aside from the chewing and scratching, it is perfect for pets. Most rattan furniture has seat and backs cushions that can easily be cleaned or replaced if a pet has an accident. Rattan is also termite proof, something you can't say for most woods.

- **Avoid upholstered furniture**, especially in very light colors (which

Mike Sidney photos

Flooring is important when you have multiple pets. Forget carpeting and opt for a bamboo (top photo) laminate or other wood laminate. Tile works well too, but choose a dark grout that is easy to clean. An even better idea for island homes: acid-washed cement with a non-skid coating (bottom photo). Many island homes are built on cement slabs that can be finished this way. Hair doesn't stick to a leather chair (middle photo) and Betty's accidents wipe away, but long nails can damage leather. In Hawai`i's rainy areas, mold can also be a problem with leather.

show dirt) or dark colors (which show hair). Avoid nappy or textured fabrics that trap hair and can be difficult to vacuum. Choose a tightly knit fabric that claws can't snag.

- **Consider leather** furniture, which easily wipes clean, if you live in a dry part of your island and have a small pet. However, if you have a large dog, his sharp claws may scratch or puncture leather. If you live in a damp area, avoid leather entirely; it can attract mildew. You may want to try Ultra-suede upholstery, warm for our climate, but tough enough to resist pets.

- **Use washable throws** or mats to cover your pet's favorite places. I use a patterned sheet over Archie's favorite chair. He has learned that when the sheet is in place it's okay to nap on the chair. When the sheet's not there; we are probably having company and the chair is reserved for humans.

Bedding

- **Mattress covers.** If your pets sleep on your bed, use a plastic mattress cover. Some versions are plastic on the underside with quilted fabric on top, more comfortable than the totally plastic type.

- **Avoid bulky quilts** (hardly necessary in most parts of the islands)which are difficult to clean. Use washable blankets instead. Avoid thick or ornate bedspreads that can be difficult to clean. Consider using a stylish sheet instead of a bedspread; much easier to wash.

Accessories

- **Make it removable.** Use several throw pillows for a casual, comfortable look that you, your pet and your guests will enjoy. But be sure the covers are removable and washable.

- **Choose coffee tables** of Plexiglas, granite, acrylic or marble-like compositions that can't be chewed. Avoid putting knick-knacks, flower vases, and especially candles on coffee or side tables where a curious cat or a tail-wagging dog can cause a disaster.

Include your pet

- **Give your pet his own spot** near the center of family life. His own thick throw rug (washable, of course) placed near your favorite chair or a cedar pet pillow next to the television makes your dog feel included and may keep him off the furniture.

- **A cat shelf** perched in a window near the couch or her own soft bed placed on a chair near the center of activity will let your cat feel like part of the family. A folded towel, placed on top of a bookcase or somewhere high in the room, can also make a pleasant, safe "perch" for your cat that lets her maintain her privacy.

To keep pets off furniture

Most dogs and cats respond to a "Down" or "Get off!" command, but that doesn't mean they won't hop back up on the couch the minute you leave the room.

- **First, try a scent product**, available at most pet stores and through catalogs. Sprayed on the furniture, scent products discourage pets, but are odorless to people.

- **Next, try a trick.** If a scent product fails, try this rather extreme measure: put an upside-down mouse trap on the couch or chair and cover it with a piece of stiff paper, such as that from a brown paper bag. When the cat or dog jumps on the couch, the trap leaps up, sending the paper crackling and flying and the pet scurrying away. You will probably only have to use this trick once or twice: pets remember it.

- **Discourage scratching** by keeping your pet's nails trimmed and providing a scratching post for your cat.

- **Wrap a paper bag**, secured with tape or string, around the table or chair leg your cat or dog likes to scratch. Eventually your pet may overcome the fetish.

Housing

It's not just a matter
of finding a place
to live; it's choosing
a home where you
and your pet will be
welcome and content.

*A house cat,
reflected in a
mirror, stares down
from a window
of an apartment
at the Villas at
Eaton Square
complex on Hobron
Street in Waikiki.*

Suzette's story: For rent; no pets

Suzette had always wanted to live in Hawai`i, and she gambled all of her savings on "the move of a lifetime" to Maui a few years ago. Complete happiness for Suzette meant bringing along her two canine companions: Brewster, a shepherd, and Henry, a mixed yellow Lab.

Suzette followed to a tee Hawai'i's quarantine guidelines for incoming pets. Brewster and Henry received their examinations, shots and microchips in Arizona, so they would be confined at the O'ahu animal quarantine center for only 30 days, the shortest confinement at that time.

'I felt like I was climbing a steep hill, taking a few steps and then always sliding back again.'

Suzette spent about $2,200 to ready the two dogs, ship them to the quarantine center and house them there. Financially, it was a stretch, especially with all the other costs of moving, but her pets were worth it. While the dogs were confined, Suzette arrived on Maui and began searching for work and housing. She easily found a job as a housekeeper at one of South Maui's many hotels; next she sought permanent housing. Suzette's dream included living in rural Upcountry Maui with its beautiful valley views, so she answered several newspaper advertisements for rental housing. She disregarded ads that said "no pets," but after several phone calls, she realized that even landlords who accepted pets balked at two large dogs. She finally found a small cottage with a big yard. The property included two other cottages and a main house, all somewhat dirty and in disrepair. The $950 monthly rent seemed high, but Suzette was weary of looking and rented it.

Even though Suzette could not afford to go to the O'ahu quarantine center to visit her dogs during their confinement, Brewster and Harry came through the ordeal with flying colors. Suzette happily welcomed her dogs to their new home, but soon problems developed. The yard was shared with two other sets of tenants who did not appreciate her large, playful dogs' barking and roughhousing. So each evening, after driving 20 miles home from work through nerve-wracking traffic, Suzette put her dogs in the car and drove a few more miles to a large field where they could run and play. Big dogs, after all, need plenty of exercise.

The traffic and the cost of gasoline, coupled with a rent beyond her budget, soon became stressful. When Suzette realized she would have to work an extra job to make ends meet, the logical thing to do was to move to Kihei and eliminate the drive. The hotel she worked for offered subsidized housing, but they did not allow pets.

Kihei is a town of condominiums and Suzette soon found that most condo complexes also barred pets. The few that would accept pets either accepted just one pet or limited the size or weight of the pet. Suzette finally found a small cottage in Kihei, but the landlord wanted an additional deposit and an extra $100 in monthly rent for the pets.

"I felt like I was climbing a steep hill, taking a few steps and sliding back again," she says. Eight months after she arrived, a disheartened Suzette shipped her animals back to Arizona where they would live with relatives. Aside from the heartache and stress to both Suzette and her dogs, the episode had cost her more than $3,000 and a lot of heartache.

The lesson of Suzette's true story is this: if you are moving to these islands, weigh carefully your decision to bring your pets. Realize that owning a pet will limit your choice of living conditions and may add to your rental cost, stresses that newcomers to the islands hardly need. It may be wiser to leave the animals where they are and send for them after you have established yourself. Of course, you will have to find a relative or friend willing to care for your pet initially, as well as take it to a veterinarian several times to prepare the pet for shipment to the islands.

You may decide not to bring your pet here. Or you may be disillusioned with the islands and decide to leave, in which case you will have saved your pet a great deal of stress and yourself a good sum of money by not having brought your pet.

Pets are allowed at Haleakala Gardens in Kihei, Maui, although there is no designated pet play area. The condominium complex is popular with island newcomers and first-time buyers.

Honolulu's secret pets

Look in the O`ahu phone book under "Veterinarians" and you'll note an interesting fact. Several Honolulu veterinarians advertise that they make house calls.

How quaint! How charming! How old fashioned, you might say. Sort of like the old-time veterinarians who visited farms to help with the birthing of horses and cows.

Well, not quite.

During the past 30 years, O`ahu, where 70 percent of our state's population resides, became an island of condominiums, its residents mostly apartment dwellers. The same thing happened in fast-growing tourist areas on other islands: Kihei, Wailea and Ka'anapali, Maui; Kailua-Kona, Hawai'i; and Princeville, Kaua'i. And most of those apartments don't allow pets.

"That's why I make house calls," says one Honolulu veterinarian. A major portion of his business is conducted in condominiums and

Some Honolulu buildings include small dog runs for tenants' use.

Toni Polancy photo

apartments and many of his clients are cats and small dogs who live secret lives hidden behind shut doors.

"Many of them never go outside, never leave the building. When they get sick or need their shots, it's much simpler for me to come to the owner's apartment to care for them than for their owners to sneak them out," he says.

The truth is, most of the other residents of the buildings probably know the secret pet is living there, but as long as the pet does not cause problems, and as long as the building manager can look the other way, it seems to work out.

What happens when the owner wants to go on vacation or needs to be away?

"Well," says the vet, "pet sitting is a thriving business in Honolulu. Pet sitters visit each day to feed the animal and play with it. Or maybe a friend comes in, or even lives in, while the owners are away."

While living a whole life in one apartment may not be your idea of a perfect pet lifestyle, it may be all the pet has ever known and so the pet doesn't realize what it's missing. Cats and miniature dogs seem to exist very well this way, the vet adds. "In fact, if these animals get regular exercise playing with each other or with their owners, they usually live long lives because they don't encounter some of the dangers and diseases outdoor pets do."

But secret pets can be dangerous, says Cynthia Keolanui, manager of community outreach at O'ahu's Hawaiian Humane Society. Administrator for the Pets In Housing program, which encourages the creation of pet-friendly buildings, she says it would be much better for everyone concerned if all those secret pet owners could acknowledge their pets.

"Apartment managers need to know when an animal is kept in an apartment," she says. "Suppose the manager needs to enter the apartment for some reason, some emergency, and suddenly finds a dog there? Or doesn't know and lets the dog loose? Or say there is a fire in the building and firemen have to go into the apartment. It's just not safe."

How 'pet friendly' is your building?

Many of Hawai'i's apartment complexes are "pet-friendly." That is, pets and their owners are allowed to live in the building. However, "friendly" is a relative term. How "pet-friendly" is your apartment complex?

- **Can you simply** walk your dog in and out of the building on a leash? On any leash? Or are you restricted to a leash of a certain length?

- **Are you allowed** to walk your dog on the complex's grounds?

- **Is there a space** provided for you to run your dog off leash?

- **May your cat** play outside in your garden or lanai if you so choose?

- **What if another resident** complains about your dog barking or your cat causing an odor?

- **What procedures govern** your move in? Your lifestyle? How are rules enforced?

The answers to those questions vary. Will you choose a building with strict rules that are tightly enforced? Or one wih a more laid back, less formal approach?

A large complex

Queen Emma Gardens is a large Honolulu complex: 587 apartments in three buildings surrounded by five acres of gardens and walkways. Would-be residents with pets are given a four-page Pet Policy and Procedures packet. Created with the help of O'ahu's Hawaiian Humane Society, the policy covers almost any circumstance that could arise, from the length of leash a dog must wear to how often a pet should be exercised. Among the rules:

- **Residents may have** a maximum of two pets per apartment (including birds, aquariums and rodents). Moving in requires a health report from the pet's veterinarian, an interview with the pet policy committee, and a pet photo session. The photo will be kept on file. If the pet is a puppy or kitten, a photo will also be taken when it is an adult.

- **All animals must** be spayed or neutered.

- **They must be on** a flea and tick prevention program.

- **Animals in transit** (in elevators, hallways or on grounds) must be on a leash not longer than six feet; retractable leashes cannot be used.

The policy further states that pets should be exercised daily and prohibits any commercial activity regarding pets: no breeding, no pet sitting.

Dogs are not allowed in some areas including the pool, barbecue, playground, koi pond and tea houses. Dogs are allowed, on leash, in the rest of the huge garden area; there is no specific dog run or area where a pet can play off leash.

The policy tackles safety and possible annoyances, such as barking. It quotes the Revised City and County Ordinance 90-55: Pets "who make noise continuously and/or incessantly for a period of 10 minutes or intermittently for one-half hour or more to the disturbance of any person at any time of day or night..." are subject to discipline.

Making the rules stick

Most importantly, the Queen Emma Gardens rules provide for enforcement. Complaints must be in writing. Violators face the following action, fair by anyone's estimate:

1st violation:
Friendly reminder notice

2nd violation:
Written warning

3rd violation:
Notice of violation
and $25 fine

4th violation: Notice of violations and apartment association board or pet committee action which can include a $50 fine and revocation of pet privileges. In other words, the resident would be asked to get rid of the pet or move. He has 30 days to remove the pet; he may be required to move if he does not.

Queen Emma Gardens, near Honolulu's busy financial district and across from Foster Gardens, has a program in place to deal with potential pet problems.

Toni Polancy photo

A smaller complex

Pi`ikoi Towers, a smaller condominium complex near downtown Honolulu, presents a less formal atmosphere, and not only welcomes pets, but provides a long, narrow fenced "dog run" where animals can play off-leash.

Scott Iverson, resident manager, lives on-site with his medium-sized poi dog. He says the rules at the 120-unit complex are simple and basic, and pet owners follow them, leashing pets when they aren't in the run and cleaning up their pets' waste. Pets are not allowed in the recreation or pool areas, but there are no written rules and no committee to enforce the system.

"We have responsible dog owners in this building," Iverson says. "If we didn't, I'd let them know. And it's not just because of the building; it's because I care about dogs and want to see them treated right."

Iverson says the "dog run" (approximately 8 feet by 30 feet) was actually designed as a plant nursery for the Towers, but the chain link fence made it safe and the gravel bed could be easily hosed clean, ideal for a dog run. He also occasionally sprays the area for ticks and fleas.

Residents who don't pick up after their dogs face a $50 penalty, says maintenance man Kent Contrades, but it has never been necessary to enforce it.

"We just tell people if something is offensive," he says.

The Towers has become popular with potential tenants because pets are welcome, but Iverson warns that the apartments are individually owned and it's ultimately up to the owner whether pets will be allowed in an apartment. There are 20 to 25 pets in the building, including cats, Contrades says.

"The apartments (all one bedroom, about 600 square feet) are small, so most of the animals are pretty small. We have a couple of larger dogs," comments Iverson.

Pets have presented no problems, the men say. A female pit bull made some of the tenants nervous for awhile, "just because pit bulls have that reputation of being aggressive." The dog soon proved to be lovable, and is now popular with the tenants, Contrades says.

Pi`ikoi Towers in Honolulu has a secluded dog run where owners can exercise their pets or sit and watch them play. A sign reminds residents to clean up pet's waste and offers "if you need a bag, ask an employee of Pi`ikoi Towers."

Toni Polancy photos

"When people want to rent and ask me about pets I tell them to try to talk it over with the apartment owners," Iverson suggests. "Don't just take no for an answer. Tell them you will pay an extra $200 deposit in case the carpet needs cleaning or there's damage."

Convincing a landlord to say 'yes'

Here, from a longtime landlady, are some suggestions for convincing a home or apartment owner to say "yes" to your pet.

- **Develop a rapport.** Whether your first meeting is in person or over the phone, establish yourself before you mention your pets. Do this by asking and answering questions openly and honestly with an upbeat attitude.

- **Be positive.** After you and the landlord have both decided the apartment might be a good fit, say something affirmative and positive—"I'd be really happy to have this apartment because it is close to work"—then bring up the topic of pets, but don't be apologetic. "I have a 4-year-old cat that I've had since it was a kitten."

- **Listen to the landlord's concerns.** If the apartment owner or manager balks, try to get him (or her) to talk about concerns. Ask politely and calmly what the objection is. If he or she answers specifically, you can address that concern and, perhaps, eliminate it.

  For example, the apartment owner might say "Cats smell." You would try to get the owner to discuss that issue. Did he have a previous tenant who had a cat that smelled? A friend who had a pet that smelled?

- **State your case.** Eventually, you will point out that your cat is trained to a litter box and never misses. And you change the box faithfully each day. And new litter is available that eliminates odors.

  Or the apartment owner might comment that he once rented to someone with cats and "the cat was out at night making noise and messing around."

  You would assure the landlord that your cat is neutered and, anyway, will be kept in the apartment and not allowed out.

  Or the landlord might say, "A dog bit my nephew once. I just don't want to take a chance."

  Here's another good chance to draw him out. Ask when? What kind of dog? Was the child badly injured?

Tip

If you have a well-paying, steady job–always a plus on these islands–don't be shy; say so immediately. Landlords everywhere appreciate tenants who can pay their rent on time.

A checklist for landlords

The following is a list of questions to use when you are interviewing prospective tenants. These questions should help you become acquainted and assess how responsible the tenant is in regard to his or her pet. Most of the suggestions come from the Hawaiian Humane Society's Pets In Housing program. O'ahu's humane society suggests that you meet the pet, especially if it's a dog. A well-groomed, well-behaved pet is one of the best signs of a responsible pet owner.

Questions to ask all pet owners:

1. What type of pet do you have?

2. How long have you owned your pet?

3. Do you have a letter of recommendation from your veterinarian stating that each pet is in good health and up-to-date on its vaccinations?

4. Do you have a written reference for your pet from your current landlord?

5. Have there been any complaints about your pet at your current address? If so, did you pay your landlord for any damage done?

6. Does your pet have any medical or behavioral problems? If so, what treatment or training is it receiving?

7. What type of products do you use to treat or prevent fleas?

8. How often do you treat your pet for fleas and ticks?

9. Would you object to my visiting you and your pet after you move in to see how your pet is adjusting?

10. For how long each day will you be away from your pet?

11. Who will care for your pet when you are away for a long period of time, such as a vacation?

For cat owners:

1. Has your cat been spayed or neutered?

2. Do you keep your cat indoors?

3. Does your cat use the litter box that you provide?

4. Does your cat wear visible identification?

5. Does your cat have a microchip or tattoo?

6. Is your cat registered with the humane society?

For dog owners:

1. Has your dog been spayed or neutered?

2. Is your dog housebroken?

3. Is your dog licensed?

4. Do you keep your dog on a leash when you go for walks?

5. Do you always make a point of immediately cleaning up after your dog?

6. Have you and your dog completed a dog obedience class?

7. How much time does your dog spend alone each day?

8. How often do you exercise your dog?

9. How and where will you exercise your dog after you move in?

- **Introduce your pet to the landlord.** You might assure the landlord that your particular breed of dog is known as being gentle (if that is true) and that your dog is mild-mannered and well-trained. Suggest that you bring the dog to visit the landlord or that the landlord come over to visit your house and see the dog.

Among the other encouragements you might offer:

- **Provide references** from your last landlord verifying that you were a clean and caring pet owner.

- **Provide health certificates** from your pet's veterinarian, certifying that the pet is on a flea control and health maintenance program.

- **Offer to obtain liability insurance** for your pet in case your pet bites or injures someone.

- **Offer extra security deposit** or a slight increase in the monthly rent.

- **Offer a trade.** If the landlord is paying for lawn cutting, watering or simple yard cleanup, offer to take over some of those chores. In effect, you'll be trading your sweat for the ability to keep your pet, a real benefit for a home or small complex owner.

- **Cite the benefits that animals provide**. Dogs discourage rodents and prowlers; cats can eliminate rats and mongooses.

A Maui landlord, originally concerned about renting his rural cottage to a couple with two cats, says after two years he is delighted with the arrangement. He notices fewer rodents around the property, resulting in less damage to his avocados and bananas, as well as to his electrical wiring.

Other important advice:

- **When you receive your lease,** make sure it does not contain a no-pets clause (most leases do). If it does, cross out the clause and ask the landlord or his agent to initial the modified lease. At the bottom of the lease, write in a clause stipulating whatever you have agreed upon and noting any additional security deposit you have paid. Hawai`i law does not allow a landlord to collect a security deposit larger than one month's rent. If you have lived in the apartment for at least a year you should not be responsible for any wear and tear that results from normal living. However, you may be responsible for any damage your pet has caused, including spotting and odors.

- **Before you move in**, walk through the apartment with the landlord or rental agent and note any existing damage. Write it into the clause you've added to your lease. For example:

  Inspected apartment with David Smith, owner, on (date). Noted four spots about six inches across on the rug under living room window. Also 8-inch scratch on door to master bedroom.

  Sign it and ask the landlord or apartment manager to sign too.

- **Get everything in writing.** If you have paid extra security deposit or made any arrangements with the landlord regarding your pet, detail your agreement and add it as part of the lease. It is important to make specific notes. Typically, landlord/tenant relationships are friendly during move-in, but can deteriorate quickly when problems occur. In Hawai'i, rental managers change frequently and owners often sell apartments, so you may be dealing with a different person in a few months. Get everything in writing.

It's the law: pets allowed in public housing

During the early 1990s, makers of pet food and pet advocacy groups lobbied the United States Congress to allow public housing residents to have pets. They argued that pets enhance the quality of life for their owners and can even add years to an elderly pet owner's life. So, in 1998 Congress passed a mandate saying all public housing complexes must allow residents to own pets.

The mandate states that if you live in a federally subsidized housing project supported by the Housing and Urban Development agency, you may have a pet or perhaps two pets. But the mandate does not cover all subsidized housing. For example, if you rent from a private owner and receive financial help with your rent under the Section 8 program, your landlord can set his own rule about allowing pets. (Section 8 pays a major portion of a low-income tenant's rent directly to the landlord.)

If your complex is subsidized by county or state funds, you may or may not be allowed to have pets. To complicate the issue, every

The barking dog case

A public housing official tells this story: He responded to a call about a dog barking continuously. He found a 30-plus-pound puppy, soon to be a 65-pound hunting dog, chained outdoors on a four-foot leash without food, water or protection from the sun and rain. The owner had been away for several days, leaving the pet uncared for. The housing authority official called the humane society to pick up the dog.

When the owner returned he was furious and confronted the housing official in his office. After several frightening moments, the pet owner cooled down and admitted he had gone to Las Vegas and left the dog unattended. The conversation ended with the owner commenting he "never wanted the dog in the first place" and could not afford to keep it.

"Pets are a big responsibility. Between food, health care, flea control–having a pet is a big financial burden for any family. For people in subsidized housing it's a real stretch," the official commented.

government agency seems to have its own rules.

Many managers of housing units opposed Congress's mandate, according to an Associated Press report, and the policy has already posed problems throughout the U.S.: abandoned pets, abused pets, flea infestations, feces left in walkways and cats spraying or using gardens and play areas as bathrooms.

In Hawai'i, public housing officials face an additional problem: high density populations. In many areas of our islands, people live in cramped apartments or in houses on small parcels of land.

Administration of the mandate is left up to the individual housing authority. Some housing authorities let residents vote on whether or not they will allow pets, then form a residents' committee to set rules and enforce them.

Each housing authority decides how many pets will be allowed, how large the pets can be and how to deal with the problems that arise. If you live in public housing and want to keep a pet, be sure to ask about the rules for that particular complex. You may be asked to pay an additional security deposit. This is legal. You will get the deposit back if you or your pet have not damaged the apartment beyond reasonable wear and tear. You will not receive the deposit if your pet has defiled the apartment in any way, including leaving odors.

You may also be restricted to living in an area of the complex where pets are allowed, or you may be asked to move to that area.

So, who am I to complain?

Many problems can arise even in a pet-friendly housing complex. A year after his building voted to allow pets, the chairman of a pet committee at a small, 42-unit elderly housing complex sent this report to an island housing authority. Names and apartment numbers have been changed to protect residents' privacy.

- Sally Conners, apartment G-7, was allowed to have a tamed grown feral cat. She had the cat neutered/spayed, got shots and a license but never kept that cat in her apartment, as is the rule. Since it has no litter box, this cat defecates in our flower and vegetable beds on a regular basis. It sometimes gets in a cat fight with the other cat that is also not kept in and occasionally yowls for four hours a night. Even though numerous complaints have been made, you (the housing authority) did nothing about this serious breach of the rules. (The cat stalks our bird feeders and bird baths killing many birds, says a petition signed by residents.)

- Tako Kanishiro, apartment A-10, has an old Hawaiian myna bird that she has owned since it was a baby. This bird causes no one any trouble.

- Anna Cavalho, apartment E-3, got a cat soon after Conners got hers. It also was a grown tamed feral cat. Anna never has kept this cat in the house. We really did work with her, right down to buying a leash and a little box and litter to teach her how to care for her cat. This cat is very territorial and urinates at everyone's yard and doors on that end of the compound. Sometimes the smell of cat spray is disgusting. This has also been a problem that you (the housing authority) have not taken care of. She never abided by her commitment. (She says she cannot control the cat at night because it gets mad if she will not let it out and scratches her, says a petition signed by numerous residents and presented to the housing authority, requesting unspecified action).

- Pua and Sandy Kamamoto, apartment D-5, have a small dog. Do they have permission to keep the dog? She is no problem to me. Neighbors complain to me and I tell them to call the office if they have a problem with it.

- Clyde Dagdag, apartment D-3, is feeding a stray kitten so it will catch his mice! This I object to, but if everyone else gets away with not minding the rules who am I, at this point, to complain?

Not all pets cause problems; some are welcomed and eventually become an asset to their buildings. A visitor to Ma'alaea Kai condominium complex on Maui tells of a cat who rode the elevator several times each day and became a mascot for the building. "Snowbirds," visitors who return each winter, would ask about the cat as soon as they checked in. He had become part of the reason they looked forward to their Hawai'i visit.

Finding apartments

These are the islands of *aloha*, but it's not easy to find an apartment or home rental where your pets are loved or welcomed. On O`ahu, you'll get specific help from the Hawaiian Humane Society which produces a list of pet-friendly buildings and lets landlords post available apartments on a shelter bulletin board.

On neighbor islands you'll have a greater challenge. Pet-friendly apartments are especially difficult to find on neighbor islands because so many of the buildings are used for vacation rentals. But Hawai`i's future may hold more pet-friendly apartments, a housing specialist notes. As the number of available rentals increases and the number of tenants decreases, owners tend to become more lenient about allowing pets.

In researching this section, we found that nearly every complex that accepts pets has restrictions as to number of pets or their sizes. If you have a large dog or more than one pet, you may find it doubly difficult to find housing.

On O`ahu

More than 600 O`ahu apartment complexes accept pets. That's too many to print here, but the Hawaiian Humane Society offers a

Get a list of O`ahu's pet-friendly buildings

The Hawaiian Humane Society has a Pets in Housing program to:

- Help you find an apartment or home where you and your pet will be happy and welcome.

- Encourage landlords and condominium boards to open more apartments to pets.

- Help condominium boards and landlords set up and enforce rules to make living with pets less problematic.

The society offers a helpful, free packet that includes a list of 600 pet-friendly O`ahu apartment buildings, listed by area. You can access a copy in one of 3 ways:
Write or visit:
The Hawaiian Humane Society, 2700 Wai`alae Avenue, Honolulu, HI 96826

Phone: (808) 946-2187, ext. 222, to have one mailed to you.

Log on to the website:
www.hawaiianhumane.org

The Pets in Housing program, developed over several years, has been adopted by The Humane Society of the United States and may become a model for the nation, says Cynthia Keolanui, manager of community outreach.

"Guide to Pet-Friendly Rentals on O`ahu" which includes the list. See the accompanying story.

The list of pet-friendly rentals is helpful when used in conjunction with newspaper "for rent" ads. You will know which complexes or buildings allow pets and you can call for apartments only in those buildings. Immediately ask if the individual apartment's owner allows pets and whether there are any special limits or procedures for acceptance.

On the Neighbor Islands

The following are some of the pet-friendly apartment complexes on the neighbor islands. The information was gleaned from realtors, apartment managers and office assistants. Every effort was made to assure its accuracy, but the list may be incomplete, be outdated, or an apartment complex may have changed its rules from the time we received this information until it was printed.

Additional information, when available, is listed to show the variety of restrictions and contingencies.

WEST MAUI

Lahaina: Lahaina Residential, Puamana (must have written permission of owner).

*Ka`anapali:* Maui Ka`anapali Villas; Masters at Ka`anapali Hillside (pet owners must have liability insurance).

Honokowai: Mahinahina Beach (only cats and small dogs allowed).

Kahana: Kahana Reef (this is primarily a vacation rental complex, but a spokesperson says they are "flexible" about animals); Pohailani Maui (cats allowed; not dogs); Kahana Gateway (declawed cats only); Kahana Village (small pets only.)

Napili: `Alaeloa (pet allowed if board approves).

Kapalua: None of the apartment complexes allows pets. Private homes may have pets.

SOUTH MAUI

Wailea and Makena: Polo Beach Club; Wailea Ekahi; Wailea Elua Village; Wailea Ekolu Village; Wailea Fairway Villas; Wailea Point (various restrictions apply at all Wailea complexes).

Kihei: Boardwalk, Haleakala Gardens (35-pound weight limit when pet is adult); Island Surf; Kalama Terrace (one pet dog or cat not to exceed 20 pounds as an adult), Keonekai Villages (no weight limit); Kihei Resort (no dogs; two cats or two birds are okay); Kihei Villages (one pet, 80 pound limit); Maui Banyan; Maui Gardens (cats only); Maui Sunset (cats allowed); Pacific Shores (pets under 25 pounds); Southpointe (two pets allowed); Sugar Beach Resort (permanent residents/owners may have pets).

*Ma`alaea:* Hono Kai, Kanai A Nalu, Ma`alaea Yacht Marina, Milowai, Makana A Kai.

Wailuku: Ali`i Koa (small dogs, no cats); Iao Parkside, Mount Thomas; Puuone Tower (must contact manager for approval).

Kahului: Harbor Lights (one pet); Hale Mahaolu (elderly housing; one dog or cat not to exceed 20 pounds).

LANA`I
Terraces at Manele Bay
The Villas at Koele

MOLOKA`I
Nani Maunaloa

KAUA`I
Kailua: Kailua Gardens
Kalaheo: Kalaheo Pali Kai
Po`ipu: Makahuena; Regency at Poipu; Poipu Kai (a few units do allow pets; most of Poipu Kai complex does not).
Lihue: Kalapaki Villas (pets must be kept inside apartments; no dogs leashed outside); Halelani Village at Puhi (pets must be kept on leash); Sun Village (pets must be small enough to carry); Hanauma Condominiums; Village at Puhi (on leash);
Kapa`a: Kawaihau Sports Villas; Lae Nani.
Princeville: Alii Kai; Hale Honu condominiums; Kamahana; Puamana (you must obtain board approval); Sandpiper; Villas on the Prince (cats and small dogs). In addition private home owners at the Princeville Resort may have pets.

> **Tip**
> A realtor or apartment rental agent can make your search for pet-friendly housing simpler. Many renters assume they will pay more for an apartment managed by a realtor or rental firm--and, depending on the rental market, they may. But that's not an absolute. Realtors and rental companies handle a variety of properties and their knowledge may be worth the extra cost, especially if time is a factor.

BIG ISLAND
Of the 20 condominiums and apartment buildings we called, only three welcomed pets, and two of those were complexes for the elderly. An apartment manager explained that there are relatively few apartment

buildings on the Big Island; by far most people live in homes. And judging from the few pets in buildings that allow them, there is not a large demand for pet-friendly apartments.

"Anyone with a dog will have better luck looking for a house to rent. Many landlords allow pets in houses," the agent suggested. Here are the pet-friendly apartment buildings we found:

Hilo Side

Waiakea Lagoon View Apartments: Of the 130 pet-friendly apartments in this complex only two contain pets. Pets must be housetrained and the owner must prove it via a certificate from a training class, says a building representative.

Kamana Elderly Apartments: Of the 62 apartments in this complex only about 20 have pets. A cat or dog is limited to 20 pounds in size. Bigger dogs were once allowed but are now banned because they damaged the premises by jumping and chewing, a resident manager says. The complex is on seven acres and there is plenty of room to walk a pet on a leash. A $100 pet deposit is required.

Kulaimano Elderly Apartments: Of the 52 units in this complex "not even a handful" have pets according to a manager. Those who do want pets are allowed one pet per unit and they must be small, "no monsters and no billy goats." A $50 deposit is required and vet records must show all current shots. The pet must be neutered or spayed.

Remember: Finding a pet-friendly building does not necessarily mean your pet will be accepted in a specific apartment. In Hawai'i, most apartments within a building are individually owned. Even if the building's by-laws allow pets, the apartment's owner may reject pets.

Kona Side

Alii Villas: small animals only.

Kona Coffee Villas: An assistant manager says all cats are accepted as well as dogs under 15 pounds. Larger dogs must be approved by the board. All owners must abide by house rules and make sure their pets are cared for and do not bark excessively.

Playing With Your Pet 6

Hawai`i's a great place to enjoy nature with canine and feline friends. Here are some places to play and ways to play it safe.

Two friends, two dogs and a kayak equal fun in the ocean off Maui.

A man and his dog enjoy a day of play off Hawai`i Kai on O`ahu.

Places to play
(with leash and without)

A few years ago I walked my dog along Keawakapu Beach in Wailea, Maui, one of the state's most beautiful—and expensive — areas. I carried a plastic bag. When my dog messed near a patch of *naupaka* plants, I scooped it up. Suddenly I heard clapping, and looked up to see the resident of a multi-million dollar estate standing on the *lanai* (patio) of his home, applauding. Having caught my attention, he made an exaggerated bow. I'm not sure whether the gesture was meant as a compliment or as a comment that some owners do not clean up after their pets. A few years later, at another South Maui beach, a resident actually came down from his house to tell me that I should run my dogs at a park, not on "his beach."

Hawai`i is proud of its high quality of life for humans, boasts that all shorelines are open to the public, cordons off beaches for beached seals—yet domestic pets are sadly neglected. Too many beach and park signs announce just where pets fall in the list of public priorities, warning that drugs, alcoholic, and animals are forbidden. And even if there are no signs, the number of multi-million dollar houses lining beaches makes running your dog uncomfortable.

O`ahu has two "bark parks," both too small to run with your dogs, and there is no place to play with your animals off-leash *legally* on any of the neighbor islands. Still, hard-core pet lovers like myself do find places to run our dogs. We ignore warning signs and laws that threaten fines, and traipse through fields and forests, much of it "government land," with our dogs off leash. Or we choose some of the rapidly disappearing undeveloped stretches of sand or search out little bits of beach or lava flow where our dogs can let their inhibitions go and splash through the waves. In some less-touristy areas, on unguarded or seaweed-strewn beaches, authorities are inclined to look the other way unless bathers complain.

• MAUI: an unsanctioned bark park

Dog owners congregate in late afternoon at Keonekai Park, between the Pi`ilani Highway and South Kihei Road. This is not an official off-leash park and, in fact, signs say leashes are required, but well-trained dogs chase balls and each other here, unencumbered by leashes. There are trash receptacles and plastic scoop bags, provided by the pet owners who use the park, and a hose with drinking water. The two-acre piece of grass is shared with non-dog park users, including many children. The

'Pet owners deserve places to run with their dogs just as much as tennis players deserve public courts, ball players public fields and swimmers, their beaches and lifeguards.'

—Pam Burns

combination of rambunctious dogs and eager children could be dangerous, but dog owners here watch their pets carefully and everyone seems to have a good time.

• KAUA`I: keep searching

Things are somewhat better on Kaua`i, which boasts many beaches and trails, some still secluded and wild enough for owners and their pets to play freely. Yes, Kaua`i's beach parks all wear those "no animal" signs, but on this laid-back island, no one seems to care.

• HAWAI`I: nobody's *kuleana*

Surprisingly, things are more restricted on the island of Hawai`i. You'd think a place nicknamed the Big Island would have plenty of room for its pets, but Hawai`i has been plagued with abandoned dogs. Dog attacks in the past few years have made Big Islanders wary of canines. Scarce beaches are strictly reserved for humans. Members of the Kailua Coast Kennel Club hold matches in Waimea because no parks on the Kona side of the island permit pets. Dogs are allowed on leash in some parks in other parts of the island. Still, the Big Island is so big, says one *kama'aina* (longtime resident), you can run your dog in a forest or field and "who's going to see? Who's going to know? It's nobody's *kuleana* (responsibility)."

• O`AHU: creature beaches

On O`ahu, Pamela Burns, Hawaiian Humane Society executive director, is making places for pets and people her *kuleana*. She is adamant about setting up parks where dogs can run off-leash.

"I don't like to call them 'bark parks' like some people do," she says. "That sounds like the dogs are noisy, a nuisance, and they're not."

Her dream is to create "creature beaches," certain beaches designated as dog-friendly, or at least set aside a certain time of day for pet owners to walk with their pets on those beaches.

"Fifty-six percent of O'ahu households own pets," she recites, "and 37 percent have a dog. There are 102,500 pet dogs on the state's third largest island.

"Pets have become a part of people's social and recreational life," she points out, "and pet owners deserve places to run with their dogs just as much as tennis players deserve public courts, ball players public fields and swimmers, their beaches and lifeguards.

"All parks should have areas for dogs," she says. "And many of those, where it's feasible, should include off-leash areas."

A pet owner sitting under a tree at Diamond Head's Bark Park agrees. It comes down to this, he says. "We pay taxes, a lot of taxes, and we pet owners deserve our share of the tax money that goes for parks and beaches. Period."

So far, O`ahu, with nearly 70 percent of the state's population, is the only Hawaiian island to have "bark parks." There are two official off-leash dog parks, both privaely funded. One is near Diamond Head and the other is at the humane society. Weekends some pet owners travel all the way across island to visit the parks.

"During the week I walk my dog in Kailua," says the owner of a Basenji at the Diamond Head park, "but I try to bring him here every weekend just to socialize with other dogs. He has so much fun."

In 2001, the city council agreed that several more off-leash parks are warranted, but two years later, as this book goes to press, none of them has opened.

Thousands of dogs live in condominiums and apartments in Honolulu and, despite the lack of sanctioned parks, you will sometimes see the smaller pets off-leash, frolicking happily and illegally in downtown parks like Thomas Square. At Hawai`i's most famous park, Kapi`olani near Waikiki, pets are banished to a tiny triangle on the Diamond Head side and must remain leashed. After all, pets do not buy tourist trinkets, stay in posh hotels or dine on $100 dinners.

The solution, say pet owners on all islands, is to get your dog up and out early, before tourists hit the beaches. On O`ahu, we whisper locations, swap them like trading cards:

A man jogs with his dog along Diamond Head Road. The dog is on leash, abiding by strict laws.

Signs tell the story. A park in Kapa`a, Kaua`i, bans animals competely.

Toni Polancy photo

- "Below Diamond Head, you know, near the Doris Duke estate, except you'll have to walk. No parking."
- "Go to Makapu`u, out past Sandy Beach and just keep going. There's some lava rocks out there that jut into the water and no people. Good place run dogs, yeah? Except for the glass. Watch out for broken glass."
- "Lanikai Beach. It's illegal, of course, but it's such a big beach you can get away with running your dog early mornings, when no one's around."
- "Go Leeward, yeah? Nobody care if you run dogs. But be careful. Watch out for big dogs maybe fight."
- "Top of Tantalus. A real nice hike. Everybody does it."
- "Hau`ula Beach is so beautiful! Just perfect. But go weekdays, when folks working."

Places to play on O`ahu
ON-LEASH

Dogs are allowed on leash at:

District I: Hawaii Kai to McCully

Ala Wai Parkway, along Ala Wai Canal; Kamanele Square; Kamole Mini Park; Kapiolani Park Triangle; Manoa Triangle; Mauumae Nature Park; Moiliili Triangle; Nehu Mini Park, off East Hind Drive in Aina Hina; Pukele Mini Park; Puu O Kaimuki Mini Park, 951 Koko Head Avenue; Waikiki Playground; Wailupe Valley Playground.

District 2: Makiki to Aiea

Aiea District Park; Alewa Neighborhood Park; Archie Baker Mini Park, Makiki Heights Drive at Round Top Drive; Auwaiolimu Neighborhood Park; Hoa Aloha Neighborhood Park, Salt Lake; Kalihi Valley District Park, 1911 Kam IV Road; Kalihi Waena Neighborhood Park; Kamamalu Neighborhood Park; Loi Kalo Mini Park; Makalapa Neighborhood Park; Moanalua Community Park; Mother Waldron Neighborhood Park; Na Pueo Mini Park; Thomas Square.

District 3: Pearl City to Waianae to Wahiawa

Honowai Neighborhood Park, Waipahu; Iliahi Neighborhood Park, Wahiawa; Manana Neighborhood Park; Mililani Waena Neighborhood Park; Newtown Neighborhood Park; Pacific Palisades Community Park, Pearl City.

District 4: Wai`alua to Waimanalo

Enchanted Lakes Community Park; Heeia Neighborhood Park; Kaelepulu Mini Park, Kailua; Kamananui Neighborhood Park; Kaneohe Civic Center Neighborhood Park; Kaneohe Community Park; Kawai Nui Neighborhood Park; Pohakapu Mini Park, 1329 Kailua Road near Castle Medical Center.

• "Kahana Bay! Don't tell anyone, but for a real treat I take my dogs there. A man was fined and had to go to court for just having his dog on the beach, you know, and the dog was even tied up. But it's okay, if you go early enough. If you don't get caught. If there are no dog-hating bathers around..."

If... now the state talks about cleaning up Makapu`u, planning a huge people park some day.

Dogs frolic at Bark Park on Diamond Head Road, Honolulu, where a drinking fountain is designed to serve both dogs and humans.

Toni Polancy photos

"Too bad," says a young woman. Mother to two small dogs, she hikes at Makapu`u often. "That means dogs won't be allowed and they have so much fun there."

At Wai`alae Beach in Honolulu's posh Kahala area, a standoff has arisen between beach goers and owners who play with pets on the beach in this multi-million dollar neighborhood. After several months of talking, a neighborhood board came up with a solution of sorts: volunteer rangers, many of them pet owners, keep an eye on dog walkers, making sure they clean up excrement and don't endanger beachgoers in any way. Meanwhile, a state Department of Land and Natural Resources conservation enforcement officer said he has been doling out warnings to pet owners who let their dogs off leash there, but would instead begin issuing the mandated $50 fine.

Legally, there are two places you *can* play with your dog off leash on busy O`ahu:

Off-leash parks

- **Diamond Head Bark Park** at 18th Avenue and Diamond Road, near the cemetery at the back of Diamond Head. This two-acre piece of fenced property teems late afternoons with dogs and their owners socializing. The pet lovers at Bark Park helped build the park, on land leased from the state, and maintain it and staff it with green-vested park "rangers" who maintain safety and peace. Bark Park is open from dawn to dusk daily.
- **McInerny Dog Park** at the Hawaiian Humane Society, 2700 Wai`alae Ave., near King Street, is one-third acre, beautifully landscaped and squeezed between the backside of an apartment building and the H-1 Freeway. All of the labor and materials for the park were donated. Dogs enjoy frolicking in a lovely waterfall. Prettier than some of the "people parks," McInerny is a great place for dog owners to sit and chat. Hours: Monday through Friday from noon to 8 p.m. and weekends from 10 a.m. to 4 p.m.
- **Other dog park locations** have been promised and projected. At this writing one was to open, eventually, some day, at Moanalua Community Park in central O`ahu.

Pets have their own pool at McInerny Dog Park at Honolulu's humane society. Rules, gently enforced by volunteer rangers, govern both off-leash parks.

BARK PARK
RULES & REGULATIONS
ENTER AT YOUR OWN RISK

1. PET OWNERS MUST ACCEPT FULL RESPONSIBILITY FOR THEMSELVES AND THEIR PETS WHILE IN PARK.

2. PUPPIES AND DOGS MUST BE PROPERLY INOCULATED, BE HEALTHY (HAVE NO CONTAGIOUS CONDITIONS OR DISEASES), AND BE PARASITE-FREE (BOTH INTERNALLY AND EXTERNALLY).

3. DOG OWNERS MUST CARRY A LEASH. PLEASE BRING DOGS TO AND FROM THE PARK ON LEASH. DOGS SHOULD WEAR THEIR LICENSE OR IDENTIFICATION.

4. DOGS SHOWING AGGRESSIVENESS TOWARDS PEOPLE OR OTHER DOGS MUST BE LEASHED IMMEDIATELY.

5. NO DOGS KNOWN TO BE AGGRESSIVE TOWARDS OTHER DOGS OR PEOPLE (OR EXHIBITING ANY THREATENING BEHAVIOR) MAY ENTER THE PARK.

6. DOGS MUST BE UNDER VOICE CONTROL AND WITHIN SIGHT OF THEIR OWNERS. PLEASE CONTROL EXCESSIVE BARKING.

7. OWNERS MUST CLEAN UP FECES DEPOSITED BY DOGS.

8. NO BITCHES IN HEAT MAY ENTER THE PARK.

9. PARENTS SHOULD REFRAIN FROM BRINGING TODDLERS AND SMALL CHILDREN UNDER 10 YEARS OF AGE INTO THE PARK, UNLESS THEY ARE WILLING TO KEEP THE CHILDREN OUT OF HARMS WAY AND ACCEPT FULL RESPONSIBILITY FOR THEIR SAFETY.

10. DO NOT BRING RAWHIDE, PIGS EARS, OR FOOD INTO THE PARK AS DOGFIGHTS MAY RESULT.

11. AVOID OVER EXERCISING YOUR DOG ON VERY HOT DAYS.

Very furry or hairy pets can suffer in Hawai'i's heat. Puma and Mochi enjoy several fans their O'ahu owner supplies in summer.

Bob Fijal photos

Handling the heat

You've probably noticed that your pets tend to nap in the afternoon. There's a good reason. Nature wisely tells animals to conserve their energy during the warmest time of the day, and in Hawai'i that's from about 10 a.m. to 3 p.m. or later. Heat exhaustion and heat stroke can occur quickly in our very warm weather, especially in dogs that play on hot sandy beaches, are locked in stifling cars or apartments, or play, run and frolic with their owners during the warmest part of the day.

Some animals are particularly susceptible to heatstroke; for example, overweight dogs or short-nosed breeds like boxers and pugs, and thick-furred animals lsuch as Persian cats and rabbits.

Today's pampered pets may be more susceptible to heat stroke than their ancestors simply because they are not as accustomed to heat, says a story in *USA Weekend* magazine. Our darling dogs and catered-to kitties—like those in Honolulu's many high-rises—spend their time snoozing in front of air conditioner vents, not outside in sweltering temperatures as their "great granddoggies" did.

Treat your pet to a cool down
Freeze a chicken boullion mixture in an ice-cube tray and give the tasty popsicles to your pets as treats to help them cool down during hot summer months.

It's easy to overlook the signs of heat exhaustion. Many dogs breathe heavily and salivate with the slightest activity, and a canine caught up in a vigorous game of fetch or a hike on a mountain top is too excited to notice that something is wrong with his body. Cats tend to be private animals; a cat suffering from heat exhaustion may go off into a corner of an unshaded concrete yard and die without its owner even noting its stress. It's up to you to watch for the signs of heat exhaustion.

Do:

- Air condition at least one room of your home, where your dog (and you) can retreat during our hottest days. Turn the air conditioner on to medium or low, but don't overdo the cold air.

- Use floor fans to provide relief, but be sure little paws, especially kitten or puppy paws, can't reach through the grating.

Heat stroke versus heat exhaustion

HEAT EXHAUSTION: An animal with heat exhaustion will breathe more heavily than usual and have a rapid heart rate. He may vomit, collapse, have muscle cramps, tremors, and/or muscle weakness. But his body temperature may not be much higher than usual.

HEATSTROKE: Unless action is taken to cool down the animal, the condition can progress quickly, within minutes, to heat stroke. The animal will have a marked elevation in body temperature. Control of body temperature is gone and cell damage may begin. There may be kidney and/or liver failure. Heart failure can occur. Pets can die quickly from heatstroke.

Don't:

- Don't run your dog during the hottest part of the day, from 10 a.m. to 3 p.m. Instead, save walks for early morning and late afternoon, when temperatures are cooler.

- Don't shut your dog or cat up in a hot automobile. An open window may not be enough ventilation for your pet.

- Don't leave your dog or cat outdoors without shade and plenty of water. Be sure that your tied-up dog has access to both shade and water at all times.

- Don't keep your dog or cat indoors in a very warm apartment for a long time without adequate ventilation and plenty of fresh water.

- Don't shave your dog or cut a long-haired dog's coat very short. Hair can act as a kind of air-conditioning for dogs, protecting them from sun and heat.

Our tropical climate makes dehydration a real danger for pets. In many of the islands' warmest, driest areas, pet water dishes simply dry out. The water evaporates into the atmosphere. Here are some tips for keeping your pets' water bowls clean and healthy... and full.

- **Use two water bowls.** If you are going to be away from home for more than a couple of hours and your pets will be alone, use two sturdy water bowls so there is always a backup in case one spills or you are gone from home longer than you anticipate.

- **Purchase heavy ceramic water dishes**, rather than using simple plastic. They are less likely to tip and may keep the water cooler longer. Fill both bowls with fresh, cool water at least twice daily. (Some pets seem to appreciate a tray full of ice cubes dumped into their bowl.)

- **Hike with water**. Pets can also become dehydrated simply playing a game of fetch, running at the park, hanging out at the

HEATSTROKE
WHAT YOU'LL SEE

Cats: High temperatures are much more difficult for cats to tolerate than for people or dogs and death occurs more quickly. A cat suffering from heatstroke will breath rapidly trying to cool itself. She may drool and lick herself all over, attempting to cool her body. This may progress to noisy breathing. Her tongue and mouth may grow bright red and she may vomit. Unless helped quickly, the cat may stagger and flop, have diarrhea and grow weaker. Her lips may become grayish, a sign that coma or death is near.

Dogs: His eyes may be glassy with pupils dilated. His tongue may hang from his mouth. He may be panting or may have actually collapsed.

Rush your pet to a veterinarian.

ON THE WAY TO THE VET:
If your pet experiences any symptoms of heatstroke, take him into a cool environment quickly. Douse him with cool (not cold) water to bring down his body temperature, cover him with a wet towel, and rush him to the veterinarian. If you don't have access to a great deal of water, for example if you are on a hike, dab cool water on any exposed skin, especially his nose, but also his gums, his belly and the inside of his ears (without letting it run inside his ears).

IF YOUR DOG OR CAT SHOWS SIGNS OF DEHYDRATION such as excessive salivation, panting and exhaustion, gently pour some cool (but not cold) water over his muzzle and offer drinking water. Careful! If he gulps too much at once, he could vomit. Make sure your pet takes small amounts over the course of the next hour or so.

beach or on hiking trails, so carry plenty of water along with you. Some pet stores sell a portable nylon water dish that can be folded and carried in your pocket. Or tuck a small lightweight plastic bowl into your knapsack. Or teach your dog to drink directly from a water bottle. In a pinch, just take a plastic bag along. Use your hand and the bag to form a bowl for water. On a hike at Makapu`u in O`ahu, I met a man who used a runner's watering system to provide drinks easily to his two large dogs. The system had a tube running from the container of water in his backpack. When the dogs seemed thirsty he just squirted a gentle stream of water directly into their mouths. Convenient and conservative—no water was wasted.

- **Be careful of critters.** All kinds of creatures in addition to your pets are seeking water: toads, sluggish snails and a variety of insects, mosquitoes, ants and especially wasps, who need water to build their nests. There's not much you can do about wasps, but rinsing the bowls frequently should eliminate any nests lurking underneath. You can attempt to confuse vermin and toads by moving the dish often. If your dog must stay outdoors for long periods of time, consider a watering tube, available at pet stores.

Hot sidewalks can be tough on little paws. This pet's owner has carefully tied on two pairs of booties, making an afternoon stroll near Waikiki more comfortable. Such booties are available in various sizes at pet stores.

- **Watch out for toads.** B*ufo marinus*, Hawai`i's fat toads, emit a toxin that can kill your pet. If a toad lands in your pet's water dish, remove it from your property, and change the water in the dish immediately. **Visit page 210 for details.**

A tip from the Aussies

The sun is bad for humans and it can also cause painful damage to pets. White cats and dogs and pets with pink noses and ears are especially susceptible to sun damage and skin cancer, but all animals should avoid Hawai`i's hot sun. The danger is so great that Royal Society for the Prevention of Cruelty to Animals and Greenpeace Australia issued warnings, urging owners who take their pets outdoors at those times to butter them with sunscreen and tie hats on their heads to shade their eyes. "Sunscreen is effective and works well on dogs and cats if they are trained to tolerate it on them, especially so for cats," Australian veterinary surgeon Dr. Ralph Mueller advised in an Associated Press report.

Hiking with your dog

Everybody gets excited about beaches, but ask your dog what his favorite recreational activity is and he'll probably bark "Hiking!" Many of Hawai`i's mountains are crisscrossed with paths and trails that lead to breathtaking views. Most are well-maintained and easy enough to traverse, even if you are gripping one end of a leash. And that's how it should be when you hike: your dog on a leash. It may seem mean not to let your dog off leash while you are hiking, but there are many good reasons to keep a tight rein:

- **Excitement.** Your pet is very excited by the new place and the intriguing scents all around him. In this situation, he is least likely to behave himself and, unless he's very, very well trained, may be reluctant to return when you call him.

- **Other hikers.** You are sure to encounter tourists and other hikers on the trail. If your dog is feeling very excited or highly agitated, he could attack a stranger he perceives as a foe or a danger.

- **His hunting instincts.** With all the new scents and sights, your dog can easily become disoriented, go further than he anticipates, and lose you. For example, the woods can be home to colonies of feral cats. In the excitement of "the hunt" your dog can lose his wits, or at least lose his way.

- **Hunters.** Hunters and their dog packs ply the mountains on all islands, searching feral boars. Hunting dogs, singly or in packs, occasionally attack pet dogs, even those who are leashed. See the Protecting chapter of this book, page 148.

- **Injuries.** A bird, defending her nest, nearly bit my dog Betty's ear off. Humane societies have had to rescue dogs stranded on cliffs, pet dogs have been attacked by feral boars. Your pet can be injured in an area that is difficult or impossible for you to get to, or can even be so badly injured it can't call out for help.

- **Wildlife.** Even the gentlest dog fancies himself a hunter when he's out in the "jungle." Don't let your pet cause damage to birds, small wildlife or the environment.

> ### DO IT
> ### with other dog people
> Owners and their pets take to O'ahu's hiking trails every month. Call (808) 946-2187, ext. 217, for information on Paws on the Path or travel the Internet to: www.hawaiianhumane.org

fetch
more information
Your pet can be your ticket to fun on these islands. Visit your humane society's website for a complete list of pet/owner activities. See pages 307 to 308 in the Resource section of this book.

Happier trails to you and your pet

- **Carry a small first aid kit** that includes disinfectant and gauze bandage for tourniquet and tweezers to remove burrs. See the Protecting chapter of this book.
- **Take plenty of water.** Freeze plastic bottles of water and tuck them inside your backpack to melt as you go. Carry a lightweight dish for your dog. See Water, this chapter.
- **Don't hike alone.** Take a friend.
- **Plan your trip in advance.** Even if you plan just a short hike, tell someone where you are going and when you'll be back.
- **Take a cell phone.** You may have trouble using it in some areas, but not many.
- **Wear practical shoes** like sneakers and socks. Don't wear sandals.
- **Avoid swimming in ponds and unknown waters.** See Leptospirosis, page 168, in the Health chapter of this book.

A couple, a kayak, a dog and rough seas

Janet and Jim clung to the overturned kayak;
but Koa, being a dog, couldn't cling.

Photo courtesy of Helen Milne

Life jackets like Ipo's offer at least
some protection for small dogs.
They come in a variety of sizes
and are available by special order
through most Hawai'i pet stores.

One sunny tropical morning Janet, her boyfriend Jim, and her Labrador mix, Koa, went kayaking near Olowalu on the west coast of Maui. The weather was sunny and beautiful; the ocean calm, and Janet and Jim soon found they had paddled farther from shore than planned.

By now it was nearly noon; the wind picked up and the waves whipped higher. The couple decided to paddle to shore as quickly as possible, but the waves had become so rough that paddling seemed futile. Suddenly a large wave overturned the kayak, dumping Janet, Jim and Koa into the wild ocean. Janet and Jim spent several minutes trying to right the fiberglass kayak and finally gave up. They just clung to it; but Koa, being a dog, could not cling. Koa desperately dog-paddled, heading toward shore, and Janet watched as his head, bobbing between massive waves, grew smaller and smaller, then finally disappeared.

The couple spent two harrowing hours in the ocean, clinging to that overturned kayak. Janet worried more about Koa then she did about herself, assuming fishermen or boaters would eventually pick her and Jim up. And she was right. A fisherman radioed an S.O.S. to the Coast Guard, who hauled Janet and Jim and their kayak aboard a rescue boat. Janet sobbed— from fear, yes, but mostly over the loss of her Koa.

She was overjoyed when, a few days later, Koa was found wandering in an ocean-side town a few miles from where the kayak had capsized. His identification tag was still attached to his collar and a kind person called Janet to come get her pet.

Unfortunately, water craft episodes are common here, and not all stories end as happily as Janet's. A few years ago, a young Kihei man died attempting to save his dog. He, his son and the huge, hairy sheepdog were on a catamaran when the dog went overboard.

Your dog may love the water, and you may love your dog. But unless you are on a truly sturdy craft, or very confident of his swimming abilities, love your dog enough to leave him at home. If you must take him out on a water craft:
• Make sure your pet wears a life preserver made especially for animals.
• Don't leave your pet unattended in the boat (or kayak) or in the water.
• Make sure your pet has access to shade on board the craft.

The WRONG way to play ball

What could be more natural, in our abundantly perfect weather, than playing "frisbee" or "ball" with your pet? You throw the object and your eager pet retrieves it, many even catching it in mid air. But pet care professionals say there is a wrong way and a right way to play ball with your pet.

WRONG:
Throwing the ball very high into the air or bouncing the ball so high that your pet must jump to catch it. Jocelyn Bouchard of the Maui Humane Society remembers a young dog who died, almost instantly, after its owner bounced a ball to see how high he could make his dog jump. Totally focused on the ball, the dog leaped into the air, twisted to grab the ball, and landed on its backbone, crushing its vertebrae. Young pets with developing bones are especially susceptible to such injuries.

Toni Polancy photo

RIGHT:
Keep your throw long and low, so your pet runs, not leaps, to catch the ball or frisbee. And remember not to overdo a game of catch. Some dogs enjoy playing ball so much they are almost obsessive about it and don't know when to stop, so it's up to you call time out. In Hawai`i's hot sun, give your pet plenty of time to rest between pitches so he doesn't become overheated. And, of course, be sure to have water on hand for your pet.

The RIGHT way to teach your dog to swim

You'd think, this being Hawai`i, that all dogs would just naturally love to swim. That's not the case. Some canines take to water like ducks; others like cats—which is to say they want no part of it. Whether they like the ocean or not is irrelevant. When you live on islands as we do, it's important that your dog at least be familiar with the ocean and the fact that nature made him a natural swimmer. You can gently introduce your dog to the ocean so he's not afraid of it, and then let him decide himself if he wants to become a regular swimmer. Here's how:

- **Walk into calm, shallow water** and call your dog toward you. Let the decision to try the ocean be *his*, not yours. Coax your pet with a treat or a toy; but always keep the dog within reach.

- **Have fun.** Play. Smile. Laugh. If your young pet sees you enjoying the water, chances are he'll learn to love it too.

- **Bring along a doggy buddy** who already swims. Let your dog follow his friend into the water. And don't rush them. It may take several sessions for your pet to decide whether or not he likes the water. If your dog decides he enjoys swimming, congratulate yourself. You'll both enjoy many years of healthy fun if you adhere to a few rules:

- **Don't let your dog overdo it.** The dog is using new muscles and may tire quickly.

- **Treat your dog with the same respect** you'd give a swimming human. Be careful of strong tides, large waves and hazardous shore breaks.

- **Never leave your dog unattended.** Now that you've taught him to get into the water, you should always be in a position to help him get out.

- **Check with a lifeguard** for daily water conditions. You can imagine how frightening and confusing a jellyfish sting would be to a dog who doesn't understand what attacked him.

Kula Sunn photo

Some dogs don't care for the ocean; others learn to love it.

Kai Rowland photo courtesy Maui Humane Society

Beaches

What's legal? What's not?

Laws concerning dogs on beaches tend to be confusing. Dogs are banned from most beaches on O`ahu. Officially, three beaches–Kahala, Kailua and Lanikai–allow leashed dogs on the sand; but dogs are not allowed at all on other beaches. A 2001 legal opinion by the city of Honolulu said leashed dogs may be walked *through* beach parks, even where dogs are prohibited, to get to a beach where leashed dogs are permitted, but the dogs cannot linger in the parks. Meanwhile, although the law does not address the issue of dogs in the ocean, a humane society pro says you must walk your dog across the beach on leash to the water, but your dog may be off leash when it is in the water.

Toni Polancy photo

A tranquil Sunday, a placid sea and a woman's best friend.

Matthew Thayer photo

Some pets just hate to go home.

Deborah Booker photo courtesy *The Honolulu Advertiser*

Try to explain it all to your pet: the lights and noise and why that fat man with the fake beard is wearing that stuffy red suit.

There's a pine needle in the keyhole.

It's Christmas morning. My husband, our two toddlers and I are just returning from church, laughing and looking forward to putting the finishing touches on a holiday dinner for soon-to-arrive relatives. We tromp up the steps, put the key in the lock, turn it, and the front door won't open. It seems jammed. We shove gently, then push harder. Something squishy seems to be wedged against the door.

My husband decides to throw caution to the wind and shove for all he's worth. The door opens a crack and a large tree branch pops through, hitting him in the face. Our eight-foot, ceiling-high Christmas tree has toppled over; the top half is wedged firmly against the door.

What a mess! The fat fallen tree fills the small living room. Broken branches, shattered ornaments, pine needles everywhere. The carpet is soaked with water from the tree stand and stained with dye from soggy wrapping paper. Presents are doused. Stuffed toys are squishy with water. We'll spend most of Christmas day cleaning up.

> The door opens a crack and a large tree branch pops through, hitting him in the face.

But where are our two kittens, Nip and Tuck? In the bedroom, hiding under a bed.

It didn't take much time to figure out what had happened. The night before, we had been laughing at the cats' antics. Awed by the activity, the holiday wrap and especially the big tree, the kittens had a great time batting ornaments, nibbling needles and wrapping themselves in ribbons. They even chased each other up the trunk of this tree we had so conveniently planted in the middle of the living room.

When we left for church the next morning, the activity resumed and reached a wild peak when the tree toppled. Thank heavens we had pulled the electrical cord on the lights before we left. The combination of spilled water and electricity could have started a fire. We might have returned from Christmas Mass to a burned home.

Never a Christmas passes but I remember that year. Christmas is fun and exciting, but it can also be a time of increased danger. The following pages contain tips on keeping your pets safe and your holidays sane.

—Toni Polancy

• **The tree.** Make sure your tree and other displays are strongly anchored so they won't be tipped over by a crawling cat or a dog's wagging tail. Because of the high cost of importing live trees, Hawai'i residents often use artificial trees, only slightly less dangerous to pets. Keep the tree top away from high perches or ledges such as book shelves from which your cat may decide to hop unto the tree. Consider hanging a lemon-scented air freshener or some sheets of fabric softener inside the bottom branches. The scents may discourage your cat. Leave the bottom branches bare of enticing ornaments.

• **Plants and flowers.** Poinsettia, the traditional Christmas plant, grows profusely in Hawai'i and you may be tempted to buy a few potted plants to decorate your home. Don't. The plant can be harmful. Agriculturalists don't agree on just how dangerous they can be to people and pets, but it doesn't take much to harm a curious cat. Avoid poinsettias.

• **Tree preservatives.** Those costly cut trees arrive in Hawai'i weeks early and need to be preserved in water. But, do not put commercial tree preservatives, aspirin, aspirin substitutes, or anything else that is supposed to preserve the tree's life in the water at the base of your tree. Curious pets can and *will* drink the water. Aspirin is toxic to cats.

• **Lights, displays**. As though to make up for the lack of snow, Hawai'i blooms with holiday lights and Christmas displays. Keep all electrical wires out of the way of pets and feral animals. Plastic and rubber electrical coatings are tempting to chew, but an animal could get shocked or sick from the material. Pull the plugs on Christmas lights when you leave the room. Not just when you leave the house, *when you leave the room.* Also, keep displays, especially fragile statues, etc., away from your cat's favorite window sill or napping spot. Consider the wide wagging of your excited dog's tail and move breakables out of its reach.

• **Ornaments.** Hang them high up, away from animals who may decide to snuggle under the tree or bat the ornaments—or worse, taste them. Synthetic compounds, glass, and plastic are hard to digest.

and yourself safe and sane

• **Tinsel and wrap.** Forget the tinsel. It's too tempting to your pets, especially cats and kittens. Hang any garlands high up, away from kitty's reach. Keep ribbons and wrapping of all kinds away from your pet. Swallowing ribbon or wraps could choke your pet or cause an upset stomach. A recent newspaper story quoted a veterinarian who spent the day after Christmas performing surgery on three dogs. One ate Christmas ribbon, another swallowed a spool of thread and the third attempted to digest a cassette tape, according to Copley News Service.

• **Candles.** That pleasant holiday glow cast by candles can be dangerous. If you must use candles, make sure they are in secure holders and well away from pets who could knock them over. House fires from candles are common. Never leave a lit candle in an empty room, especially when pets are around. And remember that curious cats can climb high and happy tails wag wide.

• **Food**. Don't be tempted to share Christmas treats with your pets and make sure guests don't either. **Chocolate can be fatal to dogs.** Sweet and spicy foods, as well as turkey are difficult for pets to digest. To avoid gastro-intestinal problems, maintain your pet's regular diet. Some sneaky pets will try to serve themselves when your back is turned. Be sure to put food gifts (like that holiday sausage) where pets can't reach them. Remove garbage and trash from your home quickly.

• **Craft items.** All kinds of interesting Christmas items are offered at Hawai'i's craft fairs, including those made of natural materials, such as leaves, stalks and berries, all of which are especially tempting to animals. Do not let your pets chew any decorating material. Berries can be poisonous and most materials purchased at craft stores have been treated with preservatives and/or various other chemicals.

• **People.** Holiday *luau*. Cooking *tutu* (grandmothers). Visiting aunties and uncles. There's a lot going on during the holidays. If you're having a party, alert your guests to pet safety. Post a big sign near the door to remind people to keep it closed so your pets don't get out. Or, even better, secure your pets outdoors or in a separate room during the event.

How to GIVE A PET as a holiday gift

Animals need time and attention to adjust to a new owner and a new home. For most of us, the holidays are busy—not an ideal time to bring a new pet into the household. If you want to give a pet as a Christmas gift, first be sure the recipient sincerely wants a pet and is willing to devote as much as 15 years (the life span of some cats and dogs) to the pet's care. If you are determined to give a pet, do it this way: Prepare a fancy basket with pet toys and treats. Tuck a gift certificate from a pet shop or the local humane society (and a copy of this or another pet book) inside. A gift certificate allows the recipient to choose her own pet, one that fits her lifestyle and she is sure to love. And she can bring the pet home after the holiday rush, when she can devote full attention to its training.

This purse is made of soft rawhide. Dogs can indulge hidden desires and chew up the entire purse. We found this at VCA Kane'ohe Animal Hospital at Christmas time.

From your pet's point of view

Your cat will probably find his own quiet place to get away from the hubbub, but your dog likes to be by your side all the time. The excitement could be stressful, especially for a very young or old dog. If your pet already has a special spot in your home, make sure it is not disturbed during the holidays. Or offer your pet a quiet place, away from the activity and chatter, where he can get enough rest and maintain some of his regular schedule. Spend some quiet time with him there, relaxing, petting and massaging him. You'll relax too and your holidays will be happier. Also be sure to exercise your dog regularly during this busy time of year.

A long walk before visitors come will help tire the dog and hopefully lower his excitement level.

• **Going away** for the holidays? Leave your pets with a reputable pet sitter or boarding kennel. Well-meaning friends may get too caught up in the holiday bustle to provide your pets with the care and attention they deserve.

• **Be sure** pet registration tags are up to date and all pets are wearing identifying charms with your name and phone number. Also keep up-to-date photos of your pet in case a search of the neighborhood becomes necessary.

Joan Cannon photo courtesy Maui Humane Society

"Yeah. I hate these funny hats too. But, it's only once a year. Let's humor our humans."

Q: What goes bow-wow-OW?
A: *A Hawai`i dog on the New Years Eve, Chinese New Year, and the Fourth of July*

Traditionally, Hawai`i celebrates New Year's Day, July 4th and Chinese New Year with a bang. In fact, hours and hours (and sometimes days and nights) are filled with bangs and booms. Ear-splitting fireworks explode throughout the islands, creating nerve-shattering noise, flashes of lights and thick smoke that can frighten dogs and cats and other pets, especially birds. Some pets seem to be in real agony during these sieges, others take them in stride. And the reaction does not seem to be a cultural thing; native born pets can be as bothered by the noise as newcomers.

Island humane societies are deluged with lost, frightened pets who have slipped collars, broken chains and leashes, climbed fences, dug holes and clawed through screen doors to escape their homes and yards amid the flashes and bangs of exploding fireworks. The explosions cause cats to hide, but dogs are more likely to run away and can be struck by cars.

One recent December, O`ahu's Hawaiian Humane Society had reports of 131 cats and dogs lost in just four days. The Hawai`i legislature in recent years has put some limits on fireworks so holidays have grown a bit more peaceful. Tranquilizing very nervous pets is a standard prescription for fireworks, but that can be done only when the exact time of fireworks can be pinpointed. Firecrackers and fireworks continue to explode intermittently for days. If your pet is afraid of fireworks, try these methods to alleviate his discomfort:

- **Bring your pets** into your home during sanctioned firework hours. Find a quiet, inner room with few windows.

- **Wrap the dog or cat** in a blanket and hold it gently on your lap, comforting it. If the dog is very large, spread a blanket or towel on the floor and lie down beside the pet, while stroking and talking to him. Remain calm—animals often pick up reactions from their owners.

- **If your pet is too nervous** to calm, consider keeping him in a kennel/crate during the fireworks siege. That should make a cat feel more secure and keep her from bolting.

- **Maintain your pet's routine.** If a stereo or television is usually on, keep it on as a distraction.

- **If your pet is high-strung**, tell your veterinarian who may prescribe a tranquilizer. While sedation may seem extreme, it can be kinder than making a highly sensitive animal suffer. If you decide to try this, remember: never give your animal human tranquilizers. They are extremely dangerous for pets.

- **Some veterinarians** will shelter pets in a quiet kennel environment during holidays. You may want to consider this, especially if you expect to be away from home a great deal during the holidays. But consider whether being away from you is a greater trauma to your pet than the noise itself.

- **Move.** As a last resort, remember that fireworks tend to be much more intense in some neighborhoods than others. If you love your pet and it is particularly bothered by fireworks, consider moving to a quieter area of your island.

- **Keep your pet's** tags and identification up to date in case it bolts.

It's Halloween! Do you know where your cat is?

Cats, especially black cats, should be kept indoors in the days before and after Halloween, advises the Hawai`i Island Humane Society. Some people are superstitious about cats and may try to harm them. It is also the Big Island humane society's policy not to adopt out black cats on or immediately before Halloween when they can be regarded as a costume prop or a holiday decoration.

Halloween is a scary time of year for pets, who don't know why on earth people paint their faces, wear masks, dress up in weird costumes and yell "boo!" Or why children are parading up and down the street ringing doorbells and chanting "trick or treat." Consider the holiday from your pet's viewpoint. Take these safeguards:

• Keep all candy and treats covered and away from your curious pet.

• If you walk your dog on Halloween, make sure it is securely leashed so it does not bolt. Keep tags and identification up to date in case it does run away.

• Keep your cat indoors on Halloween, even if it usually goes out at night. Purchase a litter box and introduce your cat to it.

• If your pet is high strung, confine it in a quiet room with a radio playing softly to diffuse sounds.

• Consider taking your dog for a ride or a visit, away from your home, during active "trick or treat" hours.

• If your pet is highly nervous, ask your veterinarian's advice. The vet may want to prescribe a simple sedative.

• Stay alert after the ghoulish holiday too. Don't let your pet nibble pieces of crepe paper decorations or bits of cellophane, costumes or candy left lying around.

photo courtesy Maui Humane Society

Teach your *i'lio* or *popoki* to 'speak' Hawaiian

When your pet is first being trained, all words are meaningless to him; he reacts to sounds and to attitudes, and so it is easy to teach commands in any language. You may want to teach your pet to "speak" Hawaiian, or at least to respond to a few words. Use the same tactics you would use to teach your dog any command, repeat over and over the word for a command and react positively with smiles and treats when your pet obeys the command. A word of caution: make sure your pet also knows the English version of these words so that he or she can respond to other people as well as you. Here are some commands in Hawaiian:

Robert Jonathan photo courtesy Maui Humane Society

Sit, stay
Noho

Stop it
Uoki

Come
Hele mai

Down
Moe

Behave
Noho pono

Kiss
Honi

Roll over
Ka`a

Wait
Kali

Protecting Your Pet

Keep her safe from other animals— and from cruel humans, too

Charo, a chihuahua/toy fox terrier and his owner, Gayle Lum, enjoy music at the Waikiki Bandstand. Charo's sun visor keeps her head cool and cuts glare from the hot sun, and the sling provides a safe, comfortable way to travel.

In search of a serial killer

Y ou're walking with your dogs on leash, casually strolling along a moderately busy road, when you meet a friend and start to chat. After a few minutes, you glance down and notice that your dogs are eagerly munching on something they've found along the side of the road.

"Pua! Ali`i!" you scold, "What are you into?" You and your friend trade surprised looks. The dogs are just finishing what appears to be a hunk of fresh red meat.

"Now who would leave meat in the road?" your friend asks.

"Maybe it fell from someone's shopping cart," you suggest.

Pua and Ali`i have already finished their snack and are happily sniffing the grass under a mailbox. You and your neighbor shrug your shoulders, say goodbye and continue on your walks.

'This person is very sick. He's not poisoning the animals because any one animal annoys him, but because he enjoys killing them. He gets off on it.'

A half hour later, back home, you hear a sound familiar to most dog and cat owners: your pets regurgitating. Nature has blessed some animals with a natural reflex action that can protect them from digesting harmful matter, so regurgitating isn't all that unusual. But the dogs continue vomiting. Two hours later, they are hanging their heads; they seem weak and nervous. The next morning, they refuse breakfast and are lethargic. Their eyes are glassy. They seem to have trouble breathing. You rush them to the vet, who immediately suspects poisoning and takes tests. The results verify his suspicions: paraquat poisoning. In five days, the dogs are dead.

Similar tragedies have occurred on all islands, but the episodes have been especially terrifying for pet owners in the Kanani Road area of Kihei, Maui, where a serial pet killer has taken the lives of at least 50 pets in the past 12 years. Each September, October and November, except for the years 1997 and 2000, several dogs and cats have been poisoned by paraquat-laced meat. Paraquat is a herbicide used to control the growth of grass and weeds. Authorities believe an annual visitor, an animal-hating serial killer, soaks meat in paraquat and feeds it to pets, sometimes leaving the deadly snack by the side of the road, other times throwing it over fences into yards.

Toni Polancy photos

"I have clients in the Kihei area who will no longer walk their dogs," says a Maui veterinarian who has treated several paraquat cases. "It is the most horrendous, painful death. The lung tissue, in effect, turns to leather." Survival is rare, but possible if the pet is treated immediately.

"This person is very sick," Aimee Anderson, animal cruelty investigator for the Maui Humane Society, says. "He's not poisoning the animals because any one animal annoys him, but because he enjoys killing them. He gets off on it."

Most of the poisonings have occurred near Kalani Road in this bucolic Kihei neighborhood during the same three months of the year for many years. Authorities theorize the killer could be an annual visitor. A sign outside the Maui Humane Society advertises a $12,000 reward for information leading to his or her arrest and conviction.

FOIL POISONERS

These suggestions come from animal control officers.

- **Don't give a poisoner an opportunity**. Contain your pets on your property.

- **Stay alert**. When walking your dog, keep him on a leash and under control. Don't let him pick up anything off the ground to chew or eat. Watch him closely.

- **Don't let your pet become a neighborhood nuisance**. Only a deranged or unstable person would poison an animal, but such people exist. Don't give them an excuse to strike.
  KEEP YOUR CAT INDOORS. Some people don't appreciate cat footprints or scratches on their car, or the essence of cat in their garage.
  DON'T ALLOW YOUR DOG TO BARK EXCESSIVELY

- **Report to authorities neighbors** who are allowing their pets to roam or their dogs to bark excessively. You are not being a snitch. Irresponsible owners put their own pets and all neighborhood pets at risk.

- **Know your neighborhood.** Report any suspicious cars, people or activities to police. Be especially alert for anyone throwing an object from a vehicle or bicycle or dropping an object as they walk.

Anderson conducted a door-to-door hunt for the killer, searching the neighborhood for clues. She got several tips.

"People would say, 'This person hates animals' or 'This person complained about that' or 'He's a nasty man,' but that's not enough. You have to have something concrete.

"I kept having a scary feeling I could actually be talking to the person, to the killer, but you'd have to have definite proof and that's hard to get. This killer is not going to say, 'Okay, I did it.'"

To be charged, hard evidence is needed. The most likely way to catch the killer would be for a neighbor to spot the person setting out poisoned meat, and call the Humane Society immediately.

"The frightening thing is, anybody could pick up the tainted bait," says Anderson. "A child could die next."

Paraquat is a contact herbicide. Used as it was intended, diluted and sprayed on plants, it is safe for the environment. It bonds quickly to plants, killing the part of the plant it touches, but does not affect the roots. It does not leach into the soil, but, in its concentrated form as it comes from the producer, paraquat is a cobalt blue liquid deadly to humans and animals.

The herbicide is restricted; anyone using it must pass a written test and obtain a permit from the

State Department of Agriculture. Paraquat is used on Hawai`i's farms and ranches, but not at sugar and pineapple plantations, according to a state agriculture department spokesman.

Zeneca Ag Products, which manufactures paraquat under the name Gramoxone, joined the State Department of Agriculture, the Maui Farm Bureau and private donors in posting a total $12,000 reward for information leading to the apprehension of the serial paraquat poisoner. The penalty for cruelty to animals is a $2,000 fine and up to a year in jail. However, for paraquat poisoning, additional penalties may be levied for use of a restricted herbicide, including a $25,000 fine.

They heard their pet cry in fear...

(From "Mililani hunts ways to end dog attacks" by Lori Tighe, Honolulu Star Bulletin *newspaper, Dec. 14, 1999.)*

They heard their *poi* dog, Dallas, barking, and then his bark turned to cries. Jean Seeley looked in her backyard and the doghouse started to move.

Her husband lifted the doghouse, and underneath two large hunting dogs had Dallas by the throat and hind legs. Dallas' cried turned to moans as the dogs ripped her 20-pound body apart.

Then Seeley watched in mounting horror from her kitchen window as the hunting dogs made a beeline for the neighbors' dog, Makamae, across the street.

"My heart sank as I listened to my neighbor and her son scream in terror," Seeley said.

The residents who both lost their dogs told their story at a special meeting at the Mililani Middle School to address the

Fatal Biters

These are the dog breeds most responsible for fatal bites one recent year, according to the Centers for Disease Control and Prevention and The Humane Society of the United States.

Purebred	Number of fatal bites
Pit Bull	66
Rottweiler	39
German Shepherd	17
Husky	15
Alaskan Malamute	12
Doberman Pinscher	9
Crossbred	
Wolf-dog hybrid	14
Mixed breed	12
German Shepherd	10
Pit Bull	10
Husky	6
Rottweiler	5

problem of vicious dog attacks.

After the tearful, angry, three-hour meeting, the pig hunter and owner of the killer dogs, who had been present all along, stood up and spoke. In a low, embarrassed tone the 24-year-old man told the crowd of about 50 people, "I'm sorry for what my dogs did, and I'm willing to pay for the damage." He said he had hunted too close to a residential area and his dogs escaped. "It was an accident."

Pig hunters have roamed freely in the mountains of Mililani for years, but now are being denied access by Castle & Cooke, the developer of many new Mililani homes.

Killing the wild and potentially dangerous pigs has been part of balancing ecology on the island for centuries, said a man who represented hunters at the meeting.

"Hunters are not bad people. Although this is a terrible tragedy, I ask you not to let one hunter represent us all. Which would you rather have, wild pigs coming out of the mountains or wild dogs?"

The humane society gave the dogs back to their owner immediately following the attacks because current law does not permit stronger action. Police fined the dog's owner $25 for each dog violating the leash law. The new Council bill calls for owners of dogs who recklessly attack other pets to be fined up to $2,000 and/or jailed for as many as 30 days.

The stronger law is needed to control not just hunting dogs, but domestic dogs as well. They can brutally attack other pets and children said a Humane Society spokesman.

"There needs to be some accountability among dog owners," said Mike Betz, a Mililani resident. "I have a 7-week-old son and my wife takes him walking. They wouldn't stand a chance if they were attacked."

(A year and a half after this article appeared, and after several other attacks by wild dogs or hunting dogs, the law was toughened somewhat in July 2001. That story follows.)

REMEMBER

Aside from illustrating that Hawai'i, despite its sophisticated veneer, can be a pretty uncivilized place when it comes to animals, the preceding stories highlight another important fact. You must be alert and careful, ready to react to unforeseen problems to protect your pet. You must also be watchful and cautious when exercising your pet whether on city sidewalks, deserted beaches, at island parks or on our numerous hiking trails. Suggestions follow in this chapter.

An old problem; a new law

As a pet lover, it is heart-wrenching to read these statistics: man's best friend, praised for its ability to provide companionship, good mental health and protection, will also bite about 4.7 million Americans every year, more than 60 percent of them children. More children are seriously injured by dog bites than are taken ill by measles, mumps and whooping cough combined.

Each year approximately 800,000 Americans seek medical attention for dog bites; about 18 people die, according to the Centers for Disease Control and Prevention.

It is easy to understand why parents become so concerned when we run our dogs on beaches where their children are playing. It's easy to be on one side of the controversial issue—off-leash pleasure for our dogs—and to see the concerns and rights of the other side. One mauling of one child wipes out our entire argument for pet rights.

We pet owners have a right to parks and places to run our dogs off leash—but they should be separate from places where children and families play.

A "dangerous dog" law took effect on O`ahu in 2001. The law protects both people and animals that are attacked and allows determination of responsibility through the criminal court system. If the dog in question is deemed dangerous, the county may impose restrictions upon the housing and handling of the dog, and fines or jail time for the owner, according to Pamela Burns, president and CEO of O`ahu's Hawaiian Humane Society.

Despite laws, dog attacks continue throughout the islands. Any pet owner whose animal is injured or killed by a dog should file a report with the police as well as the island humane society.

Burns also urged anyone who has a dog that exhibits aggressive tendencies to take immediate action to socialize the dog, sterilize it or confine it so it may not become a threat.

If you live in Hawai`i, with our abundance of feral animals, hunting dogs and loose pets, the question is not whether you will come face to face with an uncontrolled canine, but when. While the temperament of aggressive breeds of dogs can vary according to their training, it is absolutely essential that you take care, for yourself, your child and your pet, when any unknown dog of any breed approaches.

Protecting

At the dog park

Off-leash dog parks are great fun for you and your pet. But they can also be dangerous places. O`ahu's two official off-leash parks, Bark Park near Diamond Head and McInerny Dog Park at the Hawaiian Humane Society, usually have attendants on hand during busiest hours, but beaches, trails and public parks do not.

Toni Polancy photo

- **Stay alert. Keep an eye on your dog at all times.** It's tempting to fall into conversation with other dog owners. That's part of the fun. But something as simple as a sniff, a snarl or the introduction of a new visitor can turn a peaceful park into a battleground.

- **If your dog seems to be too excited** or is playing too roughly, call a time out. Remove your dog from the activity and play calmly with him away from other dogs, if possible.

- **If you see someone else's dog acting aggressively**, inform the attendant and the dog's owner. You're not being unfriendly; you may be saving someone's pet from a dangerous situation.

- **If your dog becomes combative** or any other dog behaves aggressively toward him, remove your dog to a quiet corner. Consider leaving the park and coming back to visit at a time when fewer or less belligerent dogs are present.

- **If dogs begin to fight**, both owners should pull the dogs apart and take them to separate areas in the park or leave the park altogether.

- **Take affirmative action**: Discuss safety issues with attendants and other pet owners. How should you break up a dog fight? How can you help make the park safer? Ask a humane society dog control officer to visit and answer questions and concerns.

When dog meets dog

What goes undocumented is the number of times dogs bite and injure or kill each other. In Hawai`i, it's not unusual to encounter large dogs and aggressive breeds, unleashed, in the back of trucks, on hiking trails, and, in some neighborhoods, simply wandering down streets or roads. Pet owners should protect their pets. Here are some suggestions.

- **Keep your dog under control,** on a leash, whenever you are off your own property. "Under control" means the dog goes where you want him to and he cannot pull you toward a dog he wants to visit or jerk and run away.

- **When your dog wants to "meet" a new friend,** first ascertain from the other dog's owner if the new dog is friendly and "safe." If the owner hedges or seems reluctant, move away with your dog.

- **Watch closely as the dogs sniff and become acquainted**. Dogs make instant decisions about relationships. The first meeting between dogs can erupt into a fight within moments.

- **Avoid aggressive breeds.** People who own guard dogs often do so because they want a canine who is a tough fighter, a good hunter, or can protect them. All are good reasons why the dog is trained to be aggressive. Therefore, it would be smartest, for the safety of your pet, to keep it from interacting with any of these breeds, even if he is one of them, until you are familiar, and feel completely safe, with the other dog's disposition.

- **Don't make your pet a sitting duck.** Don't tie up your dog in an unfenced yard where he can be an easy target for aggressive wanderers. Keep him behind a fence high enough so he can't jump out and other dogs can't jump in. Some dog behaviorists suggest you also keep your dog from seeing out into the street or watching passersby, thereby cutting down on barking and aggressive behavior.

An owner of large dogs insists that guard dogs, on the whole, are better trained than most "family" or "lap" dogs. Small breeds, she maintains, can be as aggressive as guard dogs. She makes a point: it is ultimately up to the owner to ensure that his or her dog, regardless of breed, is "fit" to interact with other dogs.

When child meets dog

Most large dogs are friendly, like this big kisser at Bark Park, Honolulu.

Toni Polancy photo

Here are safety suggestions for children from the American Kennel Club.

- Get permission from the dog's owner before you pet it.
- Stay away from any unfamiliar dog.
- If an unfamiliar dog approaches, stand still and don't make eye contact.
- Never run away from an unfamiliar dog. Instead, move away slowly.
- Never approach a dog from the rear.
- Don't interrupt a dog when it is eating.
- Never try to remove a ball or toy from a dog's mouth.
- Never roughhouse, wrestle with, or antagonize a dog.
- Don't make contact with a dog that is confined to an auto, pen or kennel.
- Stay clear of dogs that are fighting.
- Stay away from any dog that appears angry or agitated.
- Make sure your friends also follow these rules.

Socializing Wink

I was about to leave the veterinarian's office when her assistant handed me a quivering mass of stiff black hair.

"Here," she said. "You work at home. Take Violet home and socialize her."

"What's this?" I frowned. The mass of sticky hair had two huge ears and one scared brown eye. A big incision sliced across the other side, where a right eye should have been. It was a puppy, or maybe just a small dog.

"She was found wandering in a macadamia orchard in Waihe`e," the aide explained. "She was brought in from the humane society for surgery. It looks like someone kicked her in the head. We tried to save her eye, but it was so bad we had to remove it. The little gal was pregnant, too, but we had to abort the pups. She was just too small. "

"The poor thing!" I cuddled the dog to me, but she flinched in fear.

"That's what she needs," the attendant encouraged. "Affection. Socializing. She needs to get used to people. She won't look so bad once the swelling goes down. We call her Violet. You know, like Shrinking Violet, because she's so shy."

Just then, the postman walked in. Violet lifted her head, opened her one eye very wide, let out a banshee-like howl and sprinted from my arms through a door to the inner office. Shrinking Violet? Try Bolting Begonia.

The attendant retrieved Violet and handed her to me again. "Why don't you take her home and nurse her? You can bring her back if you don't want to keep her. Just help her get better."

"Well, I guess I could just hold her on my lap while I'm at the computer," I admitted. "But I'm going to the Big Island in a couple of days so maybe I should wait till I get back... "

The veterinarian joined us just then. "You can bring her back here while you're on your trip. Take her home and I'll throw in her health checkup and a year's heartworm medicine."

My other two dogs welcomed Violet as though she were a long-lost part of the family. Betty began cleaning her ears and licking her wound. It soon became clear that the pup loved my dogs, but feared humans. She spent most of her time hiding under my bed, peeked out at dinnertime, but refused to take food from my hand. I had to put it down and walk away; then she'd go to the dish and eat voraciously. *continued*

The bonding process was slow and I didn't want her to regress, so I decided to take Violet with me to the Big Island. She tucked nicely inside a large purse, as I smuggled her past valets and porters at a Kona hotel. Small though she is, Violet attracted a lot of attention. Asian tour groups would break rank to rush over and pet her, asking about her eye via interpreters. At first Violet cringed and hid inside her purse, but eventually she began to look forward to the sympathetic "ooohs" and " aahs," to the gentle caresses of numerous fingers, to strange faces bent to kiss her. Violet was being socialized, all right, and in a way that could only happen in Hawai`i. She'd had a brutal start in life, but she was learning that humans could be gentle and loving, too.

Asian tour groups would break rank, visitors rushing over to pet her, asking about her eye via interpreters.

By the time we returned home it was clear that Shrinking Violet was no longer an appropriate name for our little foundling. She greeted our other dogs eagerly, hopping joyfully. Just as pets have a way of appearing when you need them most, so do their names materialize from nowhere. When her eye healed, Violet looked as though she were winking. Her name became Winky, Wink for short.

Wink has been with us for two years now and she's come a long way. She keeps up with the bigger dogs, barks bravely at Skat the Cat, prances happily when it's time to go to the park. An eternal puppy, an eight-pound bundle of joy, Wink completes the family we didn't even know needed completing.

At Hawai`i's parks and beaches, I have encountered countless owners whose pets came to them unexpectedly like Wink came to us: surprise blessings. Lee Stack of O`ahu visits the Big Island regularly. She never meant to have a dog, but fate had other plans. Lee was picking mangos in an old orchard on the Kona side of Hawai`i when Thumper, a chihuahua mix, began following her. Three days later, Petey, who looks like a Lhaso Apso, was lying in her driveway, dirty, matted and dehydrated. Lee checked with the Hawai`i Island Humane Society and said she'd adopt the dogs if no one claimed them. Now Lee's life revolves around her two pets, who travel with her on Big Island jaunts.

Someday, surely, unexpectedly, God or Buddha, Allah or Pele, Nature or whoever you believe in, will send a pet your way. Be open and ready to accept as *hanai*, to adopt as a loved part of your family, whatever and whoever comes to you. It's the Hawaiian way.

The sun did it: its rays caused a cancer that claimed the ears of this white cat.

Sylvan Schwab cuddles a resident of the East Maui Animal Refuge, nicknamed the Boo Boo Zoo.

Bear: a hero of sorts

Deborah Booker photo courtesy *The Honolulu Advertiser*

Malia Newhouse coaxes Bear down a ramp made for him after his front leg was amputated. He managed very well on three legs, she says.

Bear, a 6-year-old Belgian Shepherd, once had a life and a job to make any animal proud. As an airport sniffer, Bear nosed his way through incoming freight at the Honolulu Airport. He had been trained by the State Department of Agriculture to hunt out brown tree snakes and he was part of a team of such sniffers. But being a sniffer is a little like being a baseball hero; by the time you're middle aged, you're getting too old for the job. So Bear was adopted by the Newhouse family of Punalu'u. In windward O'ahu, he lived a peaceful rural life.

One day the Newhouses noticed Bear had begun limping. When veterinarian Dr. Eric Pearson pressed an area on his leg, the dog whimpered in pain. Cancer was diagnosed and Dr. Pearson amputated Bear's painful leg at the shoulder. Utilizing a type of immuno therapy, Dr. Pearson had an experimental vaccine made from Bear's bone tumor, but Bear's cancer later spread to his lungs. He was euthanized, at home, several months later. Large dogs like Bear seem prone to bone cancer and some may be genetically predisposed to it, researchers and veterinarians say.

The Newhouse family is still recovering from losing Bear, but take solace in knowing they made the last days of a working hero happy and peaceful.

CANCER:
as deadly to pets as to people

It's a quiet Sunday afternoon as I write this. My three dogs are enjoying their mid-day naps. Archie, who always stays as close to me as he can, is curled on the floor near my desk. Betty and Winky are spread on the couch a few feet away. I look at them and shudder after reading these statistics:

One in four dogs will have cancer during during its lifetime; almost one half of dogs over the age of 10 will die from cancer.

Like their loving owners, dogs get breast cancer and prostrate cancer. Like their human counterparts, some forms of cancer seem to be genetic in dogs; some breeds appear pre-disposed to certain types of cancer. Boxers and Scottish Terriers may have a tendency to malignant melanoma, a certain kind of skin cancer. Large breeds are at risk for cancerous bone tumors. German shepherds are prone to tumors of the spleen. Sporting breeds face a higher rate of mammary gland (breast) tumors.

The incidence of tumors in cats is less than in dogs. However, a cat's tumor is much more likely to be malignant. Whereas about 34 percent of canine tumors are malignant, approximately 72 percent of feline tumors are malignant. Benign tumors of the skin in animals usually grow slowly; malignant tumors grow quickly and can spread to nearby tissue and blood vessels of the skin, reaching lymph nodes, liver or lungs via the bloodstream.

The most common sites for cancer in pets are skin and mammary glands, lymph nodes and other blood-forming organs, as well as mouth and bones, but cancer may appear on almost any part of a dog or cat.

Cancer of the colon, pancreas, prostate and cervix is rare in pets. So is lung cancer, but they can contract it. Since pets do not smoke, some research has shown a link between lung cancer and second-hand smoke in dogs. If the research is correct, when we smoke, we put our own pets in danger.

For many reasons, most kinds of cancers go unnoticed in pets for long periods of time, often until it is too late to save them. For example, outdoor dogs and cats who roam may get little hands-on attention from their owners who fail to notice changes in bladder or bowel habits.

Long hair can hide tumors on some cats and dogs. Nursing moms have large, swollen-looking breasts, and so breast tumors are hard to note. When did you last perform a breast exam on your dog or cat?

And of course, even if our loving pets noted a change in their own health, they could not tell us.

Cancer signs: A swelling or lump, especially in the lymph nodes, mammary glands or testicles. A sore that does not heal in the mouth or any part of the animal. Difficulty eating, swallowing, breathing, urinating or defecating. Loss of energy, appetite or weight. Bleeding from the nose, mouth, rectum, vagina or urinary tract. Offensive odor. A veterinarian will diagnose cancer after a biopsy. Treatment for cancer in pets may be similar to that for humans: surgery, chemotherapy, or radiation therapy or a combination of these.

Skin cancers: the plague of the islands

The incidence of most kinds of cancer in dogs and cats and humans is no greater in Hawai'i than anywhere else, with one exception: skin cancer. In our tropical sun, all of us are especially susceptible to melanomas. Skin cancers (malignant melanoma and squamous cell tumors) are most likely to appear on unprotected skin. On a dog or cat, the ears, nose or lips are most susceptible. Short-nosed breeds of dogs and white or light-colored cats are more likely than others to develop squamous cell skin cancers. Squamous cell tumors may vary from a red, flat sore to a cauliflower-like or a hard, flat, grayish lesion that does not heal.

Symptoms: Watch for lumps, scratches or lesions which don't heal or which change in color. If you note anything suspicious, see a veterinarian immediately. As with all cancers, the sooner a skin cancer is diagnosed and treated, the better. If the squamous cell tumor is small, says a doctor, it can often be cured by freezing or by surgery, depending on its location and size. Check your pet's ears, nose, mouth area and skin often.

What can we do? Keep your pet out of the sun during the hottest part of the day: from 9 or 10 a.m. until 3 or 4 p.m. If you must go to the beach at these times, don't take your pet. If your pet must be out in the sun, apply a sun block on your pet, but make sure he doesn't lick it off. Keep white or very light-colored pets, and especially hairless pets, out of the sun.

Pets catch colds, too

We live in paradise, where everything is supposed to be perfect. But we still occasionally catch a common cold. So do our pets. Probably at some time, or several times, you've noticed your cat sneezing, her eyes tearing and/or her nose running. Or perhaps your dog has had the sniffles or a deep cough. That may be due to a respiratory infection (cats) or bronchial infection (dogs). Although a pet's "cold" is similar to a human's, you are not likely to catch your pet's infection or vice-versa.

• Feline upper respiratory infection (cats)

Cats who are under stress of any kind are more susceptible to upper respiratory infections because their bodies' resistance is lowered. Stress to a cat could be caused by a change in his routine, loss of a loved one, a change in diet, a trip to the vet, staying in a boarding kennel or animal shelter, being in a cat show or surviving a hurricane. Increased cases of upper respiratory infections in cats were reported on Kaua`i after Hurricane Iniki. You'll notice sneezing, watery eyes and nasal discharge. If your cat's respiratory infection is of the less serious variety, it should go away within a week on its own. Occasionally a more serious condition may develop or the virus may allow a bacteria-based infection to take hold. In that case, you'll see a heavier, perhaps more yellowish discharge from your cat's eyes and nose. The cat may cough or have a fever. It's time to call your veterinaran. At what point would he or she want to see your cat?

This cat's eyes literally melted from a high fever during an untreated severe upper respiratory infection when it was a kitten. The East Maui Animal Refuge (Boo Boo Zoo) is home to four blind cats from the same litter.

Photo courtesy of Sylvan Schwab

• Kennel cough (bordetella) (dogs)

Kennel cough, highly contagious, is passed by airborne secretions from an infected dog and can take hold wherever dogs are housed near each other (kennels) or interact with each other (dog parks) and especially when they feel stressed (dog shows). Several different virus and even a bacterium can cause this inflammation of your dog's throat and bronchial tubes. A dog whose immune system is up to par may suffer from kennel cough for a week or two and overcome it. A dog with less resistance may seem a bit better, but may actually pass into a second phase of the disease, with a cough that lasts for weeks.

Like feline upper respiratory infection, canine kennel cough may be treated with liquids and plenty of rest. If the cough persists, see your pet's veterinarian.

Leptospirosis: a local killer

You and your dog have been hiking in the mountains for a couple of hours and you are both hot and tired. You come upon a slow moving stream, its water wonderfully cool and inviting and your dog is already drinking the clear water as you shed your clothes. You jump into the stream and your dog leaps in after you.

Carleen Allencastre and Zak, her Australian Shepherd, play in an island pond.

JoAnn Allencastre photo

Ah, heaven! You feel like you're in the middle of one of those Hawai`i-made movies where islanders glide through quiet mountain pools.

Sounds like a great way to spend an afternoon. Also sounds like a great way to pick up one of the islands' most serious diseases: leptospirosis. A potentially fatal bacterial disease that can damage the liver and kidneys of humans, dogs, and other animals, leptospirosis is spread by bacteria in the urine of infected rodents .and mammals. The bacteria can infect streams, fish ponds and mud holes. Hawai`i has the highest rate of leptospirosis in the nation thanks to our large wild boar, goat, mongoose and rat populations. When you or your dog swim in infected water, the bacteria can enter your bodies through mucous membranes in the eyes, ears, nasal passages and mouth, or through skin scratches, lesions or sores.

During the 1990s, more than 40 cases of leptospirosis were reported each year in Hawai`i. Seven people died from the disease. And the problem may be more serious than numbers indicate, the Hawai`i Health Department says. Mild cases often are misdiagnosed or not reported to health authorities. Kaua`i has the highest annual rate of infection, but the disease is also found on O`ahu, Moloka`i, Lana`i, Maui and the Big Island, according to an Associated Press report.

Signs of leptospirosis

Dogs. The first indications of leptospirosis are usually fever, depression, anorexia and/or, muscle pain. Within a few days, vomiting, dehydration, diarrhea or bloody urine my occur. Veterinarians examining dogs with leptospirosis may also find jaundice and abdominal pain. The disease can damage the animal's liver and/or kidneys, sometimes resulting in renal or liver failure and death. If the disease is diagnosed in time, it can be successfully treated with antibiotics.

Even if your dog frolics only in pond-less neighborhood parks, he should be inoculated against leptospirosis and many Hawai`i vets routinely include lepto inoculations in their regular pet care. Check with your

An enticing stream runs through Foster Gardens park in downtown Honolulu; the park is overrun with mongoose and a sign warns that the stream is infected with leptospirosis.

PARASITES

Giardia and coccidia
Fancy names for feline
and canine intestinal bugs

Like many of our island transplants, giardia and coccidia like Hawai'i because we don't have a cold season. These two exotic-sounding parasites attack the intestines and are transmitted to cats or dogs through infected feces or contaminated water. They are often associated with filth, and pets who contact giardia and coccidia can be reinfested from their own or other animals' feces. It is believed that giardia can be transmitted to humans.

Signs: Greenish watery diarrhea. The stool may also contain mucus. If you notice a watery diarrhea lasting more than a day, call your veterinarian.

Prevention: Don't let your pets drink water from contaminated water sources or unknown ponds or creeks. Keep your pet away from other pets' feces.

veterinarian. However, Big Island veterinarian Dr. Maria Jose warns that there are many forms of leptospirosis, and canine vaccines may not provide protection against all of them. A vaccinated dog may still be susceptible, she says, so you are best advised to keep your pet out of unfamiliar puddles and bodies of water.

Cats. Cats almost never show signs of leptospirosis and some experts believe cats have developed a kind of immunity from their long association with rodents, according to the Cornell University College of Veterinary Medicine.

Humans. The early stage of leptospirosis are similar to the flu, and are rarely diagnosed until someone is so ill they require hospitalization.

What can we do? Hawai'i has vast acres of hikeable land, waterfalls, ponds and wetlands and all are tempting. Some are safe, but some aren't. Hawai'i health officials occasionally warn people to stay out of mountain pools, but very few are marked with signs warning of leptospirosis. It's up to you to be careful that you and your dog swim only in waters you know are clean... like the relatively safe ocean that surrounds us.

Other viral and bacterial diseases

Feline leukemia

Feline leukemia virus (FeLV), one of the most contagious and deadly cat illnesses, is prevalent in the cat population throughout the world, including Hawai`i. The virus is spread by contact between cats trading bodily fluids such as saliva (in grooming), blood (fighting) and sperm (sex), as well as sneezing, urinating and defecating. Kittens can be infected from their mother in the womb or through her milk.

After being infected, cats develop a low-grade level of the virus in their blood. The infection progresses in some cats; a few, less than five percent, says one vet, can successfully fight it off. It is believed that all cats that develop the persistent infection can carry the disease to healthy, uninfected cats with which they come in contact.

When the virus first became widely known, in the early 1970s, there was some concern that it could be spread to humans. It is now believed that "cat leukemia" affects only cats, although some veterinarians still recommend limiting contact with FeLV positive cats.

The Cornell (University) Feline Health Center has this to say about possible transmittal: "Although the possibility that FeLV can be transmitted to human beings and cause disease cannot be ruled out completely, there certainly is no evidence to date that transmittal does occur despite decades of extensive research. Also, there is no known association of FeLV with Acquired Immune Deficiency

Rates very high here

How common are Feline Immuno Deficiency Virus and Feline Leukemia Virus on these islands? And how can we keep the disease from spreading? Dr. Antonio Rodrigues of the Moloka`i Veterinary Clinic tested 51 male cats on Moloka`i with disturbing results. Thirteen cats (25.49 percent) tested positive: 11 for FIV (21.56 percent) and two for FeLV (3.92%). Those figures are nearly triple the national estimate of one cat in twelve or 8.22%.

Of the cats infected, nine were male feral cats. The Hawai`i rates are especially high, Dr. Rodrigues says, because of the islands' high feral cat populations. Unneutered male cats tend to fight and spread the viruses through saliva.

The Moloka`i Humane Society, in its newsletter, suggests that neutering of the feral feline population is the first line of defense against these two diseases. An FIV vaccine, Fel-O-Vax, is available from vets.

Syndrome (AIDS) in human beings. Similarly, there is no evidence that FeLV is carried by or causes illnesses in dogs."

Signs: An infected cat's immune system is radically suppressed, making it susceptible to other infections which are often the only indication that a cat is infected with FeLV. The cat may lose its appetite and weight, its mucous membranes may become pale, it may be constipated or pass bloody stools and have difficulty breathing, coughing or swallowing. Because his immune system is affected, the cat, in the words of one veterinarian, "probably never really feels well" and may eventually develop any of several problems such as cancers, anemia, kidney disease or secondary infections which may finally cause its death. Infection with the virus is diagnosed by a blood test.

What can we do? Once a cat is infected, there is no known way to eliminate the virus from the cat's system. The only way to keep your cat totally safe from the virus is to keep him indoors. If your cat goes out, you may want to consider a series of vaccine injections and annual booster shots. Spaying and neutering cats also helps protect them, as they are less likely to roam or fight.

Some veterinarians suggest that it is kindest to euthanize infected cats rather than subject them to infections, a long slow death, or a "sickly" life that may be painful.

"We can't communicate with cats, so they can't tell us, 'this hurts, that hurts.' We don't know what the quality of life is for these cats, so we just have to watch for signs: lethargy, weakness, sores that don't heal," a veterinarian says. "The kindest thing to do may be to end their lives before they really suffer very much."

Feline Panleukopenia (Infectious enteritis) (Distemper)

Highly contagious "feline distemper" (Panleukopenia) is the leading viral disease in cats and the leading cause of infectious disease deaths in kittens. It is not related to the virus that causes distemper in dogs. However, like canine distemper, feline distemper virus is very hardy and can live for months or even years in the home of an infected animal. Not transmitted to humans, distemper is neveretheless a destructive and painful illness that will kill animals if it is not diagnosed and treated early enough. The disease may be spread by contact with an infected cat or his secretions, by exposure to contaminated dishes and litter boxes, the bite of an infected flea, or contamination of the hands or clothing of a caretaker. Distemper is common in cat populations throughout the world and is probably seen no more or less frequently in these islands. Kittens can even be infected with the virus by their mothers before they are born. Death can come suddenly, before you are even aware a kitten is ill.

Signs: An infected cat may have loss of appetite, diarrhea, a high fever, vomit repeatedly and even "moan" in pain.

What can we do? Your veterinarian may vaccinate your kitten against feline distemper in two sessions; for example, the first at age approximately 9 weeks and the second about six weeks later. After that, your cat should be vaccinated annually. Check with your veterinarian.

Canine Parvovirus

The very word "Parvo" makes kennel keepers and wise dog owners shudder. Canine Parvovirus is a deadly virus, most often fatal to puppies under 6 months of age. It is so contagious that outbreaks have occasionally required euthanizing all the dogs at kennels or humane societies on the mainland United States. And paradise holds no panacea against the deadly disease. Humane societies on all islands have experienced outbreaks of parvo.

> **REMEMBER**
> You must take any dog you suspect of having parvo to a vet immediately. Let the veterinarian know in advance that you suspect parvo so he can give you instructions about your pet's arrival and arrange for its isolation.

The disease is transmitted through the feces, hair and feet of contaminated dogs and by contaminated objects such as shoes and grass. It spreads quickly through litters, kennels, pet shops, animal shelters or anywhere dogs gather. That can include the parks and playgrounds your dog probably enjoys so much.

First discovered around 1978, parvo is believed to be a mutant strain of cat distemper. However, parvo does not infect cats or humans. Although it can affect dogs of any age, parvo most frequently attacks puppies between the time of weaning and about 6 months of age, when the natural antibodies a puppy is born with decrease below a protective level. All breeds of dog can be infected, but Rottweilers, Doberman Pinschers and, some veterinarians say, black Labrador Retrievers, are most susceptible and may have less chance of recovering.

Signs: The first indication of parvo is vomiting and lack of energy, followed by diarrhea, bloody and watery feces, rapidly dehydrating the pet. Other symptoms include depression, loss of appetite and high fever. Untreated, pups may continue to vomit and have diarrhea until they die, usually within a week or even a few days.

Cleaning up after distemper and parvo

Distemper and parvo are hardy diseases and can remain infectious in the kennel or house for as long as six months. Bleach is the only known "disinfectant" against parvo. If your pet succumbs to parvo or distemper, do not introduce a new pet into your home and yard until floors, pet dishes, beds, toys, kennels, play yards and anything the pet touched or chewed has been thoroughly cleansed with a solution at least as strong as one part bleach to 9 parts water. (Careful, too strong bleach solutions can burn your lungs and sinuses.) You must also thoroughly wash your floors, bedding, couch covers, etc. and douse your yard and all grass with the solution several times to make sure the virus is eliminated. If you cannot do this, wait at least six months before you introduce a new dog into your home.

Prevention: A parvo vaccine helps control the spread of parvo. Unvaccinated puppies should be kept away from other dogs. Most vets say vaccinations should begin when a puppy is 8 weeks old and continue until 4 months of age. Current research into parvo antibodies will determine how long we should be vaccinating pets against the disease. Follow your veterinarian's recommendations.

Itching & Scratching

Some Hawai`i veterinarians say itchy skin is the most common problem in pets who visit their clinics. An itch can be caused, among other things, by infections, mites, parasites and/or allergies.

Signs: You may notice your pet licking himself often in the same area, especially his paws, or rubbing his face or back against furniture in an attempt to scratch. Or your pet may actually be biting himself to get relief from his itching. You check the pet carefully and find little red pimples or a crust that resembles human dandruff. You may also see open sores or lesions which the tortured pet has caused as he scratches. Or you see nothing at all, but the scratching persists.

What can we do? It's important to stop your pet's itching and scratching cycle; he or she is very uncomfortable and can get an infection from the scratching. Depending on the cause, there may be some things you can do to eliminate the problem. Or you may end up at the veterinarian's. .

Mites and mange

Mites are microscopic creatures that reside on the animals' skin or in his ear canals. They cause a multitude of problems in both dogs and cats and, if left to do their worst, may develop into one of several forms of mange. You won't see the mites, but you may notice your pet scratching or see hair loss. Ear mites are found especially in cats; skin mites in dogs.

Signs: Any of these symptoms can indicate one of numerous kinds of mites: loss of hair and/or bald spots; a crusting around the eyes or ears; a dry, scaly dandruff over the back, neck and sides (mostly in dogs); sores on the skin between the toes.

What can we do? Keep your house and your pet clean. Avoid carpeting, which can harbor mites. See a veterinarian for advice on ridding your pet of the problem.

Miscellaneous allergies

Dogs or cats can have skin allergies from numerous causes. For example, he or she can be allergic to fleas, and/or to the flea collar you put on to control the fleas. Pets can develop allergies to certain food ingredients, primarily proteins. And some food allergies occur after a pet has been eating the same food for years. Your pet may also be allergic to molds, common in some areas of each island, pollens or house dust.

Flea allergies

Signs: Flea allergies are common. A pet who is allergic to fleas may break out with small crusts and bumps in the areas where fleas hang out: around the neck, between and under the ears and/or on his back.

What can we do? If the situation is not too far along, you may be able to handle this problem yourself by getting rid of the fleas. (See the section on fleas beginning on page 186.) Once the fleas are gone, the itching and scratching should stop within a few days.

Other allergies

Pets can also be allergic to insect bites and stings, the latex coating on plastic food bowls, to carpet dyes and even to some flea products.

Signs: Constant scratching and rashes in places where the pets hair is thin or absent, such as his back, chest, tummy, groin, leg, face and ears.

What can we do? If you think you know the cause of the allergy, remove the offender. If the rash does not clear up, talk to your veterinarian.

Sometimes it's just a nasty habit

Scratching and chewing can become habits for cats and especially dogs. A very active pet who does not have enough stimulation may begin scratching or chewing on his body as a release of nervous energy or out of boredom. It's important to stop the actions, which can result in infection. See your veterinarian first, to make sure there are no physical causes for the scratching or chewing. If there aren't, try these methods to distract a pet until it overcomes the bad habit:

- **Increase the pet's physical activity.** Add an extra long walk or active play time to your pet's daily agenda. A tired pet may not chew or scratch himself.

- **Distract him.** When he starts to chew, call his name, get his attention, throw a ball, offer a toy, run around and play for a few minutes, anything to get his mind off the bad habit.

- **Give him something else to chew.** A purchased bone or other chew toy may give your pet something else to chew when he feels the need.

- **Get him a friend.** If you can't be around to distract your pet, consider obtaining a second dog or cat. Having a friend will give your pet someone to play with and may keep him too busy to chew. Dogs may especially need companion pets.

EMERGENCY!

It's the middle of the night and your cat goes into seizures, twitching and writhing, eyes glazed. You can't even hold the animal, let alone administer to her. What can you do?

Obtaining emergency care for a person is easy; almost every hospital has 24-hour emergency services. But, finding after-hours emergency care for a pet can be a nightmare.

It's extremely important that you talk to your veterinarian NOW about how to handle a pet emergency. Ask these questions:

- **If my pet required emergency care after hours, say at 2 a.m., would you be available?**

- **At what phone number can I reach you at that hour?**

- **Will you be willing to see my pet immediately in an emergency?**

Most veterinarians we spoke with said they would be available in an emergency, but some stressed that you, the pet owner, must be honest in determining if the call is truly an emergency. If your pet has been sick for several days, and then seems worse in the middle of the night, you may be able to wait until morning to visit the vet.

Also be aware that an emergency visit may be more costly than one during regular office hours. If your pet seems ill during regular visiting hours and you wonder if you should take him in, you probably should.

24-hour emergency rooms

At least two O'ahu animal hospitals offer 24-hour emergency care.

- **Animal Clinic Waipahu**
  94-806 Moloalo Street
  Waipahu
  Phone (808) 671-1751

- **Veterinary Centers of America (VCA) Kane'ohe**
  45-608 Kamehameha Highway
  Kane'ohe
  Phone (808) 236-2414

Animal Clinic Waipahu is open and staffed 24 hours a day. At VCA in Kane'ohe, several veterinarians are on-call to share after-hour duties. Both pet hospitals will care for your pet no matter who its regular veterinarian is. After emergency treatment, they will refer you back to your own vet and send your pet's medical information to her or him. We were unable to find 24-hour emergency service on any of the neighbor islands. If you live on a neighbor island or an area of O'ahu far from the emergency rooms listed, talk to your veterinarian about emergency care.

Assemble a simple EMERGENCY KIT

You can assemble an emergency medical kit for your pet using many of the items in your own medicine cabinet. Keep the pet kit in an accessible area of your home, such as the bathroom or kitchen. If your pet rides in your car, hikes or swims with you, also make a version of this kit to tuck in the car trunk.

You can also purchase a pet first aid kit from a pet store or pet supply house. Check to see that it contains all the items below. I bought a complete kit at a discount warehouse for under $20 and it included a separate small kit I carry along on hikes. It proved valuable on a hike when Betty, my rat terrier, cornered a mongoose that tore her ear. If you make your own kit, start with a watertight container that can withstand a hurricane. Here is a minimal guide:

- **Gauze bandage** (for tourniquets, splints and muzzle)

- **Scissors** (to cut gauze)

- **Absorbent cotton** (for bleeding, applying disinfectant)

- **Tweezers** (to remove splinters, ticks, burrs)

- **Alcohol** (for insect bites)

- **Hydrogen peroxide** (a disinfectant for small scrapes)

- **Spirits of ammonia** (to help revive your pet if it is in shock)

- **A piece of wood as long as your pet's legs or two magazines** (to serve as splints)

- **Rectal thermometer**
  A dog's temperature is usually 100.2 to 102.8 degrees Fahrenheit.
  A cat's temperature is usually 100.5 to 102.5 degrees Fahrenheit.
  Under 100 and more than 104 degrees may be considered emergency.

- **Vaseline** (to ease insertion of rectal thermometer)

- **A sturdy twin-size or baby blanket** (to keep pet warm if it is in shock and to use as makeshift stretcher if animal must be moved)

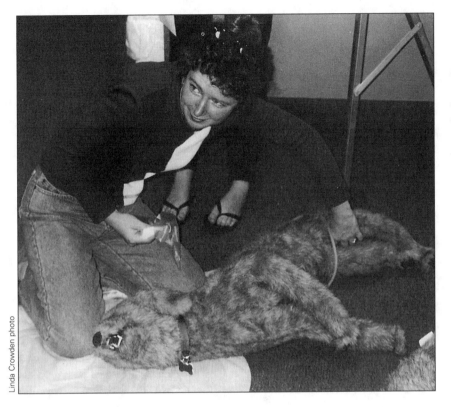

Linda Crowden photo

An instructor checks the pulse of a pet mannequin by feeling the dog's inner thigh during a Red Cross Pet First Aid class. Students learn to take pulse and temperature, practice rescue breathing to revive a pet who has choked, and apply "mouth to snout" cardiopulmonary resuscitation. The Red Cross holds Pet First Aid classes occasionally at sites around the islands. Call your local branch for information.

Learn to save your pet's life

The American Red Cross is well known for coming to the aid of people, but few of us realize that the Red Cross also helps pets and their owners. With a little effort, you can get the kind of training and information that could some day save your pet's life.

- **First Aid courses:** You'll learn important safety techniques, like giving your dog CPR, at Red Cross courses held occasionally on all islands. Call your local Red Cross office for information.

- **The Pet First Aid Book:** You need more information on pet emergencies than we can provide here. Keep this easy-to-read book on hand. Written by Bobbie Mammato, DVM, MPH, the *Pet First Aid Book* is recommended by the American Red Cross and The Humane Society of the United States. Published by Mosby Year Book, Inc., it is available from most Red Cross offices across the nation, including Hawai`i, for under $10 and also by special order through bookstores.

fetch
more information

Local Red Cross Numbers:

Hilo: 935-8305

Kona : 326-9488

Kaua`i: 245-4919

Maui: 244-0051

O'ahu: 734-2101

Alternative treatments and care

Acupuncture helped Lucy walk again

Nancy and Russ Kanady knew their miniature poodle Lucy had hip problems, but they didn't realize the extent of the problem until Lucy awoke one morning, unable to walk. She could only pull herself forward with her front legs, dragging her back legs behind, like a beached seal.

The Kanadys rushed Lucy to the Central Maui Animal Clinic in Kahului where Dr. Curtis Willauer, VMD, diagnosed a protruding disk. He recommended acupuncture and came to the Kanady's Kihei home to perform the procedure. He slid "about 20 needles" into Lucy's skin, Russ says. The procedure did not seem to cause any pain at all until Lucy, totally relaxed, rolled over on one of the needles. In all, she had six acupuncture sessions over several weeks. Before long, Lucy was walking again and her pain seems to be gone.

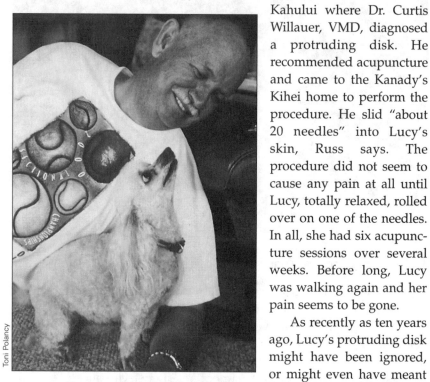

Russ Kanady and Lucy.

Toni Polancy

As recently as ten years ago, Lucy's protruding disk might have been ignored, or might even have meant she would be euthanized instead of treated. Today, pet owners are seeking a wide variety of treatments to keep pets healthy and comfortable including acupuncture, massage therapy, acupressure, *lomi lomi* therapy, herbs and/or preservative-free or home-prepared food. Dr. Willauer is one of several Hawai`i veterinarians trying alternatives to the traditional methods of pet health care.

Dr. Willauer says Lucy's success with acupuncture was "dramatic" and warns that not all alternative treatment is as successful.

One of the state's best-known holistic pet healers is Dr. Ihor Basko, DVM, who practices on O`ahu and Kaua`i. According to Basko's Web

Alternative pet care

Dr. Ihor Basko
Dr. Molly Rice
All Creatures Great & Small
Kapa`a, Kaua`i
808-822-4229

Dr. Curtis Willauer
Central Maui Animal Clinic
45 Ho`okele Street
Kahului, Maui
Phone (808) 893-2380.
e-mail: cmac@maui.net

Dr. Suellen Kotake
All Pets Clinic Waipahu, Inc.
94-366 Pupupani Street
Waipahu, O`ahu
(808) 671-7424

Dr. Carol Fujioka
Kilani Pet Clinic
810 Kilani Avenue
Wahiawa, O`ahu
(808) 622-2607

Dr. Wendy Asato
University Pet Clinic
2728 Woodlawn Drive
Honolulu
(808) 988-2111

Dr. Robin Woodley
Hawaii Veterinary Alternatives
Kapa`au, Hawai`i
(808) 889-5488

For a complete list of Hawai`i veterinarians, see the Resource section at the back of this book.

site, he helps patients develop home-prepared diets for pets including grains, protein, meat, vegetables, roots, leaves, beans and herbs, many of which are grown in Hawai`i.

Acupuncture therapy has been practiced for thousand of years in the Orient. Dr. Basko uses needles, electricity, lasers and injections of vitamins to stimulate acupuncture points and treat arthritis, paralysis, allergies, epilepsy, skin problems, geriatric problems, immune system disorders and digestive disturbances in pets, according to his website.

Related business
and organizations:
Gentle World
Non-profit organization educating people and dogs to the health and benefits of a vegan diet.
Flowers Kison
(808) 884-5551
gentleworld.org

Massage for People and Pets
Kim Mays
1151 12th Avenue
Honolulu
(808) 732-8870

Naturally Pet
This Honolulu health food store for pets includes food, treats and alternative medicinal products.
535 Ward Avenue, Suite 106
Honolulu
(808) 591-9944

fetch
more information

from the Internet:
naturallypet.com
drwoodley.com
drbasko.com

Which shots... and when?

Start talking inoculations with a group of pet owners and you are apt to get a variety of opinions about what pets should be innoculated against, and when.

"My vet recommends annual boosters for that pig disease, you know lepto something," says one.

"My vet says there's no use inoculating against leptospirosis at all because there are so many varieties of it," says another.

"One thing you need for sure is rabies shots. My dog gets his every year," advises a third.

"Every year?" comments a fourth. "My dogs get one shot every six months."

We asked Dr. James Foppoli, the state veterinarian, if the state sets any standards or recommends any particular series of shots for pets. It does not. Puppies are "historically" given a DHLP or DHLPP at the age of about 8 weeks, Dr. Foppoli says, with booster shots at 12 weeks and 16 weeks. Thereafter, most carefully cared for dogs receive an inoculation each year. Here's what those letters mean:

D-Distemper
H-Hepatitis
L-Leptospirosis
P-Parvovirus
P-Parainfluenza (colds, kennel coughs)

After the first 16 weeks, "the whole issue of when to boost gets clouded," Dr. Foppoli says. Most veterinarians follow the guidelines of the drug manufacturers, but there is some controversy in recent years about how often and when booster shots are needed. Traditional vets may simply decide to inoculate each year, others want to take blood tests first and decide if the pet needs booster shots. But this route can be costly, the doctor says. "High costs can drive people away, keeping them from seeking care when their pets need it."

There are over 300 strains of leptospirosis. Hawai'i veterinarians usually inoculate against the strain carried by wild pigs and the strain carried by mice, rats and mongoose, all common problems in the islands. There is some question about just how long lepto inoculations are effective and how often they need to be repeated: six months or a year.

Leptospiroris inoculations can have undesirable side effects for young puppies and you may want to discuss that with your vet. Cats have their own series of shots and are rarely inoculated against leptospirosis.

By the way, not every dog who encounters lepto becomes seriously ill. Some healthy dogs are able to fight off the infection.

Who will care for your pet when you can't?

If you had a child, you would probably be planning ahead, concerned about your child's future in the event that you become very ill or have an accident and cannot not care for the child. It's time to show the same concern for the future well-being of your pet.

Mentally sift through your friends and relatives and choose one who seems to communicate well with your pet. Discuss your pet's future with the person you choose. Ask if he or she is willing to be the pet's guardian if something should happen to you. Make sure the person you have chosen understands what a large responsibility caring for a cat or dog can be.

Although it is not entirely necessary, if you can afford to do so, you may want to leave some funds to help care for your pet. This is a matter for your attorney. If you can't afford to, don't worry. The care of a pet should not be so expensive that it will be a burden to its caretaker.

The form on the following pages is designed to give your pet's new caretaker all the information he or she needs to be a responsible and loving friend to your pet. Using one form for each of your pets, complete this form. Make two copies and:

photo courtesy Maui Humane Society

- **Give one to your pet's future caretaker.**

- **Place another copy with your will and/or insurance policies.**

Be sure to tell your attorney, your executor, your spouse, your adult children, and anyone else close to you about your choices for your pet's future care. Stress to them how important your pet is to you and ask them to promise to fulfill your wishes.

Future Caretaker's Form

In the event of my death, illness or any trauma that keeps me from caring for my pet, this is the information you need to love and care for my pet as I do.

My pet's name: _____
Nicknames: _____
Kind of pet: _____
Breed or description: _____
Tag number: _____
Tattoo number or ID number: _____
My pet has a microchip. ○ Yes   ○ No

If I am unable to care for my pet due to illness or death,
this pet will be cared for by:
Name: _____
Address: _____
Phones: _____

My pet's veterinarian:
Name: _____
Address: _____
Phones: _____

My pet's health:
Problems or considerations: _____
_____
_____

Medications and what they are for: _____
_____

Instructions for administering medications. How much, how often:
_____
_____
_____

Diet:

What my pet eats and how often: _____

_____

_____

Special treats my pet enjoys and how often: _____

_____

_____

Any special diet considerations: _____

_____

_____

_____

My pet indicates a need to relieve itself ("go to the bathroom") by:

_____

_____

_____

Grooming:

How often? _____

Groomer's name: _____

Groomer's address: _____

Groomer's phone numbers: _____

If no groomer is used, who cuts pet's nails and how: _____

_____

If no groomer is used, how is my pet bathed and how often: _____

_____

_____

Flea control:

Name of product: _____

How is it obtained: _____

How often is it administered: _____

How to administer it: _____

_____

Heartworm control:

Product used: _____

Where to get it: _____

How it is administered and how often: _____

_____

Licensing:

Dog (or cat) tag number: _____

When does it expire: _____

Where and how do you renew it: _____

_____

Exercise:

My pet's favorite forms of exercise and how often: _____

_____

_____

_____

His or her favorite toy is: _____

Where it is located: _____

Where I walk my pet and how often: _____

_____

History:

How my pet was obtained:

When: _____

Where: _____

How: _____

My pet's birthday is: _____

How my pet got its name: _____

_____

_____

_____

_____

Disposition:

What makes my pet angry: _____

_____

What makes my pet afraid: _____

_____

What makes my pet happy: _____

_____

My pet's favorite method of communicating with me is:

_____

_____

_____

_____

Words and/or phrases my pet understands:

_____

_____

_____

_____

_____

_____

My pet means a great deal to me. Mahalo for agreeing to be caretaker.
Here are some other things I want you to know about my pet:

_____

_____

_____

_____

_____

_____

_____

How old is your dog?

You've probably heard the old adage that one year of a dog's life equals seven years of human life. That's just not accurate. Large dogs age more quickly than smaller dogs. And all dogs age more quickly early in life and less quickly later in life.

Here, from Merial, a pet pharmaceutical company, is an approximate calculation of pets in comparison to people.

Makana Bender art

Dog	Human
8 months	13 years
1 year	16 year
2 years	24 years
3 years	28 years
5 years	36 years
7 years	44 years
9 years	52 years
11 years	60 years
13 years	68 years
15 years	76 years

Fleas, Bugs & Bites

These are tropical
islands and, yes,
we have bugs.
Lots of bugs. And
other creatures, too.

*Greta, a
dachshund,
gets up close
and personal
with a cockroach.*

FLEAS! and ticks

They love our islands and our pets,
and aren't adverse to nibbling on us

Not so many years ago, fleas were a horrible problem for all dog and cat owners, but especially for those of us who lived on tropical islands where the breeding conditions are excellent, the flea reproductive cycle is year-round, and the temperature never drops low enough to eliminate them. If you saw a flea on your pet, you could bet there were hundreds more fleas and flea eggs lurking in your carpets, your pet's bedding and in baseboards throughout your home.

In those not-so-good old days, it was common to see children whose legs were covered with the tiny itchy bites. (You can usually differentiate a flea bite from a mosquito bite by its size and number. Flea bites are smaller and fleas usually bite numerous times in one area.)

Flea problems? Move Upcountry. Fleas cannot live above 5,000 feet and are rarely seen at higher elevations.

The only way to avoid flea infestations was to bathe your pet often, spray and respray him and use flea collars, or keep the pet indoors at all times. If the home became infested, you had to set off flea bombs, leave the house for several hours, vacuum thoroughly and throw the vacuum bag away (it could harbor flea eggs). This was a strenuous and often ineffective process. And the procedure had to be repeated two weeks later when any flea eggs left in the carpet or furniture hatched.

Ah! But then a little miracle occurred. Along came wonderful new flea controls that are highly effective, safe and relatively easy to use. Suddenly, we could give our dogs and cats just one pill per month or squirt a little solution between their shoulder blades and eliminate the problem of fleas and ticks entirely.

Products like *Frontline, Advantage* and *Program*, new to the market in the 1980s and 1990s, make pet pest control a breeze. At this time, flea controls are costly, as high as $10 a dose. You will find here a story with suggestions from a Hawai'i vet to cut the cost of flea control products somewhat. The Internet offers sites where they can be bought at a discount. (See page 190 of this book.)

If you haven't done so already, put your pet on a regular schedule of flea/tick control now. Don't wait until you see little round ticks

IF YOU SEE A FLEA...

Despite using the gels and/or pills, you may occasionally find a flea on your pet, especially if you let him run with other animals or in grass or foliage. Remove the flea, if possible. If you see more than one flea, or if you choose to try to eliminate fleas without chemicals, try this effective method we used before reliable flea control was available: Work up a sudsy lather with a good flea shampoo and thoroughly wash your dog or cat. Don't rinse off the lather. Wrap the suds-soaked pet in a towel and hold him, keeping the towel around him for 10 to 15 minutes. This allows the pet shampoo to kill the fleas. Remove the towel. If your pet was infested, you should see dead or dying fleas on the towel. Now thoroughly rinse off the shampoo. Try to submerge your pet in a tub or gently hose him off. Comb through his fur with a fine-toothed comb or flea comb to remove any other dead fleas.

All that because you saw a flea or two on your pet? Isn't that overreacting? Not at all. Fleas breed and spread so quickly that your home can be infested in a matter of hours.

Janice Carr photo courtesy of the CDC Public Health Image Library

or fast moving tiny black fleas on your dog or cat. These pests can carry tape worms and blood-borne diseases. And, by the time you see them, ticks or fleas have already become a problem.

Types of Control

Three "modern" types of products for flea control are available; each has its benefits.

- **Oral:** These products can be fed directly to your pet as a pill or as a liquid or sprinkled on his food. Oral versions usually control flea and tick populations by interrupting the pest's life cycle. Fleas who bite the pet cannot lay more eggs. This helps to keep your yard pest free, eventually, and controls most pests in your animal's fur too. Unfortunately, oral pet controls may be slower to work than topical versions.

- **Topical:** With topical flea controls, you squeeze a liquid onto your pet from a small tube, usually monthly. Most versions go on the animal's skin between his shoulder blades. It's applied at least three days *after* the pet has had a bath and the pet should not be submerged in water for several days afterward, so the liquid has time to work. The oils on the animals skin help disperse the insecticide throughout his skin. Be sure to get the appropriate dose for your animal; doses are determined by the animal's weight. Be very careful to give the correct amount. Some of these products can be fatal if a dog dose, for example, is given to a cat. See the related stories, this chapter.

- **Spray:** *Frontline* offers a spray bottle version of the topical control that could be ideal for multiple pet owners who have plenty of patience. You can use the same spray on any size animal, be they cats or dogs, spraying once for every pound of your pet's weight. The nozzle of the spray is pressed close to the animal's skin. This is not as convenient as the tube or oral products and it can be difficult to use this product on a cat. Our cat bolted after the second spray and we had to do it in three sessions.

Nature's Alternatives

If you are adverse to chemical flea controls, you may want to try one of these methods, recommended by some veterinarians, pet owners and holistic enthusiasts. It should be said that these three flea "solutions" have been around for years with questionable effectiveness.

- **Fresh garlic.** A little every day, they say, will keep fleas away, and this natural plant, available in pill form, offers additional health benefits.

A tick disease (dogs)

Ehrlichiosis, a tick-borne disease that can kill dogs, is common in Hawai`i. A dog is infected after being bitten by a tick that has dined on another dog carrying Ehrlichiosis.

Signs: An infected dog may exhibit high fever and/or vomiting. He may have enlarged lymph nodes, under the jaw or behind the legs. He may be depressed, says Dr. Maria Jose, DVM, who travels across much of the Big Island as Humane Society veterinarian.

"Where we have problems," she says, "is when the infection gets into the bone marrow and infects certain types of cells. It targets platelets that clot blood. Over time the dog may have a tendency to bleed easily and may start to bleed through the rectum, nose or gums. He may bruise easily and hemorrhage.

"In practice I've seen several dogs die of this disease. There is treatment, but in later stages it can be difficult to save them."

What can we do? Prevention involves using a flea control product such as Frontline which includes a tick preventive. A tick collar called Preventic, available from veterinarians, seems to help. It's also important to clear your yard of ticks. Spray frequently with a tick repellent or hire an insect control company to help.

- **Vinegar**. Just a teaspoon of vinegar can prevent fleas and ticks? Add a teaspoonful to each gallon of your pet's drinking water. Such a small amount, almost undetectable to your pet, is said to be enough to discourage fleas and ticks.
- **Brewer's yeast**. Some dog owners say that additional brewer's yeast in the diet prevents fleas and ticks. A good source of thiamine and other B complex vitamins and relatively inexpensive, brewer's yeast is available in tablet or powder form. The powder can be liberally sprinkled over food, or the tablets given as treats. What is not absorbed in the system is excreted through the skin, and may discourage fleas. The yeast may also improve the quality of the dog's coat.

Careful! Flea control mistakes can (and do) kill pets

It was my fault. A few years ago, attempting to save money on flea control for my pets (at the time I had three dogs and three cats) I bought over-the-counter flea control products. I opened the packages, threw away the outer covers, and laid the tubes out on the counter. The phone rang and I answered it. When I came back, I never even gave a thought to the tubes of liquid I was about to squirt on my pets' backs. I simply gave the dogs theirs from the first three tubes; then applied the next three tubes to the cats. That night Hobi, my Russian Blue, went into seizures. At 2 a.m. I rushed Hobi to his vet's office where the gentle, loving cat died in my arms.

Our vet knew immediately what had happened: I had mixed the containers of flea control, giving Hobi a dog's dose. And the vet knew something else: the products were OTC

Hobi, left, died from a flea control dosage meant for a dog. Coop, was more fortunate. Her vet and a $600-plus tab, saved her life.

or purchased over the counter rather than through a veterinarian. The costlier vet-purchased products contain ingredients less deadly to pets, she explained.

Back at home, I pulled the used vials out of the trash. None of the vials were labeled, only the outer packaging indicated whether the product was for dogs or cats.

A Maui woman had a similar experience. Her two cats received incorrect dosages from an unmarked inner packet of an OTC product. The cats survived, thanks to her vet's quick work. The woman wrote a letter to the company that had manufactured the flea control product.

"I told them what happened, what I had done. I felt like the vials should have been better marked, or different colors. Something to tell them apart easily," she says.

"The veterinary bill was in excess of $650. Being a single mom, it was a lot of money to come up with. They wrote back and said to send them the bill. I did and they wrote back again and said send them the vial." Of course, I'd thrown it away.

Several veterinarians we talked to while writing this book had encountered problems from incorrectly administered over-the-counter flea control product. Flea control products represent a huge industry from which manufacturers make great profits. But flea controls vary in both their effectiveness and

ASPCA issues warning: permethrin fatal to cats

In October, 2000, an Associated Press story warned that over-the-counter flea and tick control products for dogs that contain the common chemical permethrin, can be toxic to cats. Cats exposed to permethrin through direct contact can become ill or die. Even cats that groom or engage in close physical contact with a recently treated dog may be at risk of toxic exposure.

The ASPCA says there are 18 products on the market containing permethrin and even a small amount can be fatal to a cat.

Quoting a veterinarian, a press release from Farnum Pet Products, makers of BioSpot, says "While over-the-counter flea and tick products have a wide margin of safety when used as directed, it is important for people to realize that certain flea control products intended only for dogs can be toxic to cats. A product labeled only for dog should not be used on cats, and cats that actively groom or engage in close physical contact with a recently treated dog may be at risk of toxic exposure in the first 24 to 48 hours after application."

Farnum says its packaging for cat and dog products is very different, "in hopes that consumers will carefully examine the label" of any flea and tick product before applying it to their pets.

safeness. Be careful using any of the products, and especially over-the-counter brands. Pay astute attention to labels.

For my pets' safety, I now use only vet-sanctioned flea controls and I apply them to my dogs and cat very separately. The dogs are treated one day and the cat the next day, so there is no chance of mixing vials.

Hopefully, one of the pet product manufacturers will soon come up with a less costly, safe version of flea control for our pets. Meanwhile, many Hawai`i pet owners buy flea control products over the Internet and/or through mail order, where a variety of discounts are available. But the products are still very costly for multiple pet owners.

Flea controls: Which does what?

Which flea control is best for your pet? That depends on the age and lifestyle of your pet and the severity of the flea infestation, says Dr. Maria Jose, DVM. In a column for *Paw Prints*, the Hawai'i Island (Big Island) Humane Society newsletter, she outlined some of the most popular brands to show the difference in products.

Frontline TopSpot (fipronil)
- administered topically, directly to your pet's skin
- kills adult fleas only
- also effective against most ticks
- most effective if applied every four weeks
- for use in dogs and cats 10 weeks of age or older
- available only through veterinarians

Frontline Plus (methoprene)
- this is exactly the same as *Frontline TopSpot* above, except that methoprene, a flea growth regulator, is added. It stops the reproductive stage, killing flea eggs as well as adult fleas
- can be used on dogs or cats 8 weeks and older
- available only through veterinarians

Advantage (imidacloprid)
- administered topically, directly to your pet's skin
- kills adult fleas only
- most effective if applied every four weeks
- for use in dogs and cats eight weeks of age or more
- available only through veterinarians

Tip
**Keep
surfing**
You can save by
purchasing flea
control via the
Internet, but
don't just flip
to the most
popular sites,
for example,
those that
advertise on TV.
Internet prices
vary a great deal.
Here's the
comparison for
a six-pack of
Frontline Plus
for a medium-
sized dog when
I surfed in
June, 2003:

• **My vet:** $72

• **PetMed.com**:
$61.73 plus $8
postage, a total
of $69.73

• **fleas-go.com**:
$41.96 plus $4.50
postage for a
total of $45.46.

**That's a savings
of $26**—worth
the time it takes
to keep surfing.

Revolution (selamectin)
• administered topically, directly to skin
• kills adult fleas and eggs
• also effective against one species of tick, some intestinal parasites, ear mites and heartworm
• most effective if applied every four weeks
• for use on dogs and cats six weeks of age or older
• available only through veterinarians

Bio-Spot (permethrin/pyriproxyfen)
• apply to dogs only
• administered topically, directly to skin
• kills adult fleas and contains an insect growth regulator which inhibits the flea reproductive life cycle
• most effective if applied every three to four weeks
• for use in dogs 12 weeks of age or older
• available over-the-counter

Note: The *Bio-Spot* product for cats is similar to the dog formula except it does not contain permethrin and so is not effective against adult fleas.

One Spot (permethrin/methoprene)
• apply to dogs only
• administered directly to skin
• kills adult fleas and contains an insect growth regulator which inhibits the reproductive cycle.
• for use in dogs six months of age or older
• available over-the-counter

Note: The *One Spot* product for cats is similar to the dog formula except it does not contain permethrin and therefore is not effective against adult fleas. The cat product is safe for use in cats over 12 weeks of age.

Although the products seem similar, they have completely different active ingredients and their effectiveness varies, Dr. Jose says.

"In my experience *Frontline, Advantage* and *Revolution* are the superior products for overall 'kill' of adult fleas," she writes. "In most situations, nearly 100 percent of all fleas are dead within 24 hours when these products are applied in the correct manner. This has not been my experience with *Bio-Spot, One Spot,* and other over-the-counter flea controls.

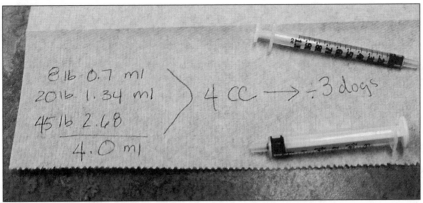

Save $$ on pet care costs

If one pet is costly to maintain, imagine paying food, flea control and medical bills for three, four, or more pets. Multiple pet owners can and should save money on food, vet bills and pet medications, says a Hawai`i veterinarian. Here are her suggestions:

- **Ask your vet for a multiple pet discount.** Some owners who bring two or more pets at the same time for a routine vet visit pay less for second and third animals. For example, your vet might charge $50 for the first office visit. He or she may charge $40 for each additional animal. If your veterinarian charges the same for each pet, request a discount. There's really no good reason a vet should charge less for additional animals. After all, it takes the same amount of time for each animal no matter how many there are. But some vets simpy recognize that you are caring for several animals and offer a discount.

- **Divide flea control capsules and worm medicines.** Depending on the size of your pets, one extra-large capsule of a premium flea control product like Frontline can be divided between two or three smaller pets or can be saved for multiple doses. Ask your veterinarian to help you calculate the dosage based on your pet's weight. Then ask him to supply a syringe for each pet, marked with the amount each pet needs. Break the capsule open and spill the liquid into a bottle cap or very small dish. Using the syringe, suction up the exact amount and apply it to your pet. These two extra steps can save you nearly two-thirds on the cost of monthly flea applications. (See photo.)

Bugs

One extra-large dog's dose of Frontline contains 4 milliliters of flea control which I divide into three doses, one for each of my dogs. Winky, my eight-pound terrier, requires 0.7 milliliters; Betty, my 20-pound mixed Chihuahua gets 1.34 milliliters; Archie, the 45-pound Airedale mix, gets 2.68 milliliters. The cost of the three doses would be approximately $30. Purchasing one extra large dose and dividing it costs me approximately $11, a savings of $19 each month.

- **You can also save** by buying Frontline in an 8.5-ounce spray bottle or 16-ounce spray bottle. Application isn't as frightening as it sounds. "Spray" seems to indicate the product fizzes all over. Actually, the spray nozzle is pressed close to the animal's skin and you count sprays: one spray for each pound of weight whether the animal is a dog or a cat. Ask your vet to show you how to figure the correct number of sprays for your pet and how to use this product. This is considerably more difficult than opening a packet of pre-measured liquid and applying (especially on an unwilling cat), but it does save money.

- **Ask for a Humane Society member discount.** Some island veterinarians and pet supply stores offer discounts to card-carrying Humane Society members. Ask before you make an appointment or buy pet supplies.

- **Seek out pet care bargains.** Call your island Humane Society and ask when they will be offering discounted inoculations, microchip implants and grooming services. Maui, for example, has "Dog Day Afternoons" when nail clipping, ear cleaning and bathing is offered for about $15 a dog. Microchipping costs a small extra amount. Some pet stores also sponsor special events with discounted microchip implants and vaccinations.

To save money on flea control, a veterinarian suggests Archie, Winky and Betty could share one large vial of Frontline.

Insect and creature bites

You and I and our pets aren't the only beings who enjoy Hawai'i's near-perfect weather. So do numerous small, nasty creatures: insects, fungi, virus and bacteria that can mean problems, disease, and even death to our pets.

Nearly every Hawai'i insect or creature that bites you or me will also bite our dogs and cats. The bite can be as painful to them as it is to us, and much sadder because, being animals, they don't understand why that bee sting hurts so much or why a mosquito bite itches.

"I practiced in California and attended school in Washington state," says a Big Island veterinarian, "and I did not see nearly the amount of parasites that we have here."

Fortunately, Hawai'i has no insects whose bites are fatal, in themselves, to man or beast unless either is allergic to the insect bites. You can treat your pet's insec[t] bite much as you would treat your own. However, unle[ss] your dog or cat lets out a yowl (for example, after bei[ng] stung by a centipede or scorpion) you may not know where, when or how your pet was bitten.

What can we do? Don't keep your pet outdoors overnight, at the mercy of mosquitoes. Don't leave him chained up for long periods during the day, a target for biting flies. If possible, make your cat an indoor cat.

> ## Pet bitten by a bug?
> ## Try these safe soothers
> For mosquito, fly, bee, wasp, yellow jacket, ant, centipede and flea bites, remove the stinger, if there is one, and apply any of these pet-safe soothers:
> - A paste of baking soda and water
> - Calamine lotion
> - Ice packs to relieve swelling and pain
>
> If the bite area continues to swell or reddens, see a veterinarian. immediately.

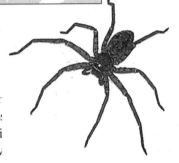

Mosquitoes

If mosquitoes are particularly pesky, try applying a safe mosquito deterrent such as Avon Skin So Soft when your pet goes outdoors. **Do not use an insect repellent.** Your animal may try to lick it off, and most insect repellents are hazardous. Some are also flammable.

Jim Gathany photo courtesy of the CDC Public Health Image Library

Biting ants

Vicious biting ants are a painful problem at many of Hawai`i's parks and a few beaches. When vibrations disturb a fire ant colony—for example, when you or your pet stands on or near a nest—these tiny but tough brownish-red creatures attack en masse and bite with blazing stings that can leave burning welts. The ants aren't fussy about their prey; either you or your pet will do just fine. I've had to rush my dog to a water faucet and scrub off ants that scurried up his legs to his soft underbelly. As I worked to get them off my yelping and confused pet, the ants clambered over my arms and legs, leaving red lesions that itched and ached for days. These are not, by the way, the fire ants that attack some part of the mainland U.S.A.

Scott Bauer photo courtesy of the USDA Agricultural Research Service

What can we do? Be careful. Keep your eyes open. Watch for small hills, holes and ants in sand or dirt or between patches of grass, anywhere you and your dog sit, walk or play. There are no posted signs to warn of active fire ants, so other pet owners (or, unfortunately, your own experience) will have to alert you to which parks, or which areas of parks or beaches, to avoid. Watch for sprayings. Community parks are occasionally sprayed to eliminate ants. Signs are usually posted alerting you to the sprayings. Stay away. The insecticides can be dangerous to your pet.

Centipedes and Scorpions

We humans think they are about the ugliest creatures on earth, but dogs and cats seem to be fascinated by fast-moving centipedes, which can grow to eight or nine inches in Hawai'i. Centipedes don't appreciate the attention and a centipede is apt to sting a dog's or cat's tender nose or curious paw. Hawai'i's centipedes and scorpions inflict nasty bites, which are painful, but rarely deadly. It's nearly impossible to keep

> ## Tip
>
> ### Ask your veterinarian
>
> in advance, at your next visit, what he or she wants you to do if your pet is bitten. Depending on the size, type, age and health of your pet, some vets may want to see the pet immediately.

curious pets away from centipedes who lurk under brush, but can appear almost anywhere.

What can we do? If your pet is bitten by either of these creatures, flush the bite with plenty of cool water. Apply one of the soothers listed here and watch the pet and the bite area. You can expect some swelling, but if the swelling seems extensive or if your pet is lethargic or acts strangely, it may be allergic. See a veterinarian immediately.

Jellyfish

Check the shoreline carefully before you or your dog goes into the ocean. If you see a bluish, slimy bubble—a jellyfish—on the shore, it's a safe bet more are slinking through the water. Stay out of the ocean and keep your pet out, too. Continue your stroll away from the beach; shores are sometimes littered with the jellyfish, still capable of inflicting pain.

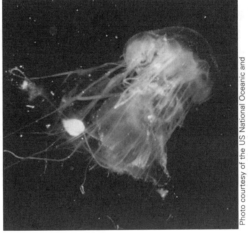

Photo courtesy of the US National Oceanic and Atmospheric Administration

What can we do? Most dogs are so hairy you wouldn't expect them to be bothered much by jellyfish, but dogs can be stung by the slimy bits of ooze. And a dog who steps on a sticky jellyfish or gets one attached to its nose has no good method of removing it, so that's up to you. You can pick up a handful of sand and very quickly and gently rub the jellyfish away. If the slime has attached to a hairless area like nose, paw or genitals, your pet will be in severe pain. A jellyfish sting burns intensely, much like a burn from heat or fire. Apply ice or ice water immediately to lessen pain. Later, apply one of the soothers listed here. The area may be painful for several days.

Worms: real problems in a tropical climate

Nobody ever told you being a pet owner would be easy, but did anyone mention that you will occasionally be checking your cat's or dog's stool for worms? Heartworms are by far the worst, but numerous other wriggling parasites can infect your pet. Intestinal worms such as round-worms, hookworms and whipworms are prevalent all over the world and particularly in warm climates. Yes, Hawai'i.

Your cat or dog becomes infected with worms in a variety of ways: by wandering in infested dirt, associating with other infected pets, eating mice or rats that are infected or ingesting infected fleas.

What can we do? Fortunately, modern chemistry has made worm problems easy to solve. Your vet will want to test regularly for worms and can advise you on the best solutions. Over-the-counter products are available at most pet stores and drug stores, but a veterinarian reviewing this book advised against OTC (over the counter) de-wormers. Talk this over with your veterinarian.

Heartworm: spread to pets by our relentless mosquitoes

As a mosquito feeds on your pet, it can spread heartworm, one of the most common and feared parasites in Hawai'i. Every animal health care professional we spoke with stressed heartworm as a very real danger to dogs and cats here.

"Heartworm is so prevalent in some areas of Hawai'i," says one vet, "that if a dog doesn't (take a preventative tablet or pill each month), he probably *will* get heartworm in his lifetime."

Mosquitoes are everywhere in Hawai'i, but they are especially rife in rainy areas such as Haiku and Olinda, Maui; the windward side of O'ahu; most of Kaua'i, and the Hilo side of the Big Island.

Mosquitoes can pass microfilaria (baby heartworms) from an infect-ed animal to healthy ones. It takes about six months for the larvae to develop into adult heartworms which take up residence in the dog's heart chambers, producing more worms. You have probably seen photos or illustrations of an infected heart in your vet's office, the heartworms looking like thin spaghetti noodles winding through the heart chambers.

Signs of heartworm: The first indications a pet is infected may include exercise intolerance and weight loss. Later signs may include coughing, vomiting and difficulty breathing. Treatment is very effective, safe and painless. Costs range is $200 to $600 depending on the severity, says a veterinarian.

Cats. Diagnosing heartworm can be particularly difficult in cats. Though cats rarely contact it, they may have more severe reactions to heartworms than dogs. The heartworms tend to live in different areas of the cat, such as the brain, lungs and body cavities instead of the heart.

Tip
For pets and people

Humans don't get heartworm, but mosquitoes can carry malaria, dengue fever and other diseases deadly to us. Keep tight screens on your windows and use an insect repellent when you go outdoors. But never use a strong insect repellent (such as those with the chemical Deet) on your pet. Some pet owners spread a thin layer of a mild product like Avon's Skin So Soft on their pet's exposed skin. Check with your veterinarian before doing this.

What can we do? Prevention is essential, veterinarians and humane societies agree. This includes giving your pet a preventative your veterinarian prescribes, usually after first testing to make sure the animal does not already have heartworms. Chewy pills such as Heartgard Plus, administered monthly, are inexpensive and effective. My dogs and cats seem to consider the pill a treat.

Tapeworms (cats and dogs)

Signs: You may see signs of them in your pet's stool or near his *okole* (rump). The short flat white "worms" look like grains of rice, but what you see are not actually worms. They are the egg packets left by the worms who live in the pet's intestine.

What can we do? Keeping your pet free of fleas is the best way to keep him free of tapeworms. Flea larvae eat the tapeworm eggs and then your pet ingests the fleas as he cleans himself. Put your pet on a flea control program. Consult your vet.

We call them HITCH-HIKERS

The rest of the world calls them burs—those rough, prickly cases around the seeds of certain plants. Here in Hawai`i we call them "hitch-hikers." Burs attach themselves to pets' fur just about anywhere—paws and faces, tails and ears. Whatever you call them, Hawai`i pets tend to be pretty cool about the nuisance, nonchalantly pulling them off a paw despite the discomfort. Some pets even eat the sharp little burrs, chewing them despite the discomfort. But burs are particularly painful for long-haired animals who may need your help, via a pair of precisely administered scissors, to dislodge an unwelcome hitchhiker.

Wire-haired pets like Wink have a difficult time with burs.

Toni Polancy photo

Ringworm (It's really a fungus).

Warm, humid conditions in parts of the islands are conducive to fungus: plant-like growths that can be difficult to get rid of. Most fungi are spread by spores in the ground, or they may pass from animal to animal, person to person, person to animal and vice-versa. The most commonly seen fungus in Hawai'i is ringworm, which affects people, especially children, as well as pets and can run rampant through children at school.

Signs: On infected pets or people you will note a scaly circle, darkish red at the edges, that spreads outward. In a pet, you may see loss of hair around the "worm". (There is no real worm; ringworm is so named because the red circle is reminiscent of a curled worm.) A dog or cat with ringworm may lick and scratch, infecting the sore even more.

What can we do? Oral remedies are available from a veterinarian. He or she will probably also instruct you to clean the house, the pet's bedding and your own bedding thoroughly, washing it in a strong bleach solution to kill the spores. Reinfection is common.

Mother Nature's Chew Toys 11

Toni Polancy photo

Hawai'i is littered
with tempting
treats for pets.
Some are fine;
others can be deadly.

*Skat the Cat
does her bit
to solve Maui's
mouse problem.
Instinctive
though it may
be, dining on
rodents is
dangerous for
several reasons.*

Mother Nature spoils Hawai'i's pets

She sends pods, beans and sticks cascading from trees; rolls mangos down the driveway; parades mice, toads and geckos across the *lanai*, all to tempt our curious cats and playful dogs. Most of Mom Nature's gifts are safe enough and some are even beneficial to our pets, but others can be irritating, toxic or deadly. You should know which bush grew the stick you throw for your dog, which tree created the pod your pet is munching. Never let your pet chew on a plant, leaf, branch or pod, or run in a field or bed of any plant or flower you can't identify. Some plants will simply upset your pet's stomach or make him itch; others can be toxic. And to confuse the issue further, it may depend on which part of the plant he nibbles, chews or touches. Here are some of the most common plants found in Hawai'i's gardens, fields and trails.

WATCH FOR DROOLING

Chewing most of Hawai'i's plants is safe fun for your pet, but even safe plants can cause problems. Watch for excessive drooling or any drooling in a pet that does not usually drool. Check your pet's mouth carefully. A bit of woody stick, burr or leaf may have lodged in its mouth. Use tweezers to remove the object and be sure to save it. Watch your pet carefully for the next few hours. A portion of the object may have remained in his mouth. If the drooling persists or your pet acts strangely, take him to a veterinarian immediately. Bring the object you pulled from his mouth.

Kiawe beans

Every dog and some cats enjoy chewing on the crispy yellow beans that drop from kiawe, the thorny wild trees that grow on undeveloped land across our islands. The beans have a slight molasses flavor, says a state agricultural agent, and in addition to being tasty and chewy, they are a good source of protein for your pet. In fact, ranchers sometimes collect kiawe beans, grind them up and feed them to cattle. Don't let your pet gorge, however; an excess can cause diarrhea.

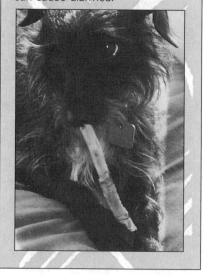

There are good plants...

Coconuts, husks and bark fiber
(right) It's hard to say whether a dog has more fun tearing the husks, chasing the rolling coconuts or chewing up the milky fruit of coconut palms. Most dogs also enjoy destroying the huge fibrous pieces of bark shed by the trees and would be delighted to have you hold tight to one end of the pieces while they pull on the other. All this is safe fun, but be careful your dog doesn't eat too much coconut meat. It's high in fat content.

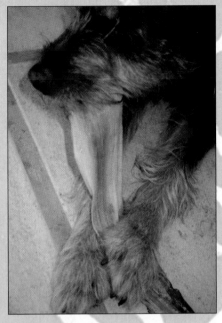

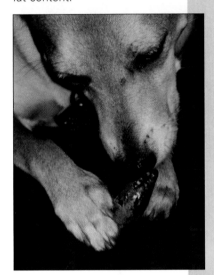

False Kamani
(left) The seed inside the pod of the False Kamani tree is tasty and harmless to people and animals. Before the pod grows brown and chewy, it is a slightly oblong, reddish colored fruit.

Autograph Tree
(right) This hardy tree graces many a parking lot where its interesting seed pod litters the ground, first as a shiny round green "fruit," and later as a crisp brown flower shaped pod. West Indians used this tree as a medicine source and it should be safe enough for a healthy pet to chew.

And bad plants

Discourage your pet from sleeping under, playing in, chewing, fetching or tasting any of these plants:

Dumb cane (Dieffenbachia)

(right) These plants are popular indoors as well as out, and your curious cat will probably encounter *Dieffenbachia* some time in her life. When any part of the leaf or stem is broken, the plant shoots out tiny needles of calcium oxalate crystals and toxins. In fact, Amazon tribes used this plant to poison darts. Dieffenbachia is a severe threat to both dogs and cats because it causes the throat to swell and can result in suffocation as well as loss of speaking ability. Hence the common name, Dumb Cane.

Kukui Nuts

(left) Chances are, you've hiked with your dog in forests of candlenut or *kukui* trees. The beautiful light green leafed tree is our state tree, but its nuts, eaten raw, are poisonous and its sap can cause a rash. Dogs have suffered painful deaths from eating nuts from the *kukui* tree.

Quick! Do this

If you see your pet chewing on any parts of these plants, take it away and rinse your pet's mouth thoroughly with water. If she has swallowed any part of the plant, call your veterinarian immediately.

Plumeria

(left) Ah, plumeria! The bountiful flower fills the island with fragrance and romance. Nearly every Hawai`i yard has a tree or bush, showering the ground with delicate petals. We use the plumeria's flower for lei, decorating our necks, our hair, our homes and our tables. But pick a plumeria flower or break a branch and a sticky white milk called latex oozes forth. Latex is an irritant that can be toxic. Although problems are rare, mouthing a branch would be very unpleasant for your pet and ingesting it could be fatal.

Koa haole (Also called hale koa)

(right) This straggly weed/bush/tree abounds on undeveloped land throughout the islands, much to the sorrow of ranchers. It takes a toll on horses and cattle if ingested over a long period of time, causing hair loss and severe damage to the hooves. Although your pet is unlikely to eat enough of the plant to cause serious problems, why take chances? Don't let them chew the dark brown bean-like seed pods or any other part.

Lantana

(left) Lantana grows throughout Hawai`i, both as a weed and a cultivated garden flower. All parts of the plant are poisonous, including its clusters of multi-colored flowers, but especially its green berries. Symptoms can include vomiting, diarrhea, weakness, staggered walk, visual disturbances, hallucinations and lethargy.

Oleander: it's everywhere!

Oleander is everywhere in Hawai'i: borders of it surround outdoor restaurants, walls of it shelter housing developments. Yet all parts of the pretty plant are poisonous and can even be deadly. One leaf is sufficient to fell a grown adult; imagine what it could do to your dog or cat. Even inhaling the burning leaves or raking the plants and sniffing the dust is toxic. Don't let your animals drink the vase water from cut plants or drink water collected at the base of the plants after watering. Never use the branches for a campfire nor the sticks for toasting marshmallows. Be careful not to throw branches or sticks of the oleander for your dog to chase. Symptoms of oleander poisoning can include irritation to the mouth and stomach, vomiting, abdominal pain, diarrhea, and possibly heart failure.

Be-still tree
(left) This tree is an ornamental shrub related to, and as dangerous as, oleander. Like oleander, it is planted by landscapers all over the islands. It's unlikely your pet will chew a seed pod since the plant tastes terrible, but don't toss a stick from a be-still tree or bush for your pet to fetch. Every part of this plant is either an irritant, toxic or poisonous, and can cause many problems, from rashes and swelling to irregular heartbeat and confusion.

Among the other dangerous plants we see in Hawai'i:

Taro plants

(left) Hard to believe a plant that was once a main food source for the islands is anything but healthy, but taro leaves contains calcium oxalate crystals, similar to Dumb Cane. Keep your pets out of taro patches and don't let them nibble the raw plants. Leaves and roots must be well cooked before becoming edible. Poi, made from taro root, is fine for your pet.

Angel's trumpet

(right) The leaves, nectar, and big inverted trumpet-shaped flowers of this spectacular, sweet-smelling ornamental shrub are toxic. Even sniffing it can cause problems. Symptoms may include dilated pupils, dry mouth, increased body temperature, intense thirst, confusion, delirium, hallucinations and pulse disturbances. Let your pet play with this plant and he could be answering an angel's trumpet... in heaven.

Poinsettia

This showy red, white or pink "Christmas plant" grows in gardens throughout the islands and wild in some higher, cooler regions. Every kama'aina (longtime resident) knows poinsettia are poisonous and should be kept out of reach of children. Interestingly, science is now deciding that the plant may not be as poisonous as once thought. Still, eating the leaves can cause irritation to the mouth and stomach upset. Your pets aren't likely to nibble poinsettia; still, keep the plants out of reach.

fetch
more information
The University of Hawai'i Press has published several books on island plants. Among them: Poisonous Plants of Paradise *by Susan Scott and Craig Thomas, M.D.*

And more: African violets, azaleas, bird of paradise, black elder, caladium, castor bean, China berry, coral berry, crown flower, English ivy, holly berries, hydrangea, Jerusalem cherry, jimson weed, milkweed, mistletoe, morning glory, periwinkle, philodendron, pokeweed, poison ivy, poison oak, the leaves of potatoes and tomatoes, Star of Bethlehem plant, woody nightshade, rubber plant, rubber weed, yew.

Visitors our pets should avoid

Like many Hawai`i backyards, mine is well-fenced. It keeps my dogs and cat from leaving the property. However, walls and fences do not protect my pets or yours from visitors who fly or crawl over, under and through them. Ants, mosquitoes, wasps, scorpions, centipedes, toads, mongooses, mice and rats visit often, usually to the delight of our pets. I am forever pulling mice and lizards from the jaws of Skat the Cat. Betty, a rat terrier, was recently shaking her head violently, holding a large gray object in her mouth. We thought it was a bird. It turned out to be a rat, almost half her size. Winky, our one-eyed dog, snaps at wasps and dragonflies. So far, fortunately, she has failed to catch any. Those unwelcome backyard guests can be dangerous to your pets. Some (geckos, lizards, snails) can make your pet ill; others (mongooses, rats, large birds) will fight back when cornered and may injure your pet. Still others (toads and the wild boars that enter some rural yards) can kill your cat or small dog. Keep your pets indoors, or keep a sharp ear and eye. Be ready to break up any backyard battles. Keep emergency supplies on hand and your veterinarian's phone number nearby.

This baby mongoose is cute, sure, but you wouldn't want to get this close to an adult. The islands are overrun with mongooses, vicious fighters. They were imported to the islands years ago to help control rodents. But rats are nocturnal and mongooses like daytime, so their paths hardly cross, and both pests live and multiply.

Photo courtesy JoAnn Allencastre

Don't let your pet eat geckos or lizards...

Toni Polancy photo

Geckos and lizards are so common in the islands that the round-toed gecko has become our unofficial state mascot. What can be quainter than a gecko, considered a symbol of good luck, scampering across living room walls or holding a dinner party near *lanai* (porch) lights? Their darting movements stir the adrenaline in both dogs and cats, and it's almost impossible to curb pets' hunting urges, especially in cats, who consider the little lizard a tasty snack. However, you should discourage your pets from eating geckos and lizards, which can cause liver flukes, a type of worm similar to tapeworms. Symptoms can include general debilitation and diarrhea.

Photo courtesy of the CDC Public Health Image Library

...or rodents of any sort

Some of our thousands of rodents may have been poisoned and can pass the poison on to your cat or dog. Clues that your pet has ingested rat poison, either directly or by eating a rodent, include: aimless wandering, confusion, vomiting, excessive uncontrolled urination and bowel movement, frothing at the mouth, labored breathing, bloody nose or mouth, and convulsions. Sudden death may occur in a seemingly healthy animal. Another concern: a rat, cornered, will fight back and your pet could be injured.

Bufo: the fat, evil toad that can kill your pet

He looks so fat and harmless, but *bufo marinus*, that big toad who thuds through our yards and rests in our pets' water dishes, is dangerous to both dogs and cats. Bufo secretions have killed many pets on these islands and elsewhere. And killed them quickly.

Attracted by the bufo's slow, sloppy hopping, your curious dog or cat nuzzles, sniffs or picks up the toad in its mouth. Threatened, the bufo first empties his bladder, then discharges toxins from ducts behind his ears. The toxins are mildly hallucinogenic. They can raise your pet's blood pressure and, in large enough doses, cause death.

Your pet probably reacts by immediately dropping the toad, but

Tip

Bring your pet's water dishes (and your pet) inside at night. Watch your pet when he goes out for his night-time duty. As much as your pet may enjoy playing with a bufo, don't let him.

not before some of the toxin has entered his mouth or been ingested. The pet usually experiences irritation of the mucus membranes of the mouth and throat and begins salivating. If your pet eats the toad or otherwise receives a dose of toxin, vomiting, seizures and death may occur in as little as 15 minutes.

Keep your pets away from bufos, dead or alive. Here in Hawai`i, we often see moribund bufos in parks, slain by lawn mowers or garden chemicals. We also see them lying in streets, flattened into pieces of leather by autos. Dogs are known to roll in carcasses, absorbing what they perceive as a great scent. A Hawai`i health department official warns that an encounter with a bufo carcass can be very unhealthy because the poison remains active, even after death.

Even a toad that sits in your dog's watering dish for some time can emit enough toxin to make your pet ill. Although the toxicity varies by the amount your pet comes in contact with, the death rate for untreated animals is high. And the smaller your pet is, the more likely he will suffer from his bufo encounter.

Conduct a bufo hunt

Island agriculture departments could offer no suggestions for getting rid of bufos short of conducting a bufo hunt. Here's how: chase the toads, use gloves to capture them, put them in a pail with a screened lid on top and release them into the wild, far from your property. Bufos can be harmful to pets, but they are beneficial to have around. They eat insects and balance the environment. Nature just happens to have given bufos an extremely anti-social way to defend themselves.

Ask your vet NOW

Bufo poisonings tend to occur at dusk and later, when mosquitoes and termites, bufos' favorite cuisine, are active. That means bufo poisonings are most likely to occur after veterinarian offices are closed. So do many other pet traumas. Prepare now for an emergency. Ask your vet how you can reach him after hours.

> **QUICK! DO THIS**
> If you suspect your pet has tasted a toad, flush its mouth with water and make sure it does not swallow any of the water. Wipe teeth and gums with a rough cotton towel. Continue rinsing for several minutes. The toxin is slowly being absorbed into the pet's membrane and you want to remove as much as possible. Rush your pet to a veterinarian.
> If you act quickly, your vet can administer medication to control the seizures, salivation and heart irregularity that can lead to death.

If your child shouldn't taste it, neither should your pet

If you had a toddler in your home, you'd make sure dangerous items were put way, up high where the child couldn't reach them. You'd lock up the cleanser, keep insecticides hidden. Cats, kittens, puppies, and even some adult dogs are a lot like youngsters. They tend to snoop and sniff, taste and try anything that's new, anything they haven't experienced before. Here are a few tempting items, often found around island homes, that you should keep away from your pets. If your dog or cat does inhale or swallow any of these, call your veterinarian immediately.

- **Antifreeze:** Pets, especially cats, are particularly attracted to automobile antifreeze, which is sweet. They seem to like the taste and smell of it and even a tiny amount can be fatal if ingested.

  Antifreeze? In Hawai`i's warm weather? Yes, antifreeze is also a summer coolant. It lowers the boiling point in radiator water, which is ideally 50 percent water, 50 percent antifreeze. Keep antifreeze in your radiator, and out of your garage where a pet could taste it. Watch for radiator leaks on your garage or carport floor and wash them away quickly and thoroughly with plenty of water.

  Signs: Cats who have eaten antifreeze may exhibit a drunken, staggering appearance within an hour of exposure, followed by renal failure, vomiting, depression and coma.

Keep all insecticides, including sprays, far from your pet's reach. Pet exposure to insecticides is usually the result of improper storage or disposal, spilled mixture or containers left open. Keep lids tightly closed and shut cabinets that contain these products. Pets have also been known to ingest citrus oils and insect repellents. Dogs and cats may also chew flea collars and tick collars.

Other toxic household products: Dry cleaning fluid, cooking fuels, lighter fluid, kerosene, diesel oils and house heating oils, fertilizers, furniture polish, perfumes, laundry bleach, matches, mothballs, shampoos and window cleaners.

Death from heart failure can follow in 12 to 24 hours.

- **Batteries:** The acid in batteries could burn your pet's mouth, esophagus and stomach. Batteries, including small watch batteries or AA or AAA type batteries commonly used in clocks, games, phones and toys, contain lead. Make sure your pet does not chew or play with batteries of any kind.
  Signs of lead poisoning can be vague. You may notice occasional vomiting, depression, constipation, anorexia, diarrhea, thirst and convulsions.

> ## QUICK! DO THIS
> If your pet swallows any of the products mentioned here, wash his mouth out with cool, clear water. Read the product label regarding poisoning and follow its directions. In some cases, you should NOT try to induce vomiting. If your pet regurgitates on his own, fine. But if he's swallowed solvents, cleaners, acids, petroleum products or sharp objects, inducing vomiting may do more harm than good. Get your pet to a veterinarian immediately. Take the offensive product along so the vet can determine the best course of action.

- **Ant and roach traps:** Hawai`i is inundated with ants and roaches, and ant and roach baits. Those small round plastic or metal ant and roach baits are especially attractive to curious cats and dogs, who may like to chew them. If you use traps, be sure to place them in closed cabinets or tucked far behind appliances where your pets can't get to them.

- **Molluscacides:** Snail-eliminating agents are dangerous to cats who often find snails particularly attractive and may eat a poisoned snail. And dogs have been known to die quickly after eating snail bait. Avoid these agents if pets use your garden. Beer makes a safer snail bait, advises a pet lover. Placed in small containers, it attracts snails, who drink it and die. (Before your try this, make sure your pet isn't also attracted to beer.)

- **Rat poisons:** Most rat poisoning of pets is the result of careless placement of baits, overuse of baits, failure to discard poisoned rodents and malicious poisonings. Cornell University's School of Veterinary Science states the rodenticide sodium fluoroacetate or "1080" should never be used around animals. It is very toxic and there is no therapy for it.

A true lizard tale

Don't underestimate the power, will and tenacity of some of Hawai`i's quickest little creatures: lizards and chameleons.

I lived in Central Florida for a while, where large Hawai`i-like lizards and chameleons hung out nights on our windows and occasionally entered our homes.

One day my cat Cookie let out a howl and I ran out to the yard to find a large lizard, about eight inches long, attached to her nose. The cat was panicked, flopping around on her back and sides and batting at the lizard with her paws, trying to dislodge it, all the while yowling in pain. The lizard was clinging tenaciously and painfully with his teeth, his sole weapon in a battle that he was clearly winning.

What to do? If I took hold of the lizard, he might whip around and attach himself to me. I grabbed a towel from the clothesline, wrapped it around my hand and pulled the lizard off the cat. It required quite a tug. Cookie stopped howling, and crept off to lick her wounds and soothe her pride. Imagine! A cat bested by a lizard.

Meanwhile, I tried to figure out what to do with the lizard. My first choice would be to release it outdoors to go on its merry way, terrorizing other cats. But as I unwrapped the towel, the lizard dropped, limp, to the ground. Obviously, I had smothered it with the towel. Somewhat relieved that he was dead, I lifted the lizard by its long green tail and deposited it into the trash can next to the kitchen stove. He'd go out with the garbage after dinner.

A half hour later I was frying hamburgers when I heard a small thud. The reincarnated lizard, bright-eyed and very alive, was perched on top of the stove near a burner. He glared at me like a demon from hell.

Shaking in fear—after all, he'd come from the dead—I grabbed him with a pair of long barbecue tongs, ran to the swamp behind our house, threw him in, tongs and all, and ran back. I never saw him again, except in my nightmares.

Our plentiful Hawai`i lizards, with the exception of the Jackson chameleon, seem to be smaller than their Florida relatives. But don't underestimate the will, strength and tenacity of even the tiniest lizard.

Some folks say
animals know
when a great wind,
a monster wind,
is coming.

*Kaua`i photographer
Tom Tamura caught
this photo of a
cat, confused by
the destruction
of his home after
Hurricane Iniki.*

For pets and owners, lessons from a hurricane

You cannot imagine a hurricane unless you have lived through one. Ask the people of Kaua`i who have survived two. "As a hurricane approaches," says a Lihu`e man, "you wait, your stomach in your throat. You pray that it will turn. You pray for the best and you prepare for the worst."

On Sept. 9, 1992, as Tropical Storm Iniki danced offshore of the Hawaiian islands, residents of the Big Island, Maui and O`ahu watched confidently, sure the winds would turn away. Not Kaua`i residents. They remembered Hurricane Iwa, ten years before, and they had much work to do.

Kaua`i residents took pictures from walls, filled as many bottles and jugs as they could find with drinking water. They stood in long lines at supermarkets to buy canned foods, flashlights, matches, first aid supplies and batteries and all the canned and dry pet food they could find. Nearly every family on the island has a dog or two and more than one cat, and some have birds and rabbits.

The next day, September 10, Iniki, ranked as a tropical storm, stalled off O`ahu. The atmosphere was eerily calm. It was hard to believe disaster breathed a few miles off island, a sleeping giant, snoring lightly. But the animals knew something awful was going to happen.

"They seemed nervous," a Kilauea man remembered. "Our cats kind of paced, not sleepy like usual. And the dog wanted in and just stayed close and looked at us with big eyes like he was already scared."

Kaua`i is a sparsely populated, wide-open island with plenty of land. On farms and ranches where animals roam free, some folks conducted roundups of their animals, brought horses and cows and sheep into barns and lean-tos and considered how strong those bits of shelter might be. Dogs and cats who rarely saw the inside of a house were snuggled next to their owners' beds and wondered why they were suddenly so blessed.

Kaua`i awoke Friday morning, Sept. 11, to sirens bleating across the island. Overnight, Iniki had changed its course; now it was pointed straight at Kaua`i, moving fast, a gun aimed at a target, its trigger cocked.

Residents who lived in oceanfront condominiums and homes gasped at the angry waves, at civil defense workers pounding on doors, ordering them to evacuate. Animals were not allowed at emergency shelters. Pet owners forced to evacuate had two choices: leave pets in crates or kennels inside cars parked outside emergency shelters or lock them inside their homes or condos, at the mercy of the storm. Those who brought their pets to emergency shelters left car windows cranked open a bit for air, even as winds grew ominously stronger, as rain blew in sideways and small tree branches flew by. Residents who lived a safe distance from shore could stay in their homes, crouched in closets and bathrooms and windowless hallways. As the winds grew louder, nervous dogs began to bark and wail. Cats hid under beds, hissing in fear, or cuddled closer to their owners. One family hunkered down in a hallway, two cats in one cage between them. The cats usually hated the cage, but now, as though they sensed danger, they slinked in easily. A few doors down, another couple sat in a bathtub, a large dog on a leash huddled between them, a mattress over their heads to deflect falling debris. Some pet owners did foolish things. A woman put her cat in an outdoor dryer and shut the door, figuring the machine would protect her pet. A man used a sturdy rope to tie his dog to a fence, outdoors.

> Some pet owners did foolish things...

> A women put her cat in an outdoor dryer and shut the door, figuring the machine would protect her pet.

The Westin Hotel in Lihu`e had many animals, including a stable of horses. Since the Westin was close to the ocean, it was decided the horses would be safest in a pasture near the hotel. There, a story goes, the horses, sensing danger, formed a circle, heads together. And all the colts were in the center, protected by the older horses.

At Kaua`i's old humane society, three decrepit buildings on a few acres of land near Hanapepe, they knew what to do. One of the workers had survived Iwa ten years before. The society had about 40 dogs and at least as many cats in kennels and cages, but it also included many abandoned farm animals who lived outdoors in pens. Now those animals had to be brought in. Sherry Hoe, then Humane Society director, doubled up on dog kennels, putting two or three friendly mutts together, and moved massive, sluggish pigs and bleating, skittish goats into the kennels, stacked rabbits in cages, put a swan in the bathroom. And as the winds grew louder, she prayed.

> A man used a sturdy rope to tie his dog to a fence, outdoors.

For the next five hours, Iniki blew 175 mile-an-hour winds at Kaua`i, its eye passing directly over the little island, and spitting out gusts of over 200 miles an hour. It sent huge shingles and pieces of metal roofs, sheds and fences hurtling through the air, ramming against houses where families huddled. It wreaked the worst damage along the coasts. Its waves sucked furniture from apartments, sent refrigerators bobbing in the ocean. But Iniki spared no part of the island. Windows in nearly every home blew out, shooting glass shards through the air. Church steeples tumbled. Roofs blew off houses and families stared in awe, up into a darkening sky. In Kapa`a, a family fled to a neighbor's house theirs collapsed. As they crossed the road, their grandfather was struck by debris and killed.

'The worst was the quiet. It was deadly still. No birds. No animals sounds.'

Where were the animals in all of this? Who could think of them now, at the height of the storm? Dogs and cats panicked. Cages blew over. Pets who had been left at home broke loose as roofs flew from houses, as walls crumbled. Dogs ran away. Cats hid. In the parking lots where animals were left in cars, trees collapsed, cars swept into each other. Some animals died; others escaped.

As darkness set in, the winds stopped and people began to crawl out of their hiding places. They saw a world violently altered. Every leaf was gone from every tree and bush. The Garden Isle's lush green had gone dreary brown.

Electric poles were down throughout the island, making roads unsafe to travel. Towns and neighbors a few miles apart were isolated from each other.

"But the worst," says one survivor, "was the quiet. It was just deadly still. No birds. No animals sounds."

Farmers who had sheltered cows and horses in lean-tos and sheds found the structures blown apart, their animals peppered with nails and bits of wood; some dying.

The woman who had put her pet cat in the outdoor clothes dryer couldn't get home for days. Flood waters drowned the cat.

The family who sat huddled with their dog felt it slip from their hands, then watched it run through a shattered window in terror. They never saw it again.

In its panic, the dog tethered to a fence was choked to death.

The two cats in their cages survived.

Over the next days and weeks, stunned residents stood in more lines,

Sheila Heathcote Arthur photo

for water and food and gas, to use a makeshift phone, to get a loan to rebuild, to find a new place to live, to find jobs because old ones were gone, blown away. So much rebuilding to do. Not just of homes. Of lives.

Many pet owners left the islands, at least temporarily, to live with relatives or friends on the mainland or on other islands. Some would eventually return; many would not. Others resided at shelters or with relatives. It would be weeks before they could even think about their pets.

At the height of the storm the pets had fled, terrified; now dogs and cats wandered, dazed and confused. Animals, even pampered house pets, depend on scent for much of their survival. But the scents were strange; the views changed.

> Pets who had been left at home broke loose as roofs flew from houses, as walls crumbled.

Miraculously, Iniki almost ignored the little Humane Society, maybe because its buildings were so poor and insignificant. The only real damage was to some big old banyan trees behind the shelter; their downed limbs blocked back entrances to the shelter. No big deal.

A big deal was water. You can manage without electricity and phones, but water sustains life. Humans stood in long lines at distribution centers for scarce water; pet needs took a back seat. The humane society's director, Hoe, found a secret spigot in Lihu`e that still spat out the precious liquid and for weeks a humane society truck spent the entire day, every day, transporting garbage cans full of water from the county seat several miles to the animal shelter.

Shelter employees used buckets instead of hoses to wash out animal feces. It was important; after flooding or a hurricane, disease runs rampant. Within weeks the Humane Society would be battling leptospirosis in animals that had guzzled contaminated stream water. Ringworm was common. Feline leukemia doubled. When deadly parvo broke out, employees cleaned the kennels and lawns with a strong bleach solution.

> Former lap dogs and loving cats reverted to a feral state, hissing at those who would help them.

In the first days after Iniki, supermarket employees conducted shoppers by flashlight through darkened aisles, giving away much of the perishable food from freezers. New supplies were slow to come and pet food was low on the list of necessary items. Many pets who still had homes learned to eat rice, noodles and whatever food their owners had.

For the humane society, help came from several sources. An unsolicited $25,000 check from the North Shore Animal League, Long Island; 50 pet carriers from The Humane Society of the United States; 25,000 pounds of canned dog food from KalCan company and various donations of feed for the farm animals.

Sherry Hoe geared for a huge influx of stray pets, but they were slow coming; scared wild, they were difficult to catch. Traumatized by the storm, former lap dogs and loving cats reverted to a feral state, hissing at those who would help them. Others ran and hid, terrified. Some died of their injuries; others from starvation.

The humane society invested in a net gun and trained two officers to use it. The gun shoots a net out to gently capture fleeing animals. It helped, but only a little. Only about 2,500 of Kaua`i's estimated 50,000 dogs were licensed before Iniki, but addresses are of little help when homes and their owners are gone.

"Officers would bring in a dog with tags and be so happy because the dog had an owner," Hoe says. "Then we wouldn't be able to find the owner."

Humane society workers hung notices all over the island on shopping center bulletin boards and the telephone poles still standing. Plasticized to withstand the never-ending Kaua`i rains and Iniki's mud, the notices were marked either "lost" or "found" and included pictures of animals. The society also placed newspaper ads.

Through the months that followed, the number of animals brought in to the humane society climbed. Before Iniki, about 5,000 animals a year came to the tiny shelter. A year after Iniki the numbers rose to about 12,000, Hoe says. Whereas the shelter usually held a maximum of 150 animals; now it was hosting 350 to 400 at a time. Kennels built for one or two dogs housed six or seven. Many of those were puppies and especially kittens. Unneutered cats and dogs, once someone's pets, were breeding in the wild. Left to roam, cats seemed to produce four litters per year instead of the usual two or three.

> The dogs' faces came alive whenever they heard a truck. But there are many trucks on Kaua`i, an island of trucks...

Dogs sat waiting at the Humane Society for their owners to come get them. Accustomed to the sound of pickup trucks, the dogs' ears perked up, their faces came alive whenever they heard a truck. But there are many trucks on Kaua`i, it is an island of trucks, and the dogs were continually disappointed.

The Humane Society stayed open seven days a week, longer hours. They kept healthy animals longer than most shelters might, three to six months, before euthanizing them. Still, the number of animals euthanized was up from 200 before Iniki to about 600 a month, Hoe says. She started a program called Aloha Angel Escorts, sending pets with travelers to the mainland to be adopted from West Coast shelters.

By 1994 Kaua`i began to recover, at least a little, from Iniki. Most homes were rebuilt, some jobs returned and families were willing to adopt pets again. Many who visited the Kaua`i Humane Society went home with two or three pets. Along with new houses, the island got a new animal shelter. Big and bold and strong, hurricane proof, with its own generator and water well.

A wind like Iniki clears out the mind and heart, blowing away what's not important and making us remember what has real value. For the most part, amid the shock, a peaceful appreciation of life was born in Kaua`i. There are lessons to be learned from Kaua`i's disaster, for people and their pets, and we are all still learning them.

A shelter for pets and people

"We learned from Iniki that people will not go to a shelter without their pets," says Dr. Rebecca Rhoades, executive director of the Kaua'i Humane Society. That's why Kaua'i's new Humane Society is the first shelter in the nation to allow both pets and their owners.

From Kaumuali'i Highway north of Lihue, the society's new $3 million building looks like a fort: sterile, cement-walled, set on seven acres and surrounded on two sides with parking lots. The American Red Cross and state Civil Defense-approved facility contains 30,000 square feet of concrete and a 5,000 square foot basement. The shelter has its own well, assuring a water supply after a disaster, as well as a generator, drainage system, hurricane shutters on windows and hurricane doors bolted in three places.

When a disaster looms, pet owners can come to the shelter, ideally bringing their pets in kennels or crates, Rhoades says. During the hurricane, pet owners will stay in the basement and pets will be in their crates stacked in hallways and rooms.

She acknowledges that pet owners would like to cuddle next to their pets during a hurricane, soothing them. But realistically, pets will be more secure in sturdy crates, safe from flying debris or other hurricane hazards and unable to bolt in fear. To make the pet more comfortable, the crate can include some of its owner's clothing or a favorite toy.

Evacuees going elsewhere for shelter can also leave their pets at the Humane Society. After the disaster, the society will continue to house the pets if necessary, Rhoades says, giving owners time to find more permanent shelter or to repair damaged homes without having the added stress of worrying about their pets.

Kaua'i, ravaged by Iniki and knowing well the horrors a hurricane can unleash on pets and people, is the only island so far to offer pet/owner shelters. But the facility may become a model for the nation, according to Glenn Lockwood, director of disaster relief services for the Hawai'i chapter of the Red Cross. Out of devastation, comes a better way.

Other natural dangers

Devastating as hurricanes can be, they at least give us hours, and even days, of warning. Not so with another of the island's natural enemies, flash floods which occur often, even several times a year in some parts of each island.

Sudden violent storms or days of prolonged rain can turn parks and roads into temporary lakes.

Human lives have been lost on all islands in flash floods, torrents of rushing water pounding down our steep mountains during and after strong or prolonged rains.

What can we do?
Information on the following pages will help you protect your pet in major emergencies. Protect them during and after major rainfalls, too.

- Bored as they may become, keep your pets in during heavy rains or unusual weather.
- Construct a litter box and keep your cat indoors, even if it usually goes outdoors.
- Don't take your dog out unnecessarily. Avoid its usual play outings. When you must go out, keep dogs on a leash.
- Make sure licenses, microchip IDs, and other identification tags are up to date. If your pet becomes lost, they will help him get back home.

A soggy lesson

It had rained for three days in desert-like South Maui, and my three dogs were edgy and eager to be out. It was still cloudy as Archie, Betty, Wink and I hiked across our favorite park. The rains had turned low lying areas of grass into shallow lakes and I yelled at the dogs to keep away from them. They minded, and ran happily 40 feet ahead of me, to an open field where they often play. A ditch separates the park from the field. Archie and Betty leaped down and then came up over the other side of the ditch soaking wet, but Wink did not emerge. I ran to the ditch and gasped in horror. Rains had turned the ditch into a small, raging river of murky brown water, four or five feet deep. My mind barely registered "Wink's drowned!" before I heard a whine. A few feet away, her *okole* submerged in the rushing water, Wink clung to a bush, her one wide eye beseeching me. I clamored down to the beach and waded into the ugly water, getting as close as I could. I was nine or ten feet away when the skinny 8-pound dog bravely let go of her bush and swam toward me. It was a lesson I won't forget: nature can change quickly, radically. Keep pets near by and on leashes after storms.

The following information is from the O`ahu Civil Defense Agency, O`ahu's Hawaiian Humane Society, the Kaua`i Humane Society, The Hawai`i Island Humane Society and other sources.

Plan NOW for an emergency

Our islands are subject to dangerous year-round hazards such as flash floods, hurricanes, tsunamis and earthquakes. You, your family and your pet should be prepared and being prepared includes realizing just how damaging a natural disaster can be. In the case of a hurricane, you may have several days or at least several hours notice before the winds grow violent, but a flash flood or a tsunami comes with almost no warning. And an earthquake, common on the Big Island, happens in seconds.

REMEMBER: Pets are not permitted in most public shelters, so you must make advance preparations to ensure their safety. Have a plan NOW and rehearse it with your family; you may not have time to prepare one when a disaster strikes.

Before a disaster

- **Find the safest place** in your home for you and your pet. The place you select should be away from windows and mirrors and free of breakable objects that could fly or fall. A windowless bathroom, with mirror removed, may become your in-home shelter. Or the bottom of a windowless staircase or interior hallway. Noise of high winds and objects being hurtled at your home during a hurricane is particularly frightening to animals. If possible, stay in the center of your home where outdoor noise will be a little less intense.

- **Place your dog or cat inside its carrier** before the winds pick up. Keep your pet there until the emergency is over.

- **Familiarize your pet with his crate now.** Keep pet crates on hand for each pet. Crates should be large enough so your pet can stand up and turn around inside. Take time now to acquaint your pet with the crate. Put it in an area where your pet likes to hang out, even if that is the living room. Leave the crate's door open. Use a soft pillow, your pet's favorite toy, or a treat to entice your pet inside. Encourage your pet to sleep there. If he becomes familiar with his crate now, staying there will be less traumatic in an emergency.

- **Evacuation.** If you live in a low-lying or coastal area subject to ocean waves, high winds or flooding, you may have to evacuate. Make advance arrangements for yourself and your pet to stay with friends or relatives who reside in a safer area. Familiarize your pet with that home now, so he will be less stressed during an emergency. When the time comes to evacuate, go early so you and your pet avoid jammed roads and are settled in before the actual disaster.

- **If you must leave your pet alone** in your home during a disaster, be sure to put him in his crate and place the crate in a sturdy, high place, such as a counter top, in case flooding occurs.

- **Be sure your pet wears identification** at all times. Both dogs and cats should wear properly fitted collars that include a tag with your name, phone number and address. Include the name and phone number of your pet's veterinarian. "We write our names on books, coolers, and other items that are not nearly as important to us as our pets, and can't wander off on their own," notes Pamela Burns, executive director of O'ahu's Hawaiian Humane Society.

- **Keep your pet's county dog or cat tag** up to date—vital if it becomes lost after a hurricane or flood.

Emergency Checklist

Make sure you have the following items ready to ensure the safety of your pet in an emergency or natural disaster:

- Pet carriers or cages: large, tough, safe
- Well-fitted collars, identification tags and leashes
- Two-month supply of dry pet food
- A month's supply of any prescribed medication
- Your pet's health records
- A two-month supply of heartworm pills and flea control
- Sturdy water dishes and plenty of water, at least a three-day supply
- A two-week supply of kitty litter
- Newspapers, plastic bags, paper towels, detergent to clean up after your pet

For more information contact:

Hawaiian Humane Society
2700 Wai`alae Avenue
Honolulu, Hawai`i 96826
(808) 946-2187

O'ahu Civil Defense Agency
City & County of Honolulu
650 South King Street
Honolulu, Hawai'i 96813
(808) 523-4121
Recorded info: (808) 527-5372

Kaua`i Humane Society
P.O. Box 3330
3825 Kaumuali`i Highway
Lihu`e, Hawai'i 96766
(808) 632-0610
fax (808) 632-0727
Mobile number during
an emergency: (808) 639-2149

Kaua'i Civil Defense Agency
4396 Rice Street, Room 107
Lihue, Kaua`i, Hawai`i 96766
(808) 241-6336

- **Tattoo or microchip your pet** as a permanent identification that can't be lost. Collars and tags can come off. A microchip can't.

- **Keep clear, sharp photos of your pet** with you. If your pet is lost in a disaster the photo may help you find it. The photos should be suitable for a "lost" poster or for Internet "lost and found" sites.

- **Have plenty of your pet's medications** on hand; a two-month supply is recommended.

- **Keep your pet's inoculations up to date**. Disease can run rampant in the moldy mess left by a hurricane or flood. You want to protect your pet, who will be stressed and more susceptible to infection. After a natural disaster, leptospirosis and heartworm cases can increase significantly. Leptospirosis is a bacterial disease found in streams; heartworm is spread by mosquitoes.

- **Have your pet's health records handy**. If your home is unlivable after a disaster, you may have to board your pet in a commercial kennel for a time. Most boarding facilities require proof of current inoculations.

- **Stock up on pet food** and kitty litter as well as newspapers, plastic bags and cleansers to handle pet wastes.

- **Prepare your family**. Make sure your entire family knows the emergency routine. Your family may be separated or, for example, an older child may be alone at home. Review plans and scenarios. Discuss where to hide or where to evacuate, how to care for yourselves and your pets, where to meet and how to communicate after the emergency.

- **Ask a neighbor to help**. You may have some warning and time to prepare for a hurricane, but other disasters, like floods, can happen quickly. You may not be able to reach your home. If your pet is routinely left alone, ask a nearby friend or neighbor to care for it in an emergency. Read the rest of this article, decide your course of action, and discuss your plan with the neighbor.

- **Consider housing your pet at a kennel** during and immediately after an emergency, especially if you have other pressing responsibilities. Check with your local veterinary clinic or kennel now and locate boarding facilities that will care for your pet in an emergency. Make sure the kennel also has an emergency evacuation plan and is out of the hazard area. It should be located far from the ocean and away from flood zones.

During a disaster

- **Bring your pets indoors early**, well ahead of a natural disaster. This should include rabbits, chickens, birds and outdoor pets. Do NOT leave your pet outside or tied up. An approaching storm may frighten him, causing him to flee and become lost. Or your pet may become confused and get tangled in its tether. Horses, cattle and other large farm animals should be secured in barns or garages.

- **Do not house animals together** in crates, even if they are normally friendly. Fear may cause unusual reactions. Keep small pets like rabbits, birds and mice away from cats and dogs and cover their cages with a towel to make them feel safer.

- **Do not put animals in appliances** such as dryers and washing machines during a storm as some pet owners did in Kaua'i during Hurricane Iniki. They could suffocate, and at the least they are very traumatized.

- **Have sturdy water containers** on hand that will not spill, and plenty of dry pet food. Pet food should be stored in strong plastic jugs that won't tear or come open. Animals should be provided with food and water in dispensers that can hold at least a two-day supply and will not spill. Fill two bowls or containers with water in case one spills.

- **If you must leave your house** because it is considered unsafe, it is also unsafe for your pet. If you could not arrange to shelter your animal elsewhere, as a last resort your pet can stay in your car parked at an evacuation shelter. Keep the pet in its crate or carrier. This is essential and may be the key to whether he survives. High winds may hurl debris at the car; a frightening experience for your pet. The kennel will keep him from bolting. Provide plenty of food and water in heavy, sturdy dishes. Include a favorite toy or blanket or an old piece of your clothing with your scent on it. This may provide some comfort. Remember to leave a car window slightly open to provide ventilation and park in a protected, shady area.

After a disaster

Attend to your pets as soon as possible. After Hurricane Iniki, some animals died because pet owners left them tied up, forgotten for days or weeks. Please remember that your pets will be disoriented and in need of care and reassurance. Be extra gentle with them and remain calm.

- **If you are injured and cannot care for your pet** for some reason, call your local humane society.

- **The outdoors will be dangerous** after a hurricane or other emergency and especially dangerous to your pet. There may be downed power lines, fallen trees and debris, shattered glass and wire. Cats and dogs rely on scent for much of their perception, and familiar scents and landmarks may be altered, causing your pet to become confused and

Sheila Heathcote Arthur photo

lost. Consider carefully whether your pet should be allowed out alone, even on a leash, even in your yard.

- **If your pet comes in contact with a 'hot' electrical line,** do not touch him. The pet's body can act as a conductor of electricity—-in fact, fur is especially conductive—and you could be shocked if you touch it. Call the power company to remove the line.

- **Clean up broken glass and debris** around your home as soon as possible. They can puncture your pet's paws.

- **Look for small cuts and wounds** on your pet and attend to them as soon as possible. Clean them with an antiseptic; infections from small cuts are common after a disaster.

The stress continues, for animals too

Because animals cannot understand what has happened, why scents and sights in the world around them have changed, they are particularly traumatized after a disaster. Busy as you will be in the aftermath of a hurricane or flood, take time occasionally to console your pet with a hug, some petting or a gentle massage.

Cats: Cats endure a special trauma during any disaster. Your cat may become very skittish and/or hide for several hours or even several days. Or the cat may be trapped by debris. Check the house and yard carefully. Call the cat's name or use "Here, kitty, kitty," that universal cat call, and listen for any soft mews. Continue to put dry food and water in an area as close as possible to where your cat usually found his food. Alert neighbors to watch for your pet. Call and keep dropping by your local animal shelter to check for your pet. Pray.

Dogs: Dogs always want to be near their owners. After the trauma of a disaster, that is particularly true. When you must leave your dog alone, keep it in its crate, inside the house where it will feel most secure. Because they were stressed and upset after Iniki, some dogs strangled themselves on leashes and objects not normally considered dangerous. If you must tie your dog outdoors, do not tie it close to a fence or any object with which it could become tangled.

Working or hunting dogs: Often bred or trained to be tough, these dogs are nevertheless as susceptible to trauma and fear after a disaster as pet dogs. If you own working or hunting dogs, please bring your dogs inside during a disaster, follow the suggestions above and give your dogs the special attention and care they deserve.

Feral cats: There are thousands, and some estimates say hundreds of thousands, of these cats, often sick and hungry, wandering Hawai`i's fields, forests and vacant lots. There may be hundreds more after a major disaster. If you live in an area where these cats are visible, consider that they will be even more in need now. If you can, help feed them by leaving fresh water and dry cat food. Check vacant lots and undeveloped land for trapped, wounded or dead feral cats or other animals.

After Iniki, a teddy bear lies abandoned in the rubble of a Kaua'i home.

Sheila Heathcote Arthur photo

Deborah Booker photo courtesy of *The Honolulu Advertiser*

5 days? 30 days?
120 days?
Or none at all?
Here's how to
make your pet's
incarceration
shorter and happier

The choices

Same-day release

Requirements: Two rabies vaccinations, microchip ID, blood test showing rabies antibodies, 120-day pre-arrival waiting period to assure pet is rabies free, health certificate within 14 days of arrival. For same day release, all documentation must be cleared with quarantine center 10 days prior to your arrival. You and your pet must also arrive at the Honolulu airport during daytime hours when an inspector is on duty.

What happens: Your pet is examined at the airport pet holding area. If all criteria is met and documentation was received ten days prior to your arrival, your pet is released to you the same day.

Cost: $165.

5-day or less release

Requirements: Same as above, but without verification 10 days prior to arrival.

For 5-day or less release go to this Internet site. Follow requirements and timelines preceisely. Do not arrive in Hawaii early.
    http://www.hawaiiag.org/hdoa/pdf/aqs–checklist–5.pdf

What happens: Your pet is taken to the animal quarantine center in `Aiea for up to five days while the documentation is verified.

Cost: $165 to $224.

30-day quarantine

Requirements: Same as above, but 120-day pre-arrival waiting period before coming to the islands is reduced to 90 days.

What happens: Your pet spends part of the pre-arrival monitoring time in quarantine. A post-arrival blood test is eliminated.

Cost: $655.

120-day quarantine

Requirements: Health certificate only. No microchip required.

What happens: Your pet is quarantined for four months. Tests and screening is done at the quarantine center.

Cost: $1,080.

Bob Fijal photo

Dog kennels stand in a neat row at the state's animal quarantine center near H-1 in Aiea, O'ahu.

Quarantine and your pet

Coming to Hawai'i? Hoping to bring your pet? You have a few decisions to make. Hawai'i has a stiff animal quarantine law designed to keep rabies out of the islands.

Rabies, a viral disease that attacks the central nervous system and will eventually affect the victim's brain, is the number one viral killer in undeveloped countries. With Hawai'i's high feral cat, mongoose and boar populations, health officials say the disease could quickly run rampant here.

In 1912, worried by an onslaught of rabies in California, Hawai'i set up strict regulations to screen incoming pets. They included a four-month-long quarantine in an O'ahu facility. The confinement and isolation could be traumatic and difficult for both pets and their owners. Some pet owners said dogs and cats became ill or died at the quarantine facility and argued that modern vaccinations and testing eliminate the need for quarantine.

In 1997, the Hawai'i Department of Health eased restrictions and instituted a program to allow for only 30 days of quarantine if pre-entry qualifications are met. In 2003, the state health department further eased the process by instituting a five-day-or-less quarantine.

- **The good news:** Quarantine efforts seem to have worked. Hawai'i is one of the few places in the world that has no rabies virus, neither in domestic nor feral animals.

- **The bad news:** It is still difficult to bring dogs and cats to the islands. You must send for quarantine information and begin readying your pet at least five months prior to its arrival here. Your pet must be inoculated at least 120 days before it leaves for Hawai`i and undergo other procedures. You must obtain latest information from the state quarantine center and precisely follow guidelines. Dogs and cats face quarantine as long as 120 days if all qualifications aren't met.

- **The good news:** With enough planning, several visits to your mainland veterinarian, and careful attention to requirements, it is possible to avoid quarantine completely. You have a choice of plans under which your pet will be quarantined for 120 days, 30 days, less than five days or, if you follow guidelines exactly, released immediately at the Honolulu airport.

- **The bad news:** All those pre-arrival vet visits are costly. So is quarantine. Including pre-arrival vet visits, cost of flight and travel kennel and quarantine costs, the cost of bringing your pet may total $1,000 or more no matter which plan you choose.

- **The good news:** Easing of restrictions in 2003 means Hawai`i residents who keep their pets inoculations up-to-date and have the documentation to prove it, are able to travel out-of-state with their pets and return without quarantine. So can Hawai`i's many "snowbirds," part-time residents. Breeders may take their animals to out-of-state shows. Residents are hoping to eventually have a kind of "pet passport." Meanwhile, it is vital that you get information and follow it precisely. Timing of inoculations, for example, is crucial, according to Dr. Isaac Maeda, program manager at the quarantine center.

- **More bad news:** Avoiding quarantine may still be impossible for military members who do not have enough advance warning of their move to ready their pets under the guidelines.

- **More good news:** Where once animals could be quarantined only at the state facility on O`ahu, it is now possible for neighbor island pets to spend 30 days or 120 days quarantine on their home island. The Big Island has a large private facility. Kaua'`i's humane society includes a quarantine section. Several Maui veterinary clinics have limited quarantine space. Details follow.

The Journey

Flight tips

Once a pet is pre-qualified for quarantine, it can be shipped to the island of O`ahu on most airlines. O`ahu is the only approved port of entry for dogs and cats coming into quarantine.

- **Make sure the flight your pet is on goes directly to O`ahu.** Your pet's plane cannot stop on an outer island first. One pet owner was not informed of this by his travel agent, was about to depart with his pet on a flight from Los Angeles to Maui and was told he could not take the pet. The experience cost him $1,100 for a last-minute, direct airline ticket to O`ahu.

- **Consider the time of year** you are planning your move. Some airlines will not ship animals during hot summer months. Address this issue with your airline. Is the cargo hold air-conditioned? How uncomfortable will your pet be?

- **Confirm your pet's flight**. Some flights can accommodate only a very limited number of animals. After the airline confirms that your pet can travel on your flight, buy your ticket.

First, get the facts

Before you read any further, go on the Internet or phone and order from the Board of Agriculture a free packet of information, including current restrictions and requirements.
Animal Quarantine Station
99-951 Halawa Valley Road
A`iea, Hawai`i 96701-5602
(808) 483-7151
Fax: (808) 483-7161
hawaiiag.org/hdoa/ai_aqs_info.html

Important: Be thorough. Be careful.

It is vital that you contact the Animal Quarantine Station at least five months before your pet's journey to Hawai`i. You must fill out numerous forms and follow detailed instructions perfectly. Make sure your pet's current veterinarian follows procedures meticulously. A slight variance can throw your pet into 120 days of quarantine.
Stories in this chapter are designed to help you decide whether to bring your pet; and if you do bring it, which quarantine procedure best fits your needs. If you are moving to the islands, you should also read the story about housing on page 98 before deciding whether to bring your pet.

Up to $10,000 fine; 5 years in jail

Don't even think about sneaking a pet into the islands

- A friend, whom I will call Ethel to protect her identity, swears she snuck Arthur, her miniature poodle, into Hawai`i during the Thanksgiving season many years ago. She had a mainland veterinarian sedate Arthur. Then she shaved him, wrapped him in butcher's paper, tucked him into a cooler, and told agents at the airport check-in that he was a Thanksgiving turkey she was taking to her family.

- In Waikiki I met a woman who vows she sedated her small dog, strapped him to her belly, pretended she was pregnant and went through airport checkpoints with nary a comment.

Pet owners have for years been trying to bypass quarantine. It's impossible to say how many have actually avoided incarcerating their pets by sneaking them into the islands, but it's dangerous business: at least one plan ended in the death of a dog who had been over-sedated and died. And anyone who attempts to avoid state quarantine laws and is caught faces stiff penalties: prosecution, up to $10,000 in fines, and five years in jail.

The Honolulu Advertiser records two failed attempts. In 1946, the wife of a Navy officer threw her cocker spaniel dog overboard from the ship Mariposa shortly before it docked. The dog swam to shore and was picked up by two of the woman's friends. However, officials were on to the scheme and refused to let her have her luggage unless she produced the dog. She did, and the swimming spaniel served his time.

Over the years, pets have been stolen from the quarantine center several times by their owners. In 1963 a woman disguised herself in a blond wig and kidnapped her Pekingese dog. Arrested, she declared "I can't live four months without him." She said she would go to jail rather than pay a fine and predicted, "[Hawai`i's] jails are going to get very crowded with dog lovers, and then maybe they'll do something to change this stupid law."

The "stupid law" has been changed twice in recent years, although not totally to the satisfaction of pet owners. In 1996 confinement was reduced to 30 days for pets who first undergo a complicated criteria of examinations, shots and microchip indentification implants. In 2003, the law was eased to allow pets to avoid quarantine completely if all criteria is met.

Hopefully, the new rules mean pets are no longer being smuggled into Hawai`i. Although we may never know. History records only the failed attempts to avoid quarantine.

- **Double-check information.** For flights from anywhere to Hawai`i, medium and large-sized pets must spend several hours in a waterproof "crate" container that you supply. Most airlines charge under $100 for trans-Pacific flights for animals that travel with you as freight. If the pet travels alone, the cost can be much higher. Get exact, detailed information from your airline or travel agent, but be careful. Many airline employees and travel agents do not know the full rules regarding pets and Hawai`i's quarantine laws. Get complete information regarding flight and arrival from the Quarantine Center Web site: hawaiiag.org/hdoa/ai–aqs–info.html.

At the Honolulu airport your pet will be taken directly to a pet holding area where animal quarantine agents will review paperwork and either release him to you or take him to the O`ahu quarantine station.

If your pet is to be quarantined at a satellite facility on another island, he must still arrive at O`ahu and spend two days at the quarantine facility there. (See accompanying story for details.)

At the quarantine station

Your pet will undergo an examination by a vet. One of the forms you signed and returned to the quarantine center weeks before your arrival allows the state to collect a blood sample and to sedate the animal for the test if necessary. If test results indicate antibody levels fall outside the established parameters, your pet must be quarantined for 120 days. It will go to one of hundreds of clean kennels lined up neatly on grassy lawns dotted with rows of small palms. The place is remarkably clean considering the number of animals. Kennels are completely cleaned each day. There was no animal odor on any of the several occasions we visited.

The kennels

Cat kennels are approximately five feet wide, ten feet long and include platforms for the cat to sit up high. There is also a roofed outdoor area for each cat and your Puffy can sit in her private *lanai* (patio) to drool over birds on the lawn outside her kennel and frown at dogs caged across the path.

Dog kennels are assigned to the dogs according to their size. Kennels are approximately seven feet high, six feet wide and vary in length from 14 feet to 25 feet. Very small dogs may be housed in a kennel similar in size to a cat kennel. If your animal uses bedding, you must supply it and wash it frequently.

Kennels are large enough for owners to sit inside and play with their pets.

Bob Fijal photo

The animals have no contact although they can see and hear each other through the chain link fences. The pets seem to hunger for human attention; people walking past ignite an explosion of barking, jumping and begging.

Each kennel has a bench or chair for you to sit on when you visit your pet. On weekends, families bring lawn chairs, balls and toys and spread out inside or next to their pet's kennel, making a holiday of the visit. It's not unusual for owners who plan to end up on neighbor islands to take a temporary apartment near the quarantine center so they can visit their animals daily. Animals are not allowed out, but some owners manage to play fetch inside the cage in an attempt to provide some exercise. Visits are every day except Monday and Friday. Pet treats are allowed and there's a small snack/gift shop on site that maintains a selection for both people and pets.

Overall, the facility is about as pleasant as it can be considering that it serves so many animals and their owners. The greatest problem seems to be a lack of exercise area. It's a hardship for large dogs to be penned without exercise for 30 days, let alone 120 days.

Food and care

The center provides a "nutritionally complete and balanced commercial dog or cat food for adult animals," according to its brochure. If your pet is not full-grown or is on a special diet, you may supply your pet's food, including instructions.

Your pet can be groomed by you or by a professional of your choice. Grooming allows your dog to leave his kennel and walk several yards to an outdoor grooming station. (Some pet owners schedule weekly grooming just so their dogs can get out and walk a few feet to the bathing areas. Either you or a grooming professional may care for your pet.)

If your pet is diabetic, the shelter will provide insulin shots at $1 a day, very reasonable when you consider the effort involved.

Only one animal is allowed in each kennel. That is so caretakers can monitor the pet's eating habits, bowel movements and urine to make sure it's healthy. You are responsible for your pet's health while in quarantine. While you are visiting and playing with your pet, examine him for any ticks, skin or ear problems. If you spot a problem, let the staff know and a veterinarian will examine your pet.

Two pets together

A program called Complete Care lets you keep two buddy pets together, but it's not easy. The pets must be of the same species (for example, both dogs or both cats) but need not be the same breed. You must assume total responsibility for your pets' care, on hand to feed the pets and clean their kennel twice a day. If you have more than one pet at the facility in separate kennels, you may be able to let them visit together while you are present. The brochure explains procedures and rules.

Freedom day!

You'll need to bring your picture identification when you come to pick up your pet and be able to pay your bill in full. If you wish to pay by credit card, you must present your card in person. Be sure to bring a leash or carrier for your pet. And be ready to be devoured with love by your elated pooch or pussycat. One dog was so happy to see his owner he broke his tail; the enthusiastically wagging tail hit a door.

Exempted from quarantine

Animals coming into Hawai`i from Australia, New Zealand and Great Britain do not have to undergo quarantine, but they must meet certain other conditions.

Gian's story: 'It was tougher on me'

"Pets are like family. They are your children; you love them that much," says Gian Volanti, "father" to two dogs and an elderly cat. When he moved from Oregon to Maui two years ago, the minimum quarantine was 30 days. Gian made a special trip to the island of O`ahu to see Hawai`i's pet quarantine facility.

"That was the deciding factor," he says. "If I didn't think my animals could stand the quarantine, I wasn't going to move to Hawai`i."

Gian's pets are all Oregon humane societies' foundlings whom he feared might have sad memories of kennels, and he didn't want to "jail"

Gian Volanti and family.

them again. He also dreaded putting his animals through the pre-quarantine rigors: microchip implants for identification purposes, inoculations and tests that can cut the quarantine time.

When Gian arrived at the quarantine station, just off busy H-1 in Halawa, he was impressed by the clean, odor-free, spacious indoor-outdoor kennels lined up on the center's carefully mowed lawns. Although the facility was busy, he was able to persuade an aide to give him a tour.

His impression of the quarantine facility at that time? "I felt that the staff was impersonal. It was like 'These are the rules. Don't ask any questions. Come back when you have money,'" he said.

Gian decided his three pets could endure a quarantine of 30 days if the dogs were housed together. He began to plan his move nearly a year in advance of coming. Eight months before moving, he obtained the quarantine center's packet with full details. He made sure his veterinarian in Oregon kept in close contact with the O`ahu facility to properly prepare his pets so they would qualify for the shorter 30-day stay.

Gian says the total cost for bringing his three animals to Hawai`i was about $3,500, including $350 each for pre-quarantine veterinarian visits, $100 a month each for pills and medication for three months preceding the trip, $100 each for microchip implants, and housing that cost $655 each for their quarantine facility stay. Also $50 to $100 each for pet "crates," fiberglass kennels, used on the plane.

Since he was moving to Maui, a stretch of ocean away from O'ahu, Gian took advantage of the quarantine center's VIP (Volunteers Interested in Pets) program. Volunteers visit pets, usually twice a week, administering human attention and love. Because Gian wanted his two dogs housed together, he had to accept full responsibility for their feeding, clean up and care. Although that goes beyond the scope of their duties, a volunteer agreed to care for Gian's pets. She was thorough and caring, Gian says. He did not pay her a specific amount, "just tipped her well in cash," he adds, declining to specify the amount.

The caretaker "sprung" his pets after they had served their time, Gian says, and even accompanied them to the Honolulu airport where they were put on a plane to Maui. Were his pets adversely affected by their quarantine? Gian says his cocker spaniel barked a great deal throughout his quarantine stay and upon being released did not "speak" for several weeks. The dog eventually began to bark again. Basically, he says, his pets were none the worse for their ordeal.

Gian shakes his head. "It was tougher on me than on my pets."

Stay near your pet?

When retirees Tony and Nancy Fisher moved to Maui from California with their dog Archie-Boots, they stayed on O'ahu during his 30-day quarantine rather then let him face confinement alone. Tony located an enclave of small residential hotels across from the Pearl City Shopping Center, just a few minutes drive from the quarantine center in Halawa. The Fishers turned their O'ahu stay into a mini-vacation, playing with Archie-Boots for several hours each day and also visiting nearby Pearl Harbor and other sites.

Here are some residential hotels near the quarantine center. If you must stay at the hotel with your pet after it completes quarantine, discuss the hotel's pet policy with the manager.

- **Harbor Shores Apartment Hotel**, 98-145 Lipoa Place, A'iea. (808) 488-5742 or toll free 800-227-8796.

- **Shoreline Apartments.** 98-135 Lipoa Place (808) 488-4900. shorelineathickam.com

- **Harbor Arms Apartment Hotel**, 98-130 Lipoa Place. (808) 488-5556 or toll free 1-800-360-5556.

- **PepperTree Apartments**, 98-150 Lipoa Place, Aiea. (808) 488-1993 or toll free 1-877-488-1993.

What other pet owners say

It isn't easy to qualify for shortened quarantine periods, but it is crucial. More than 40 people whose pets had endured both 30-day and 120-day quarantines were interviewed for this book. Their responses made it clear that a reduction in quarantine time means a reduction in animal trauma.

A humane society employee said she brought a dog through four months of quarantine several years ago and "it was awful. I would never do it again."

A woman who brought two large dogs in 1994 said that during four months of quarantine one dog had his tooth broken and suffered a rash from sprays used on the grounds. Her dogs were also infested with ticks, she says.

Problems were much less severe in pets who spent 30 days in quarantine. In the previous story, Gian noted that his dogs did not bark after quarantine. However, several owners whose dogs has been quarantined for 30 days commented that their pets barked more than usual after being released. That may be because at O`ahu's quarantine center, most of the dogs bark every time someone walks by the kennels.

Overall, cats seem to survive the ordeal somewhat better than dogs, perhaps because cats are more solitary animals. Six people reported that their cats were nervous and hid for a few days after coming "home" from quarantine, but four of those people noted that the home was new to their cats and they would probably have reacted that way even if they had not been quarantined. One owner said his cat never recovered and continues to be nervous.

A man who brought a cat and two dogs through 30 days of quarantine claims his large dogs survived better than small dogs would because small ones are more nervous and active. Large dogs tend to be mellow and take changes in stride, he maintains.

Other owners say the confinement is more difficult for large dogs because they require more exercise. A veterinarian commented that quarantine might be painful for dogs that have arthritis because they do not get the exercise necessary to alleviate their condition.

Both a veterinarian and a quarantine center volunteer mentioned ticks being a continuing problem. Be sure your quarantined pet is getting a flea inhibitor that includes tick repellent. And, if time allows, make the effort to cut your pets quarantine stay to, at most, 30 days.

Toni Polancy phot

Quarantine on a neighbor island

When it comes to putting your pet in the state-mandated quarantine, you'll feel as though you don't have choices, but you do. Where you choose to quarantine your pet has a great deal to do with how you and your pet will be treated. In addition to the O`ahu quarantine station, it is possible to quarantine pets at satellite sites on the Big Island and Kaua`i. If your pet has a medical need, it can stay at a veterinary clinic on Maui.

It's not simple to use neighbor island quarantine centers, and it is more costly. If you want your pet quarantined on a neighbor island, you must first make arrangements with the quarantine center in O`ahu. Your pet will go to the Honolulu airport where quarantine center aides will pick it up and transfer it to the O`ahu quarantine center to be identified, examined and undergo blood tests. After about two days, center aides will transport your pet back to the Honolulu airport to be shipped to the neighbor island quarantine site. An attendant from the neighbor island site will pick your pet up at that island's airport and transport it to an on-island quarantine site.

In addition to veterinary or kennel fees on the neighbor island, you will pay the O`ahu center about $300 for testing and processing for a 30-

An owner playing with her pet in a grassy yard? Can this be a quarantine station? Yes. It's the cuddly Big Island version of quarantine. At Bar-King Kennels, a satellite quarantine site, there's plenty of play time and even small swimming pools for confined pets.

day quarantine and $50 for a 120-day quarantine. (Less testing is required for a 120-day internment, so it costs less.)

The atmosphere

We visited all quarantine sites except one of the two veterinary sites on Maui where a veterinarian refused us entrance. Here's what you can expect at each site. We've used a dog as an example throughout, with reference to cats.

Big Island

The Bar-King Kennels, on the Hilo side of the island, is a small, friendly facility. Your dog will spend his confinement in a kennel

At Bar-King Kennel satellite site, dogs are taken to fenced play areas to exercise.

Toni Polancy photo

somewhat smaller than those on O`ahu. An attendant—he same one every day—will take him at least twice daily to a yard where he can run, play and do what comes naturally. You can visit him daily, playing with him in one of several small, enclosed, grassy yards, complete with plastic dog "swimming pools." If you plan to spend the day, you can bring your lunch to a kitchen set aside for pet owners. Some owners even bring cots and take afternoon naps with their pets. You cannot stay overnight. You may keep your cat and dog together in the same kennel. In this friendly atmosphere, the attendants will probably know you and your pet by name and chat about your pet. An attendant lives on site. Cost of the 30-day confinement is the same as on O`ahu: $650. But it costs an extra $300 to have him processed first in O`ahu and brought to this kennel. You must pay one-half of the fee in advance.

If you have plenty of money, you can even spend $300 extra to house your pet in a tiled, air-conditioned V.I.P. room with its own play yard and pool.

You do not have to live on the Big Island to house your dog at the site, but reservations must be made several months in advance.

Kaua`i

Kaua`i's new $3 million Kaua`i Humane Society is a satellite quarantine center as well as the nation's first people/animal disaster shelter. (See the Hurricane section of this book.)

The Kaua`i satellite quarantine site can accommodate 48 quarantined pets: 24 dogs in indoor/outdoor kennels and 24 cats, says Rebecca Rhoades, Humane Society executive director. Owners, who must be Kaua`i residents, can take dogs, one at a time, to one of four grassy outdoor exercise areas to "run loose and chase Frisbees," Rhoades says. Cats have two outdoor visitor areas. Kennels are about the same size as those at the O`ahu quarantine center. Cost on Kaua`i is $15 a day while the pet is there—plus about $300 in fees for tests at the O`ahu center.

We visited the Kaua'i site a few months after it had opened. The quarantine area was filled and booked several months in advance and The Humane Society was lively and busy with owners visiting their pets.

"This has been so great," Rhoades said. "It brings people to the Humane Society and does the staff good to see the loving, happy side of pet ownership."

Maui

If your pet has a medical condition and you can prove it, you may house your pet at one of three veterinary sites on Maui. Maui has no full-scale satellite quarantine site primarily because of zoning restrictions, says Dr. James Foppoli, state veterinarian.

Since this is a medical confinement, you'll pay extra. Overall, counting about $25-a-day kennel fees, $100 transportation fee from the airport on Maui, and additional examination and registration fees, it will cost about

On Maui you can keep your pet at Kihei Veterinary Clinic if the pet's current vet certifies that it has a medical problem. You may walk your pet in an outdoor fenced area (next page). It will be kept in a cage at other times.

Toni Polancy photos

$1,300 to quarantine your pet on Maui for 30 days, including the $300 fee for processing in O`ahu before coming here. These are the three Maui sites.

- **At the Kihei Veterinary Clinic,** your pet needs a medical reason to spend his quarantine time there. Here, pets stay in cages. If your pet is a dog, you can take him to a narrow play area or walk with him around a side yard, part of a wetlands area. This is quarantine and although three owners were playing with their dogs in the yard the day we visited, pets are not supposed to touch each other. If your pet is a cat, he stays in a small cage that is a far cry from the spacious indoor/oudoor kennel on O`ahu.

  This pet hospital is a friendly place, and a full time quarantine manager is available to answer your questions.

- **At the Kahului Animal Hospital,** Dr. Terry Smith refused to let us visit the quarantine area, which he said is located on the second floor above his storefront office. "I take quarantine seriously," Smith said. "I have a responsibility to the state. I can't just have people walking through." Smith said he had three cages, 8 x 8 x 8 feet and 2 x 4 x 8 feet in size. A person whose dogs were quarantined there said she was satisfied.

- **At the Central Maui Animal Clinic,** near Dairy Road and Pu`unene Avenue, quarantine areas include indoor and outdoor runs similar to those at the O`ahu facility and places to play and bathe your pet. This is also a friendly place with plenty of staff.

The procedure

To quarantine your animal at a Maui veterinary office instead of the O`ahu quarantine facility, it must have some medical problem such as diabetes. The veterinarian where you live now must write a letter to the director of the quarantine center, telling why the pet needs medical care. The director must approve the Maui quarantine. Dr. C. Chang, the quarantine center's acting director when we visited, stressed that there is no hanky-panky; the pet must actually need the attention of a veterinarian. However, quarantine site caretakers on Maui disagreed on just how difficult it might be to qualify your pet for medical quarantine on that island. One says it's pretty simple.

"All you have to do is have your current vet write a letter. Just about any perceived illness, even separation anxiety qualifies," she says. "I've never heard of a request being denied."

At another clinic the quarantine caretaker disagrees.

"You used to be able to say that your dog would suffer separation stress," she says. "Not any more. Now it's harder. The pet has to really have an illness or a condition like diabetes."

If you want to quarantine your pet on Maui, discuss details with the veterinarian or aide at the facility you choose.

O`ahu:
Animal Quarantine Station
99-951 Halawa Valley Road
Aiea, Hawai`i 96701-5602
(808) 483-7151
Fax: (808) 483-7161
hawaiiag.org/hdoa/

Maui:
Kihei Veterinary Clinic
1476 South Kihei Road
Kihei, Hawai`i 96753
(808) 879-5777

Kahului Animal Hospital
111 Hana Highway, Suite 106
Kahului, Hawai`i 96732
(808) 871-PETS

Central Maui Animal Clinic
45 Hookele Street
Kahului, Hawai`i 96732
(808) 893-2380
email: cmac@maui.net

Big Island:
Bar-King Dog Kennel
Sarah Scanlon, owner
(808) 966-8733
Fax: (808) 966-7353
email: barkingk@ilhawaii.net
Bar-KingQuarantine.com

Kaua`i:
Kaua`i Humane Society
P.O. Box 3330
3825 Kaumuali`i Highway
Lihu`e, Hawai`i 96766
(808) 632-0610

Quarantine

Make your pet's confinement happier; volunteers offer simple, sound advice

If you can't visit your pet during its quarantine, *Volunteers Interested in Pets* will help. Its 42 volunteers spend at least one hour a week showering your dog or cat with love and personal attention, monitoring his care, fluffing pillows, checking for parasites, petting and playing with your pet. Volunteers don't charge for their services; they do accept tips. Forty percent of the volunteers are retired people, says Kathy Panicek, VIP coordinator at the time we spoke. She offered this advice for making your pets confinement less traumatic:

Get your pet familiar with his crate. Before the long airline trip to Hawai`i, make the crate accessible to your pet. Most hard plastic crates open into two pieces. Take the top off and let your pet play inside the bottom. Lure him in with treats or catnip. Make it a game. Crawl in yourself if the crate is large enough. Eventually add the top.

Make a sign. Write your pet's name in big letters and attach the sign to his kennel so passersby and attendants can address your pet by his name, making him feel more secure and at home. Enclose the sign in a plastic pocket to keep it fresh and readable throughout the pet's confinement.

Watch your dog and his water bowl. Some dogs are annoyed or frightened by the water system, which sprays water into their bowls and sometimes makes hissing and clicking sounds. If your dog is annoyed or hesitates to drink, let a quarantine center attendant know. The attendant may be able to change the flow of water to a bubbling effect or will clear the water lines of air that creates noise.

Bring a pot of grass or catnip. Your cat will enjoy a little potted "garden" on which to chew. Provide a bit of extra stimulation for your quarantined cat. Sprinkle a handful of birdseed near the outdoor part of her quarantine kennel. The seed will attract birds for kitty to watch.

Keep your emotions in check. When you visit your pet, avoid over stimulating it. Keep greetings or good-byes quiet and nonchalant. Exciting entrances and sad, prolonged goodbyes confuse your pet and make him miss you more. Also, for safety's sake, calm yourself before you re-enter busy H-1 and O`ahu's dangerous traffic.

Provide comfortable bedding. Carry it in when you visit your pet at the quarantine center or send it to your VIP volunteer. An inexpensive fiberfill pillow with a case that can be washed is a good choice for dogs or cats. You can carry a fresh pillowcase in with you each time you visit your pet (or ask your volunteer to wash it occasionally). Avoid cedar or foam-filled bedding which bored pets can shred. A fiberfill comforter also works well, but avoid blankets and towels; they flatten down and provide little comfort.

Order a second blood test. The results of your pet's blood test won't come until he's been in quarantine for about two weeks. If he flunks the first blood test, order another one from the quarantine facility's veterinarian. It's well worth the $60 cost to avoid 120 days in quarantine, the usual procedure when a pet fails to pass.

Schedule dog grooming times. You, a groomer or your VIP volunteer can walk the dog to the grooming area several times a week, providing a little exercise and a break from his kennel. "You don't have to do a thorough grooming each time," Panicek suggests. "Maybe splash a little cool water on him or wash his face." By the way, you won't have to worry about clipping his nails. The kennel's cement floor keeps paw nails short.

A piece of your clothing? Panicek said owners sometimes send along a piece of their own clothing, hoping its scent will be a comfort to their pets. She has never seen a pet respond in any way that indicates he associates it with his owner. If you want to send along a T-shirt, that's fine, but it may be more comforting to you than to your dog. She usually fluffs up the pet's bedding and puts the article of clothing on top.

Add names to your pet's visitor list. The more visits, the merrier your pet will be. You must provide the quarantine center with names of anyone who has permission to visit your pet. Ask friends, relatives or caring co-workers to visit your pet and be sure to put their names on the list.

Close the door, well. When you leave your pet's kennel, make sure the door is secured. Pets have escaped because careless owners left doors unlatched.

Shi-shi in my house?

You spent a lot of time and effort housetraining your dog, teaching him to eliminate only outdoors, never in the house. Now he's in quarantine and guess what? Your pet is supposed to break all the rules he's ever learned and defecate and shi-shi (urinate) right there inside his kennel.

The process is just too mind boggling for some conscientious dogs. They get to the quarantine center and they hold it and hold it. Some get constipated or bloated.

If your pet exhibits this problem, try this solution, suggests Kathy Panicek, Volunteers Interested in Pets aide. Buy a piece of sod (a square of grass) from a nursery and put it in the outdoors part of his quarantine kennel. Some dogs connect the sod to being "good dogs" and doing their duty outdoors.

One very loving pet owner tried this solution: she collected urine from a nearby dog kennel and sprinkled it in her dog's kennel. The scent of the other dog's urine triggered the action she desired from her own pet.

Quarantine aides do monitor animal's elimination and will report any problems to the veterinarian.

After he's sprung from quarantine, your pet may have an accident, Panicek says.

"Usually dogs have one accident, not right away, but a week or two after they get out," she notes, "usually when they are playing or get excited. They just get so accustomed to doing it in the kennel they forget. You'll see them squat or lift their leg."

You, of course, will be shocked and you may even holler "No! Stop!"

That's okay. Let your shock show. Let your dog know he's done wrong. Most likely your well-mannered pet will also be shocked and embarrassed by what he's done.

"He'll look and say to himself, 'Oh, my gosh! What have I done?' and he probably won't ever do it again," Panicek says.

How often should I visit my pet? And other important concerns

Animals, it is said, have little sense of real time. They relate solely to "right now," to what is happening at the moment. When you visit your pet at a quarantine site, he is excited to see his special person; but when you leave, he doesn't understand that you are coming back and so feels abandoned again.

That is the theory of a Hawai`i travel agent who books travel plans for pet owners journeying from neighbor islands to O`ahu.

"Some go every week to visit their pets in quarantine," she points out. The ordeal, she advises, is time consuming, costly (outer islanders must also rent a car on O`ahu) and, since animals only relate to what is happening right now, it's futile, if not downright cruel to visit and leave, she maintains.

We put this question, and others related to quarantine, to caretakers who spend time with our pets while they are confined.

Q: *When I come to visit my dog in quarantine and then leave, it's so sad to say goodbye. Would it be better for my pet if I didn't visit at all?*
"People sometimes ask whether they should visit and I say, 'Yes, by all means. We encourage visits,'" says Ruth Foster, receptionist at Bar-King Kennel on the Big Island. "Visiting is important. It helps pets adjust to the kennel. They see their owners and they know, 'Well, mommy or daddy's here. It must be a safe place.' And they do know. We have dogs that get excited and bark when their owner's car pulls up," she adds.

Q: *How does my dog act inside the kennel? Does he mope? Bark? Seem ill?*
- The first week is the hardest says an attendant at Bar-King Kennel. "Some dogs it doesn't affect at all, but most dogs sort of mope. Some won't eat for a day or so; they're scared. Some get diarrhea and even colitis, with blood. But after a week or so they seem much better. They seem to adjust."

- "They bark a lot," says a supervisor at the O`ahu center, "off and on every time they see someone new. But that is normal behavior for a dog. I'd be more worried about the ones who don't bark at all."

- "They don't get ill being in quarantine," says a VIP volunteer on O'ahu. "But if they have a previous illness it can be exacerbated by the flight. Most of the pets in quarantine are very healthy and the veterinarians (at the quarantine center) are very good. I have no qualms about the care there."

Q: *Should I send along my pet's toys? Are they allowed?*
Toys and comfort treats are allowed at all quarantine sites. Bar-King suggests you send dog toys, beds and anything that's special to your dog to the kennel in advance of the pet's arrival. At the O'ahu center, you should arrange to bring the items after your dog has arrived.

Don't overdo it. Send your pet's favorite soft, cuddly toy and his favorite chew toy. You may or may not get them back at the end of quarantine, but they should serve to soothe your pet during the first traumatic days of confinement.

Q: *Can I phone in to see how my pet is doing?*
- At the O'ahu center, it is nearly impossible to get through by phone during business hours; an answering machine takes most calls. The sheer number of pets makes it almost impossible to respond to individual owners. However, pets are checked by attendants and any concerns are brought to the attention of the veterinarian. If there are any health problems, you will be notified.

- At the Kihei Veterinary Clinic, a quarantine manager is available to answer your concerns and, says an attendant, may even call you to tell you that your dog is out of biscuits.

- At Bar-King on the Big Island, "Yes, you can call in as often as you want, 24 hours a day. Owners need to do that. Then, when we have time, we go over to the kennels and tell the pets their mommy and daddy called," Ruth Foster says.

Q: *Should I tranquilize my pet to make the journey and admittance less stressful?*
"No," says Foster. "But you might want to take a tranquilizer yourself. This is much more stressful on owners than it is on their pets."

Seriously, this is an issue you will want to discuss with your pet's current veterinarian. Much depends on how far you are traveling (from the East Coast? West? the Orient?) and how long your pet will be in flight. Your decision will also depend on your pet's temperament.

14 Traveling

with and
without
your pet

On the
mainland it's
easy to take
your dog along
on a vacation
or a journey to
grandma's house,
but here...

Over the ocean and through security to tutu's *house we go...*

Traveling with your pet

On the mainland it's simple to take your dog along on a vacation or a trip to grandma's house. You pat the back seat of the car, your dog jumps in, and you're on your way. Or you pack kitty in a carrier, plop it on the seat next to you and take off. Traveling in our state is considerably more difficult, since we must fly to go anywhere beyond our own island. Unless you are one of our many part-time residents, you'd best forget out-of-state trips with Fido. Despite eased quarantine restrictions in 2003, it is still difficult and costly to bring your pet back into Hawai`i. However, with just a little planning you can easily take your pet along on "overnighters" and inter-island jaunts. Most flights are under a half-hour in length. Flying a pet is still relatively simple and inexpensive on both major state carriers, Hawaiian Airlines and Aloha Airlines.

Inter-island flights

- **Aloha Airlines.** Animals go "priority standby" on Aloha; their flight is not confirmed or guaranteed. Regulations after the September 11, 2001 terrorism attacks mandated that all luggage travel on the same flight as its owners, but that rule does not apply to pets, so your pet may have to travel on a fight different from yours. Actually, about "99 percent of pets" go on the same flight as their owners, an Aloha reservationist said.

    "We try very hard to get them on the same flight. If they don't make that one," she said, "they are

Out-of-state travel: complicated, costly

Hawai`i pet owners who travel out of state with their dogs and cats face a complicated procedure and high fee when they return. As this book went to press, the state health department was considering an easing of some requirements. Under the refined system, a *kama`aina* (resident) pet returning to the state would incur a fee of $78 if it qualifies for direct release at the Honolulu airport or $110 if it must be quarantined for five days.

For more on quarantine, see chapter 13 of this book. For current quarantine requirements and complete costs and details, visit the state health department's Internet site:

**www.hawaiiag.org/hdoa
or call
(808) 483-7157**

almost certain to make the next flight." To be sure your pet is on your flight, avoid "very early flights" and "very late night flights," when most freight travels, she advised. (Unfortunately, those are also the coolest times for your pet to fly.)

If you don't have a rigid fiberglass carrier or a soft nylon (Sherpa type) bag for your small "in-cabin" pet, Aloha will sell you a cardboard one very inexpensively. The box is six inches high, 13 inches wide and 18 inches long, ideal for a cat or a dog under 15 pounds.

Call the Aloha baggage department on your island for more information and advice as to space available for your pet on any flight. A freight handler says there is no restriction on weight, but your kennel should be a purchased one, not something you've concocted, and your pet should be able to stand up and move around in it.

"We see some," she adds, "where the dog can hardly move, and that's not right. We try to avoid that."

Cost in 2003: no charge in cabin; $25 per pet each way in baggage.

- **Hawaiian Airlines.** Hawaiian limits the total number of pets shipped as baggage on any flight. Five pets are allowed on larger planes, four on smaller ones. When you make your reservation, inquire whether your animal will be allowed on the flight you've chosen. If so, your pet has a "reservation" with Hawaiian Airlines.

  Hawaiian does not offer carriers; you must provide your own. Large animals, including carrier, cannot weigh more than 70 pounds.

Toni Polancy photo

Archie, a 45-pound dog, sits next to, from left, his large carrier; the medium-sized carrier our 22-pound Betty uses, and the nylon "Sherpa" bag that houses 9-pound Winky under a seat in the airplane cabin.

Maximum size for the large animal's carrier is 27 inches high, 22 inches wide and 40 inches long. The under-the-seat carrier for small pets cannot be larger than 8 by 10 by 16 inches. Hawaiian also offers some pet information on its website at www.hawaiianair.com.

Cost in 2003: $35 per pet each way in baggage or cabin.

The kindness of strangers

My three dogs and I fly both airlines often. Two dogs travel as cargo and one travels in-cabin and we have never had a problem. Porters, airline agents and fellow passengers go out of their way to be kind to people traveling with pets; the sight of a pet in his kennel at the airport brings smiles to weary travelers. As recently as two years ago airline agents occasionally waived the fee for cargo pets, saying something like, "You're *kama'aina* (resident)! No charge." That hasn't happened lately as the skies grow less friendly, but traveling inter-island with pets is still pleasant.

Other considerations

- **Your pet may be very nervous about this new adventure.** Be sure to let him become accustomed to his carrier well in advance (weeks) before the flight, so at least that part of the experience will be familiar to him. If you have a particularly highstrung pet, talk to your vet about a sedative. Inter-island flights are short, most less than half an hour, but since you must check in at least 90 minutes early, your pet will be in its crate for over two hours. That's a long time in a confined space.

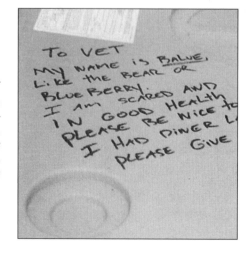

This loving dog owner covered his pet's travel kennel with helpful information.

- **Exercise your pet before departure.** A tired pet may be less anxious. Bring a leash and walk him prior to his flight and immediately after, but do it OFF airline property. That's the law.

- **Check weather conditions.** Mainland carriers restrict animal flights during hot summer weather; inter-island airlines usually don't, because the flights are so short. But sitting in a plastic cage on hot tarmac prior to loading can be brutal for your pet. Consider morning or early evening flights when temperatures are lower, even though they may be more difficult to book due to freight shipments.

- **For cats:** Pet stores offer disposable litter boxes. You can change the litter box immediately after arrival, if necessary.

- **Water:** Your pet may be without water for his entire journey. Even if you fill his kennel water dish it will probably spill. Offer water as soon as possible after the flight and/or note the tip in this chapter.

Betty tries on a "Sherpa," one of the most popular pet travel bags. Made of a soft nylon material, it is ideal for pets who travel in the plane's cabin, but cannot be used in the cargo section. The bag comes in three sizes; this one is too small for Betty. Dogs should be able to turn around comfortably inside the bag.

Toni Polancy photo

- **Air sickness:** If your pet has a weak stomach, take a morning flight and don't feed him until the flight is over. However, give plenty of water before and after the flight. If your pet seems prone to air sickness, you may want to reconsider travelling with him unless it is absolutely necessary. Talk to your veterinarian about easing his discomfort.

Trans-ocean flights

This state's quarantine laws mean you must make special arrangements to fly INTO Hawai'i with your pet. However it's much easier for an animal to fly OUT of Hawai'i. Why would an animal leave the state? A breeder might sell an animal and ship it out of state. Some newcomers return to the

Tip

Here's a clever way to provide fresh water for your pet throughout the flight. Freeze a plastic bottle of water. Puncture several tiny holes in the side of the bottle and place it in the kennel's water dish. The melting ice seeps into the dish, providing fresh water that won't spill. Your pet may enjoy the novelty of licking his own bottle of water.
(From Continental Air's Web site www.continental.com.)

Mainland or ship their pets back because they cannot find pet-friendly rentals. And some kind tourists choose pets at island humane societies and take them home. Most humane societies are savvy about the shipping process and welcome the opportunity to find a home for island animals.

Unfortunately if your pet flies over the ocean, he will be treated as freight and flown in the baggage area. He will be in his crate/kennel for hours with no human contact. Flying to the east coast of the U.S., your pet may be confined for 12 hours or more. You must be sure your pet has sufficient water for the trip and the water is in containers that will not spill. Your best bet is to buy special containers which attach to the side of the kennel and allow a small amount of water to drizzle through a tube. Use two such containers for water, to assure the animal has plenty in case of delays.

Get the details of your pet's flight from the airline representative and make sure he or she knows the airline rules. If you use a travel agent, be sure to discuss your pet's needs. Then double-check the arrangements by calling the airlines yourself. Some travel agents are not well versed on regulations regarding animals.

Pet travel blackouts

The Department of Agriculture's Animal-Plant Health Inspection

On the Web

Scanning the Internet can be great for ticket purchasing, but when it comes to hunting for information from specific airlines about pet travel, you'll feel like a dog on a fox chase. Continental and Hawaiian Air offer complete information about pet travel on line. Others sites, at this writing, ignore the issue or bury their information.

hawaiiag.org/hdoa
Complete quarantine regulations at the Hawai'i Department of Agriculture site.
continental.com
Continental Airlines offers pet travel advice
hawaiianair.com/cargo/pets
Hawaiian Airlines' pet information
hsus.org
Humane Society of the United State's site offers pet travel information, policies of several airlines.

These commercial web sites offer a variety of pet travel information:
takeyourpet.com
petsonthego.com
petswelcome.com

Call Continental Air's live animal desk at 1-800-575-3335.

Service says pets may not be checked as baggage if the animal will be exposed to temperatures above 85 degrees or below 45 degrees for more than 45 minutes on a flight. Baggage compartment temperatures are regulated during flight, but can soar when the plane is on the ground. As a result, most airlines either ban pets traveling in cargo from Hawai'i during hot summer months, or limit them to evening travel.

Ziggy's pet seatbelt anchors him safely in any automobile. The seatbelt attaches easily to a car's standard seatbelts. The seatbelt protects pets in a collision and also may help avoid crashes since it keeps pets from distracting the driver. Available in some Hawai'i pet stores for under $20.

Courtesy Hawaiian Humane Society

Keep health certificates up to date and carry them with you. Most long-distance carriers require proof of inoculations before they will allow a pet on board. At this writing, Aloha and Hawaiian airlines do not require such proof; United and American Airlines do require it.

Short-nosed dog breeds, including American Staffordshires, Boston Terriers, Boxers, Brussels Griffins, Bull Terriers, pugs, bulldogs, Shih Tzus, Pekinese and others may have breathing problems, and some airlines refuse to carry them. Other airlines require these breeds to use a kennel one size larger than usual, and to use a kennel with ventilation on all four sides.

If the kennel does not have ventilation on all four sides, modify it by drilling seven holes in the rear top and seven holes in the rear bottom of the kennel using a 3/4-inch keyhole bit, advises Continental Air.

Continental Air has a "live animal desk" with an attendant who specializes in shipping animals. Phone 1-800-575-3335. Cost is based on distance. "We don't ship pit bulls at all," says an attendant. "When they get on aircraft they get antsy and can break out of the cage."

Pet-friendly places to stay on neighbor islands

Yes, you can travel to any island with your pet.

"Wealthy and famous clients demand that their pets be welcomed," says one frequent interisland traveler. "The more high-class the hotel, the more likely it is to accommodate your pet." A recent trip took her to the posh Four Seasons Resort on Maui, where nary a word was said about her two small dogs.

A bed and breakfast owner agrees. "Who's going to say no to someone like, say, Elizabeth Taylor?"

That may be the case, but it wasn't easy for our researcher to find island hotels or bed and breakfasts that will allow pets. And breeders, who travel interisland often for dog shows, tend to keep pet-friendly accommodations secret to make sure there's room for their own pets.

"We kind of guard the locations where we stay," says one breeder. "We don't even tell each other, because most bed and breakfasts and small hotels will only take one or two dogs and they fill up quickly."

Here are some locations we found after several days of trying:

MAUI

Aloha Huelo Point Lookout
Huelo, Haiku, Maui, Hawai`i
(808) 573-0914
Toll Free: (800) 871-8645
Fax: (808) 573-0227
Email: dreamers@maui.net
Well behaved pets accepted.
Security deposit required. Cats & small dogs are easier to accommodate, but they can't be "barkers" that disturb neighbors

Haikuleana B&B
555 Haiku Road
Maui, Hawai'i
(808) 575-2890
www.haikuleana.com
A cat plays "hostess" here, so your pet needs to get along with felines.

Four Seasons Resort
3900 Wailea Alanui
Wailea, Maui, Hawai'i
(808) 874-8000
No deposit required. All sizes welcome. The hotel even provides doggy treats.

BIG ISLAND

Hawaiian Oasis
74-4958 Kiwi Street
Kailua-Kona, Hawai'i 96740
(808) 327-1701
Email: carol@hawaiianoasis.com
Deposit required; pet must be leashed.

BIG ISLAND (cont.)

The Volcano Inn
19-3820 Old Volcano Highway
P.O. Box 490
Volcano, Hawai'i 96785
(808) 967-7293
(800) 997-2292
Fax: (808) 985-7349
Email: volcano@volcanoinn.com
$50.00 deposit required

Paradise Vacation Rentals
HCR 3 Box 11020
Kea'au, Hawai'i 96749
1-800-555-8764 or (808) 982-7541
Advertised as a "home away
from home for animal lovers,"
this mini-resort offers furnished
cottages at reasonable rates
and is a few minutes drive
from Bar-King Kennel satellite
quarantine center.

Wild Ginger Inn
near downtown Hilo
(808) 935-5556
1-800-882-1887
Show dogs and possibly
well cared for medium
or smaller dogs.

Wild Orchid Inn
Mountain View
Bettye and George Wakabayashi
(808) 968-6969
wildorchid@cs.com
There's even a dog play yard.

KAUA'I

Makaleha Mountain Retreat
Kapa'a, Hawai`i
(808) 822-5131
makaleha@asis.com
Deposit required.

O'AHU

B & B Honolulu Statewide
Honolulu, Hawai'i
(800) 288-4666
www.hawaiibnb.com
Call for more information.
May be able to accommodate
statewide.

Bamboo Inn Hawai'i
44-633 Kane`ohe Bay Drive
Kane`ohe, O`ahu, Hawai'i 96744
(808) 342-1006
(800) 484-3695 PIN 8292
Email:
bambooinnhawaii@aol.com
Call for more information. $300
security deposit.

Paradise Cottage
Kailua, Hawai'i
(808) 254-3332
Fax: (808) 254-3332
paradisecottage@hotmail.com
Socialized dogs,
$10 extra per night.

Traveling without your pet

For several years, Holly Lang, a magazine publisher, worked on two islands, Kaua'i and Maui, and traveled between them every month. That meant Miss Muffy, her nine-pound poma-roodle (part Pomeranian, part Poodle) had to be packed into a travel bag each month and hauled along on the plane ride. It was always an inconvenience, but after the terrorist attacks on Sept. 11, 2001, when baggage was reduced to one carry-on item, the situation worsened.

Holly considered several options for her "baby:" A boarding kennel? An in-home pet sitter who could visit once a day? Neighbors? Friends? She was concerned that such a small dog would get lost in the shuffle of a large boarding kennel. A pet sitter would come to the home, once a day, to feed Muffy, play with her and walk her. But that still meant Muffy, an "only child," would be home alone for 23 hours a day.

Muffy's veterinarian finally solved the dilemma by producing the phone number of a woman who "baby sits" dogs in her home. The woman limits her visitors to a controllable six and accepts only small dogs weighing under 20 pounds. "The dogs can run around the home and they aren't kept in cages or kennels. Muffy seems to enjoy going there," Holly says.

Hawai`i residents tend to be very mobile, visiting the mainland or other islands to play, to keep up contacts with far-off families or, like Holly, to work. Whereas mainland pet owners think first of sending their pets to kennels, we are likely to rely on friends, relatives and neighbors.

Boarding facilities (kennels)

Boarding kennels are not as common in Hawai'i as they are on the mainland; some towns have no boarding kennels at all due to zoning, the high price of land, and the proximity of neighbors. If you live in a tourist oriented city or town, you may have to travel to a more rural area of your island to find a boarding facility.

Tip
Taking your pet to a kennel? Be sure:
- To visit the kennel in advance to be sure it meets your standards for cleanliness and crowding.
- That your own pet is clean and free of fleas and ticks.
- To bring certification from your veterinarian that your pet's vaccinations are up to date.
- If someone other than yourself will be visiting the animal or picking it up, tell the kennel keeper.

Pet sitter: I do whatever people need

Julie Hale, who lives in Kaua'i's Wailua Homesteads, has been a pet sitter for ten years. But the term "pet sitter " doesn't really explain her job. First of all, Julie rarely gets a chance to sit, except in her car, traveling the many miles between clients' homes. And then, her job isn't exactly limited to pets. She also cares for cows, horses, goats and all sorts of farm animals.

"I do whatever people need me to do," Julie says. "The price changes on how long it would take me to do."

Hawai'i's pet sitters tend to be flexible. One pet sitter holds a live insect on the end of a pair of tweezers, waiting patiently for a Jackson chameleon to whip its tongue out and snatch its dinner. Another sitter scrubs the huge amount of waste a large parrot produces. Still another walks four dogs, all from the same owner.

O'ahu sitter Vera Higashi offered to include "watering the plants" without charge when she agreed, over the phone, to pet sit for an elderly couple. She soon found that meant spending 40 minutes each evening watering a large tropical yard, swatting hungry mosquitoes.

A growing number of clients are requesting "overnighters" and Higashi brings her own bed linens to sleep near pets that need medication, special attention, or suffer from separation anxiety. One of Higashi's clients has two dogs and 14 cats and "you can see the need for someone to be there," she laughs.

Being a pet sitter means giving up your life, says Higashi, a former office worker who became a pet sitter three years ago and now works 12 to 14 hours a day. She and her husband, often recruited to help, see so little of each other now "it feels like we're dating," she says. Still, she loves the work. Pet sitters, for the most part, seem full of energy and gung-ho about their jobs.

"It's the best," gushes Debra Lusher, who was a resort concierge for many years before opening a pet sitting service on Maui a few years ago. "I found what my soul should be doing. I get to bond with pets and play with them and I don't have to adopt them. It's extremely rewarding."

Lusher visits some homes as often as three times a day, leaving a daily diary to let owners know how their pets fared. Like most sitters, she charges the same rate no matter how many animals of the same type are in the home. She does charge more if pets are mixed, explaining that "Dogs and cats have different needs."

Pet sitters rarely know how long a visit will take and must be ready for whatever the job calls for. Maui's Dawn Pasco remembers a pet visit that took her all day. A cat leaned against a loose screen, fell out of a window, ran under a deck and would not come out. Dawn and her husband spent the day coaxing the cat.

"It finally crept out after dark," she says.

There, your pet will be kept in a cage or kennel, which he may dislike, but you at least have the comfort of knowing he's getting 24-hour care. Every kennel I've contacted in O`ahu asked for my pets' health care records and proof that inoculations were up to date before they'd accept my pets. None of the few kennels on neighbor islands asked for health records.

Cost: From about $15 a day for basic service including food.

Advantages: You know your pet is confined and safe and will probably be cared for in a precise manner.

Disadvantages: Most pets hate being confined in a strange place. And they miss you.

Pet sitters

Pet sitters are very common in O`ahu, where so many animals reside in apartments. A visiting pet sitter is convenient. You don't have to transport the dog to a kennel and your pet may be more comfortable in his own home. Sitters usually spend about an hour at each home, feeding and changing the pet's water, playing with it, administering medicine if necessary, changing a cat's litter box, walking a dog and cleaning up after it. Some dog owners have sitters visit twice a day as close as possible to the times their dogs are accustomed to being walked. Pet sitters can also be hired to spend extra hours with the pet and will bring in your newspaper and mail, and change lighting so that your home looks occupied. An added advantage: they check your home daily.

Cost: From about $25 a day.

Advantages: Convenient. Pets may feel more secure at home. Sitter performs additional duties.

Disadvantages: More expensive than a kennel if you have only one pet. Pets are alone most of the day. And they miss you.

Relatives and neighbors

Well meaning friends and neighbors may volunteer to care for your pets at their homes. If you trust the person to give your pets the same kind of care and training you give them, you are fortunate indeed. Be aware that pets, like children, can quickly get on the nerves of anyone other than their "parents." You'll want to be careful that your pets don't overstay their welcome. And you should offer a volunteer caretaker the same payment you would give a pet sitter or kennel.

Advantages: Your pet gets hands-on care with someone she recognizes and you know and trust.

Disadvantages: Pets can be disoriented in a new location and may be confused about toilet habits. They may even attempt to run away from the new location, back to their "home." They miss you.

House sitters

If you have multiple pets, house sitters can be the perfect answer, especially if you are planning to be gone for an extended length of time. First put out the word to family, friends, neighbors and co-workers that you are seeking a house sitter. Most likely one of them will have a connection for you, possibly a visitor who would appreciate a place to stay. If that doesn't work, you may try this: Several months before you plan to leave, advertise in the vacation rental section of your island's newspaper. Offer free Hawai'i lodging to a pet loving person or couple who will care for your pets. You will most likely get several calls, communicating with the respondents via phone or e-mail. Look for someone who has visited your island before, comes to Hawai'i regularly, and knows his or her way around.

Be sure to check references carefully. The prospective house sitter should be able to supply you with the names of landlords on your island from whom they have rented previously. Also ask for a reference from their current landlord and place of employment. When you interview prospective house sitters, ask if they have pets of their own. You'll want someone who knows how to care for your cat or dog.

Giving a stranger access to your life

Think about it: Hiring a pet sitter or a house sitter means giving a stranger the keys to your house and access to your home, your pet, your possessions and your identification. The pet sitter will be alone for several hours during which time he or she can go through desks and drawers, and learn a great deal about you. Hiring a pet sitter is chancy, no matter where you live, but especially on these islands where people tend to be transient. Hawai'i law does not require pet sitters to be licensed, bonded or insured, so you are on your own when hiring a pet sitter.

Your best bet? Don't just take a pet sitter's number off a community bulletin board. Instead, ask your veterinarian to suggest a sitter he knows and trusts. If you can't find a sitter through a veterinarian, talk to pet owners you know for names of sitters whose services they have used and with whom they've been satisfied.

Bonded. Insured. Even though the state doesn't require it, many island sitters are bonded and insured, signs they are serious about their work.

She finds families willing to 'host' pets

You could call Babs Poei a matchmaker. Her business, Pets Are Inn, consists of finding O'ahu families willing to board pets in their homes.

Pet owners who must leave their pets for any length of time call Babs. She matches them to a family who has agreed to play host to such a pet.

Babs began her business, part of a national chain, twelve years ago. She advertises in local newspapers to find host families. "A lot of military families like to be hosts. A lot of them could not bring their pets to Hawai'i," she says, so they are happy to have a pet visit for a time.

Babs screens her host families, who have choices. Some take only dogs, others cats. Some welcome pets all the time, others "only when they feel like it."

Both Pets Are Inn and the boarding families are paid for their work.

Advantages: You can leave for an extended period of time without worrying much about your pet. Since you are offering lodging in trade for pet care, there is little or no cost to you. The right person will clean the house well just before you are due back.

Disadvantage: You must carefully check references to make sure you have "rented" to reliable people who won't destroy your home. Your visitor may leave a mess or damage. House sitters tend to spoil pets. And the pets still miss you.

Hire a neighbor, or his child

Here's another good way—possibly the best way—to assure your pets receive love and care in their own home while you're gone. See if a neighbor will care for your pets, visiting twice daily to do all the things a pet sitter does. I've allowed a neighbor child as young as age ten to do this, accompanied by her parent. The parent unlocked the door, came in with the child and checked the house, while the child performed all the pet care. It was her first job, great experience for her, and a happy time for my dogs who enjoyed having a child they knew visit. The child also brought in the mail and her parent turned on various lights in the house each night to discourage burglars.

Advantages: Pets stay in their own home and are visited by someone they recognize. A neighbor keeps an eye on your house. You will probably pay less than you would pay a professional pet sitter.

Disadvantages: Consider only neighbors and/or children you know very well and trust completely. You could end up with your home being trashed or items being stolen. The pet may not even miss you.

Give your pet's caretaker the power to make wise, humane decisions

Many years ago, our family went on a two-week trip and left our much-loved Siamese female cat at a kennel run by our pets' veterinarian. Maude seemed a little under the weather the day we left, and had rejected her supper the night before, which wasn't like her. But we felt secure knowing she was being wisely cared for by her own veterinarian.

Caught up in the excitement of the trip, we forgot about Maude. It did not occur to us to call in to the vet and see how she was faring. When we arrived home two weeks later, we learned that our beloved cat was dead. Her condition had deteriorated the day we left, our vet explained. He administered to her as best he could, but she grew worse. He decided she had ingested a toxin, which he surmised was lye. There was nothing he could do for her and, because he could not reach us, he could not legally put her to sleep and end her suffering. She had to die a "natural" death, in unimaginable pain, far from her loving family.

Make sure that the boarding facility, veterinarian, or friend who cares for your pet while you are away has a copy of your travel agenda, with phone numbers. If you don't know where you'll be, call in every two or three days to check on your pet. And complete the statement on the following page. Give one copy to your pet's caretaker and the other copy to your vet so they can legally make humane decisions for your pet.

Maude, at right, with her mate, Stanley Kowalski, and litter in an old family photo.

Caretaker's Permission

_____
(name of caretaker)

at _____
    (location of kennel or caretaker's home)

has my permission to care for my pet _____
                                     (pet's name)

in the kindest and wisest way. In the event of my pet's severe illness

or impending death, if I cannot be consulted, my permission is granted

to seek medical help and, if necessary, on the advice of a veterinarian,

to end my animal's life in a painless and humane way.

Signed _____

Date _____

Witnessed by _____

Date _____

Temporary Caretaker Form

Don't leave home without completing this form for your pet's caretaker.

In the rush of preparing for a journey, it's easy to forget small but important tasks like leaving complete information for your pet's caretaker. Fill out this form and make a duplicate. Give one copy to your pet sitter or kennel. Put the other by your phone, accessible in an emergency.

Veterinarian
Name:_____
Phone: _____
After Hours:_____
Address:_____

Emergency Contact
Friend or relative: _____
Phone: _____

My Travel Schedule
From: _____To: _____
Location: _____
Phone: _____

From: _____To: _____
Location: _____
Phone: _____

From: _____To: _____
Location: _____
Phone: _____

My pet's name & nicknames:
_____
Distinguishing markings:_____
License no./microchip:_____

My pet's feeding habits:
My pet eats: _____
Approximately how much?_____
How often and what time(s)?_____
_____
Treats:_____
How often and when?_____

Medication:

My pet takes the following medication:_____

_____

How often? _____

How much? _____

Exercise:

Walk my pet: ❑ yes ❑ no

My pet's favorite form of exercise and how often? _____

_____

Grooming:

Please groom my pet: ❑ yes ❑ no

How completely? _____

How often? _____

Please deliver my pet to a groomer? ❑ yes ❑ no

Groomers name: _____

Phone: _____

Location: _____

Additional notes about my pet's care:

_____

_____

_____

_____

_____

_____

_____

_____

_____

_____

_____

_____

Some pets travel long distances to find love

Many visitors to Hawai'i's humane societies are tourists and some of them fall in love with our dogs or cats and adopt them. It is relatively simple for tourists to adopt a pet and take it home. And what "souvenir" could be dearer than a poi dog or cat? The Maui Humane Society received this e-mail from a former guest, a gentle pit bull mix called Mahina, who may be the only dog in Germany with a Hawaiian name.

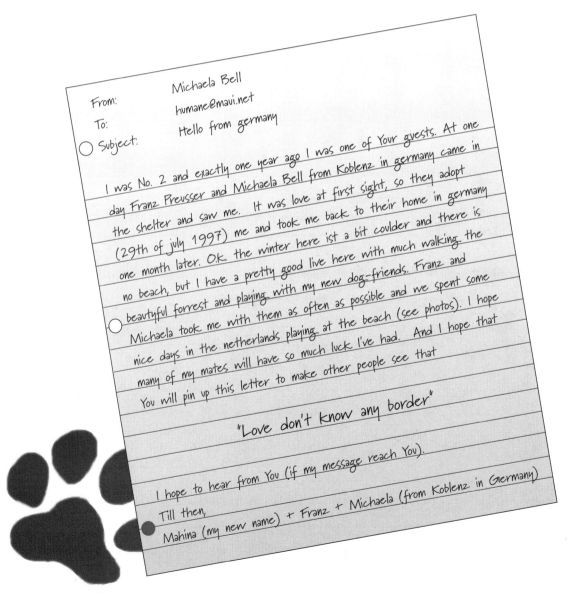

From: Michaela Bell
humane@maui.net
To:
Subject: Hello from germany

I was No. 2 and exactly one year ago I was one of Your guests. At one day Franz Preusser and Michaela Bell from Koblenz in germany came in the shelter and saw me. It was love at first sight, so they adopt (29th of july 1997) me and took me back to their home in germany one month later. O.k. the winter here ist a bit coulder and there is no beach, but I have a pretty good live here with much walking the beautyful forrest and playing with my new dog-friends. Franz and Michaela took me with them as often as possible and we spent some nice days in the netherlands playing at the beach (see photos). I hope many of my mates will have so much luck I've had. And I hope that You will pin up this letter to make other people see that

"Love don't know any border"

I hope to hear from You (if my message reach You).
Till then,
Mahina (my new name) + Franz + Michaela (from Koblenz in Germany)

Mahina ponders the hills of Austria, which surely must remind her of her Hawai'i roots.

Pets on the go

We Hawai'i folks love our pets and go to great lengths (or in the case of the stroller at left, widths) to take pets with us on our jaunts. Honolulu Advertiser photographer Deborah Booker, an animal lover, caught these conveyances on O'ahu.

Polar bears?
In Hawai'i? No.
Those are Spitz
dogs on an outing
with their owner
to a bay near
Hana, Maui,
trying to decide
whether to join
her in a swim.

JoAnn Allencastre photo

'Heaven is where all the dogs you've ever loved come running to greet you.'

Source unknown.

A young man tearfully replaces old flowers with new at a poster he hung in his Kane'ohe, O'ahu, neighborhood. His beloved Golden Retriever "Bud" was killed by a tow truck.

A graceful way of growing old

By David Shapiro

I knew my Shar-pei, Bingo, was getting old when he stopped fighting me to be first through the door. I'd read that dogs regard this as a test of macho dominance, and you should never let them enter ahead of you if you hope to ever establish discipline.So we'd battle at the doorway, throwing hips like a couple of NBA centers jockeying for position in the low post. Usually I'd prevail, and he'd slink in behind me with his ear flaps and corkscrew tail in full droop. Once in a while, though he'd slip in before me and taunt me with a victory dance that resembled a tail-wagging Michael Jackson moonwalk.

'I have to respect the dignity he projects'

When Bingo started letting me go first without a brawl, I thought he was finally recognizing my superior position in the family. Then I realized he was just getting too old and tired to fight over *manini* stuff. Unlike me, he'd gained the maturity to save his energy for more important things—like napping. Even so, his tail instinctively droops in defeat whenever he watches me enter the house ahead of him.

Shar-pei live an average of seven to nine years, and Bingo is eight-and-one-half. It's difficult to accept that the pup we've raised since he was weaned is growing old. His playful nature and good company have infused moments of joy into even our toughest times.

I used to hear Bingo running around the yard chasing butterflies and stalking imaginary prey. Now I hear only the buzz of the horseflies that chase him as he limps around on arthritic legs.

Bingo always took his watchdog duties seriously and never let anybody suspicious near our house. He's not big at 50 pounds, but he has an intimidating bark and a mouthful of snarling teeth to back it up. Some days now, he'll barely lift his head to give a halfhearted "woof" to the postman. Even while asleep, he was once sensitive to the slightest stirring on our loop. This week, I came into the house while he napped and he didn't awaken until I was on top of him, at which point he jumped up disoriented and barked at me.

"Good dog," I said, and gave him a biscuit for effort.

Lately, I've been showing some maturity of my own by letting him through the door first out of respect for his age and his superior position in the family. He knows I'm throwing him one, but can't suppress a little victory wag anyway. Even when he's looking up from his splayed nap position, swarmed by flies, Bingo still has that snooty Shar-pei way of looking down his nose at me through hooded eyes.

I have to respect the dignity he projects, and can only hope to emulate his grace as I grow old myself.

David Shapiro's column, Volcanic Ash, appears courtesy of The Honolulu Advertiser.

Saying farewell

Comedian George Carlin has a routine about pets in which he says that by acquiring a pet we are setting ourselves up for sadness. Because the life span of most pets is so short, chances are any pet owner will experience the death of at least one beloved pet and, perhaps, several.

Having lost several dear pets over the years, I remind myself constantly to fully enjoy and appreciate the four pets I have now. I know that my three dogs, all about the same age, will probably die within a year or two of each other, and I am constantly preparing myself for that by filling my memory bank with pleasant mental pictures that will console me later: Our good-morning kisses. Tiny, shy Wink leaping with joy when it's time for our daily walk. Bossy Betty's stare, the little whine she gives, asking permission to come up on the couch. Sensitive Archie wading out into the ocean and absorbing a sunset. Skat the Cat gliding gracefully from palm tree to house roof to watch the world. I am thankful for these visions now, while I have my pets.

Whether your pet dies of old age, from some traumatic incident, or is euthanized, his demise can be a wrenching experience that leaves you grieving much more than you anticipate. That grief may even sweep over you at unexpected times and for unexpected reasons for months and years to come.

PLEASE REMEMBER: You have every right to grieve. Insensitive friends who don't understand the owner/pet bond may make offensive comments, like "It's only a cat!" Ignore them. They have not had the privilege of enjoying an intense and beautiful owner/pet relationship.

Here, from a variety of articles and sources, are some methods that may help you deal with your pet's death.

Before:

- **Build memories.** Appreciate every minute with your pet and remind yourself of the happiness it brings to your life. At the same time, remind yourself how much your pet enjoys its life with you. Cherish the happy play times, the quiet cuddling. Remembering this may ease your grief when the time comes for your pet to leave you.

- **Plan for the future.** A Big Island pet lover whose three elderly dogs died within one year, offers this advice: When your youngest pet is

At home, at peace

The difficult thing about deciding to euthanize your pet, Sandra says, is that you have to call all the shots. You have to decide when your pet is to be put to sleep and you wonder how you'll know when the time is right. And then it's time and you just know, she says. You know.

For Sandra that decision came the second time a veterinarian diagnosed her dog Fendi with cancer. Fendi had survived an operation for cancer a few months before. Now the cancer had returned.

"What shall I do?" she asked the doctor. "What would you do if it were your dog?"

The veterinarian responded that he would consider putting Fendi to sleep, painlessly killing the dog by injection. But he stressed that the decision was Sandra's to make.

That decision was even more difficult because Sandra didn't know Fendi's age. She had found the emaciated Airedale/terrier/hound wandering on the beach seven years before, had taken him home with the intention of helping him gain some weight, "pretty up" and find a good home. But she fell in love and kept the mutt. She named him Fendi because he was anything but *haute couture.*

So, Fendi could be 10 years old or he could be 16. Either way, he had been happy and secure for the past seven years and had contributed quiet pleasure to Sandra's life. She and Fendi shared morning walks, romps on the beach, rides in the car.

Now, as she faced the decision to end her pet's life, Sandra spent extra, quality hours with Fendi. Longer walks, more quiet times, extra pats and caresses. "I had read," she said, "that pets can tell when you are sad, but they don't understand why." So she tried to keep a happy face and a cheerful voice. But sometimes Sandra gazed at Fendi and he gazed back and she felt as though he understood that she had a decision to make, or maybe understood somehow that they would not be together much longer.

"I kept wishing I knew how he felt, how much he suffered," Sandra says. Not knowing how much pain he was in, how much pain he might face, finalized her decision. After two and a half weeks, she called the veterinarian and said she was ready.

The doctor came to Sandra's home. First, he gave Fendi an injection to make him relax. Then, a few minutes later, he administered another injection to help him drift into sleep for the final time. The dog lay in his own bed and Sandra held his paw as Fendi died, peacefully.

five years old, introduce a new pet into your family. Your 5-year-old is young enough to enjoy a new puppy or kitten and will help train it. A rambunctious younger pet may keep your older pets more active and healthy. And the younger pet may eventually help you endure the loss of your older pets.

During:

If you know your pet is going to die, or if you must make the decision to euthanize, it may help you to remind yourself that you gave your pet this gift: a happy life. All the years you were together were pleasant for you, yes, but more importantly, they were secure, happy years for your pet.

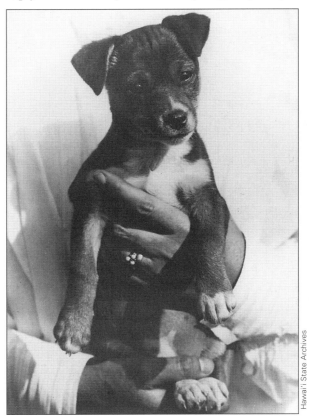

Hawai'i State Archives

Now, while your pet is lively and playful, make a video of her favorite antics. Catch her sleeping, playing, dining, kissing your children or just looking up at you. Preserve in a photo album the joy she brings. Or, create a mental video of your pet. Memorize the pleasant moments so you can recall them for years to come. Shuffle through those mental photos often now, while your dog or cat is alive, so the images will stay with you forever.

Now, it's time for the pet to leave you and you have the responsibility of deciding how and when he will take his last breath. You love your pet, you have been a wonderful owner, and now you can have the comfort of knowing you are making his death as painless as possible for him.

If you are still concerned and need help making the final decision for your pet, talk to your veterinarian about what you can do to make your pet's death the most peaceful for him. Perhaps the veterinarian will agree to euthanize at home, saving your pet a traumatic visit to the office or hospital. Your faithful friend may die cuddled peacefully in your arms, happily encircled in your love, your fingers stroking his fur. You may choose a pet cemetery, or have your pet cremated and the ashes returned

For help in your grief:

- **Pet Loss Support Group**
  meets on the first Tuesday of
  each month at the Hawaiian
  Humane Society, 2700
  Wai'alae Avenue, Honolulu. Call
  946-2187, extension 217, for
  more information.

- **Crisis hotlines.** For emergency
  assistance or if your island
  does not have a support group,
  call Hawai'i's Crisis Hotline at
  (808) 521-4555. Or these
  national pet support hotlines:

  Iowa State University
  (888) 478-7574

  **University of California at
  Davis** School of Veterinary
  Medicine Pet Loss Support
  Hotline (916) 752-4200

- **A helpful pamphlet.** O'ahu's
  Hawaiian Humane Society
  offers a beautifully written
  pamphlet, Saying Good-Bye,
  with suggestions for surviving
  your grief and a reading list
  that may help you.
  Call (808) 946-2187, ext. 223.

- **Animal Hospice of Hawai'i.**
  A team of people help with
  questions, care, prescriptions,
  supplies, counseling and
  referrals. When it is time
  to say a final farewell to your
  pet, Animal Hospice can help
  arrange in-home euthanasia.
  (808) 254-4507.

to you for burial, or perhaps to find some comfort in keeping them near. Or your veterinarian, humane society or other place of cremation can dispose of the ashes for you.

- Consider hospice care. Ruth A. Sheets, a certified family practice and pediatric nurse practitioner, was at a loss when her dog died shortly after she arrived on O'ahu. She and Letitia Course, a licensed social worker, eventually started Animal Hospice of Hawai'i.

After:

Allow yourself to grieve. You are going to grieve and the grief may sweep over you when you least expect it.

- Join a pet loss support group, even before your pet dies or before you must make the decision to euthanize. Having a circle of friends who have shared and understand this pain will help.

- Call one of the pet loss support hot lines listed here and talk to an understanding counselor. Even if you do not think your need is great enough, call. You'll be surprised how much better you will feel after sharing your thoughts with an understanding counselor.

- Preserve your memories of your pet. My dog Kula died several years ago, but knowing his ashes are tucked in a box in my bedroom somehow keeps him near. I don't understand why they are so comforting to me. Some people who have never loved a pet so much might not understand it, but that's how I feel about my dear dog. You can preserve your pet's memories in other ways, too.

- Find a friend, child or relative who shared your pet's love with you and talk about happy times with your pet.

- Find a new love. Get another pet. You may feel that you won't be ready for another pet for a long time, but remember: your new pet honors the memory of the one that is gone. And you may be surprised how soon you grow fond of your new companion.

What shall we tell the children?

When a family pet dies, it may be your child's first experience with death. Consequently, the way you choose to explain this event can lay the foundation for your child's conception of death. Try to keep in mind:

- If your children do not see you sad or upset, they may fear that their own sorrow is unnatural.

- Your child's imagination of how your pet died may be far worse than reality. If you would like euthanasia or the cause of death explained to your child by a professional, ask your veterinarian.

- Children take many statements at face value. If they are told, "Buster went to sleep forever," they may lie awake all night fearing sleep themselves.

- Children often feel guilty for things they did not do. Explain that your pet's death was not anyone's fault and that your pet is no longer in pain.

Toni Polancy photo

- Encourage your child to talk about fun times and happy memories of your pet.

- When children are ready for a new pet, they will let you know.

From the Hawaiian Humane Society's pamphlet, Saying Good-bye

Services you may need:

- Hawaiian Humane Society, O`ahu, offers cremation only. No return of ashes. (808) 946-2187, ext. 285.

- The Maui Humane Society will cremate your pet's body and you may choose private cremation after which your pet's ashes can be returned to you. Costs, from $20, are based on the weight of the pet and whether you would like its ashes returned. Or you may take your pet's body to the county landfill near Pu`unene, where a special place has been set aside for this purpose. (808) 877-3680.

- The Kaua`i Humane Society will pick up your pet's body. A donation of $35 is suggested for cremations. Private cremation, with ashes returned to you, begins at $110. (808) 632-0610.

- The Hawai`i Island Humane Society will dispose of your pet's body. Bring it to either the Kea`au or Kona Humane Society. Cost is $12.50 for a dog and $5 for cat. The ashes will not be returned. (808) 329-1175.

- O`ahu Pet Crematory offers home euthanasia, free pick-up of your pet, cremation and a selection of urns. (808) 371-7531

- Sunset Pet, Hilo, memorials and cremations as well as pickup. (808) 959-7956.

- Ash Scatterings at Sea, O`ahu, provides a one-hour ocean cruise with captain, crew and short service. Designed for humans, but the company will also perform pet burials. (808) 326-6000.

- Valley Pet Memorial Gardens offers pet burials and cemetery plots. 47-200 Kahekili Highway, Kane`ohe, (808) 239-8811.

Never too soon

By MEG SKELLENGER

I didn't think much about it when I woke in the middle of the night to the sound of cats arguing in the neighbor's yard. Half asleep, I barely registered that Marbles, our beautiful silver tabby cat, wasn't in his customary place next to me. Mocha, the tortoiseshell female, was sleeping on the bed as usual; I went back to sleep myself. It wasn't until the next morning, when Marbles didn't show up for breakfast, that I recalled the night's commotion and knew something was wrong.

With a heavy heart, strangely certain of what I would find, I left our property and walked along the side of the fairly busy street that bordered the yard. It wasn't long before I spotted Marbles' lifeless body in the grass next to the road. Though my eyes were blurred by tears, I could see no blood, no obvious injuries. It looked as though he had died instantly, and suffered no pain, but it was cold comfort.

Although I was heartbroken, I wasn't altogether surprised. Marbles had always been an irrepressible character, escaping the house and yard at the slightest opportunity to satisfy his feline curiosity. He was fearless — and careless. As my sister later said, "He was a bright flame, and bright flames burn out quickly." I suspect that he had annoyed a neighborhood cat that night, and fled or was chased into the street, where he was struck by a passing car. My husband Rick arrived a bit later to help me bury Marbles, and he held me closely while I wept for the fun-loving cat whose life was cut off too soon.

"Tomorrow, you'll go to the shelter and pick out a cat," Rick said. Taken aback, I protested, "But it's too soon! I can't just replace Marbles!"

She sat calmly next to me, as if we had known each other forever, not demanding my attention but grateful for it.

Rick looked me straight in the eyes and solemnly replied, "We are a two-cat family, and Mocha will need a friend."

Despite my misgivings, I took his advice. As soon as I entered the Maui Humane Society's cat house, I spotted a young, silver-gray female with apricot-colored specks who was just waking up from a nap. As I sat down on a bench, she came to sit beside me. I stroked her soft fur as I checked out the other cats in the "sunroom," where cats and prospective adopters can interact.She sat calmly next to me, as if we had known each other forever, not demanding my attention but grateful for it. I liked her looks and her quiet, unassuming manner, and although I made a pretense of meeting other cats in the room, I knew immediately she was the one for us.

When I started to get up to go to the front desk and fill out the adoption papers, she laid a velvety paw on my arm and looked up at me with sweet, round eyes, as if to say, "You are my human now. I know you'll come back for me." And I did.

She laid a velvety paw on my arm and looked up at me with sweet, round eyes, as if to say, "You are my human now. I know you'll come back for me."

Molly was very shy at first; she had been with us for more than a week before she emerged from the spare room where we had placed her food and litter box. One evening, she suddenly appeared in the living room and jumped up to join me on the couch. Our other cat, Mocha, had left Molly alone until then, seeming to understand that the new addition needed some time to adjust. That evening, however, Mocha literally took Molly under her paw, giving her a complete tongue bath from ears to tail, welcoming her to our family. They have been best friends for nearly seven years now.

We planted a flowering shrub over Marbles' final resting place before we moved to a secluded valley, far from traffic, where the cats can play in safety, though Molly, still the shy, quiet type, tends to stick close to home. I'll never forget my lively friend Marbles. But adopting Molly and helping her overcome a harsh kittenhood to become a wonderful companion for us all helped me as well. We helped each other.

(Meg Skellenger helped research and edit this book. A creative consultant, she lives with her husband Rick, two cats, Mocha and Molly, and numerous tropical fish in a quiet valley on Maui. She is the project coordinator for a prominent designer, as well as a freelance editor and proofreader.)

A prayer for the animals

Lord, we thank you for our animal friends;

for their waggle tail welcomes, their sedate curls

around our ankles, their morning songs.

Thank you for those people whom these animals have:

protectors, feeders, caregivers, comforters.

Bless those animals who have no people friends.

Those who are here waiting for a friend to come,

Those who are out in the wild, dealing

with their loneliness, hunger, disease, all alone.

Bless them all we pray in the name of Him who made us all.

Amen.

(From Cause for Paws,
 the Maui Humane Society newsletter,
 with thanks to Pastor Bill Pifer)

Resources 16

A guide to vets, clinics, kennels, pet sitters, humane societies, Internet sites, and pet-related businesses and services.

John McMinn of Makaha took George and Mabel to a Hawaiian Humane Society "Pooch Party Picnic" at Thomas Square in Honolulu.

About this section

This book is written as a non-commercial guide for pet owners. The resources printed here were collected from a variety of sources and were deemed correct at time of publication. Changes may occur, and probably will occur, over the life of the book. Readers are invited to alert us in writing to any errors or changes for future editions of this book.

These listings are solely for the convenience of readers. Listings do not represent an endorsement from the writer or publisher and should not be considered as such. Pet owners are advised to seek references and talk to their veterinarians or other pet owners before contracting any services or purchases.

No person or business was charged for the service. If you are aware of a business, service or place that is not listed here and should be, please notify us by email or letter and we will consider including it in a future printing.

Barefoot Publishing, Inc.
32 U`ilani Road
Kihei, Maui, Hawaii 96753
tpolancy@cs.com
bookshawaii.com

AID DOGS

Training dogs to assist
handicapped persons

Big Island

Assistance Dogs of Hawaii
P.O. Box 474
Hawi, HI 96719

Maui

**Hawaii Canines
for Independence**
P.O. Box 790626
Pa`ia, Hi 96779
hawaiicanines.org

O'ahu

Hawaii Fi-Do Service Dogs
59-790 Kamehameha Highway
Hale`iwa, HI 96712
(808) 638-0200
hawaiifido.org

Give yourself
a happier birthday

Big Island resident Ter DePuy
celebrated her birthday in a
unique way. She threw a party,
hired a band, reserved the Lava
Lounge at Kilauea Military Camp
in Hawai`i Volcanoes National
Park, and invited everyone she
knew. In lieu of gifts she suggested her guests donate to the
Hawaii Island Humane Society.
Nearly a hundred guests danced
the night away and contributed
more than $1700. The funds
helped provide more low-cost
spay/neuter coupons to the
public, which should result in
fewer homeless dogs and cats.

BOARDING

Also see pet sitting

Big Island

All Creature Comforts
Mountain View
(808) 968-8497

Alpha K-9 Kennels
P.O. Box 37
Hakalau
(808) 963-6000
www.vomyounghaus.com

Bar-King Dog Kennel
P.O. Box 1184
Kea`au
(808) 966-8733
*James & Sarah Scanlon, proprietors.
Boarding by appointment. This is also
a satellite quarantine site. See
Quarantine chapter of this book.*

Hilo Holiday Pet Hotel
Hilo
(808) 937-4621

Hilo Veterinary Clinic Inc.
711 Kanoelehua Avenue
Hilo
(808) 961-3486

Kona Paws & Klaws
78-6977B Mamalahoa Highway
Kailua-Kona
(808) 324-6410

BOARDING

Also see pet sitting

Big Island

continued

Lucky D. Inc.
Onipaa Ranch & Kennel
Kailua-Kona
(808) 325-7553

Paws University
Kailua-Kona
(808) 325-6436
Tammy Goodreau-Daniels and Allen Daniels offer non-traditional boarding stressing exercise and socialization, includes letting dogs play together all day and "retire to their personal dorm room at night." Also doggie day care, grooming, pick up and drop off.

Su Lin Kennels
Amy Wong
Hilo, Big Island
(808) 938-0881
sulin-kennels@hawaii.rr.com
Dogs only. Quiet non-barkers, please.

Kaua`i

Alyssa's Pet Care
Kapa`a
(808) 822-0979

Auntie Debbie's Kennels
Deborah Corpuz
Wailua Homesteads
(808) 822-0296

Coco Paws
Jo King
Dog and cat hotel
(808) 821-2486
joking@hawaiian.net
Also longterm boarding, care of handicapped dogs.

Kapa`a Animal Clinic
4-1571 Kuhio Highway
(808) 822-9791
Cat boarding only.

Kaua`i Animal Hotel
Yvonne Corpuz
Lihue
(808) 634-5555
All animals, including farm animals. In-home or boarding. Pasture available.

Pet Patrol
6370 Kalama Road
Wailua Homesteads
(808) 823-6031

Whiskers Resort
Moksha McClure
(808) 826-0376
Play room with television for dogs; six-foot scratching post for cats.

Maui

Makawao Boarding Kennel
Makawao
(808) 573-0080

No Ka Oi Basenjis & Kennels
Rita Webb
Kula
(808) 878-3455
Nurse practitioner boards
all breeds; also teaches pet care.

The Ohana Animal Inn
Malia Boteilho
Kula
(808) 878-6788
All kinds of animals: cats,
dogs, birds, etc.

O`ahu

Kailua Animal Clinic, Inc.
111 Hekili Street
Kailua
(808) 263-8863

Kitty Bed and Breakfast
Becarine Cattery
Beth Pagel
Kailua
(808) 262-4291

Ko`olau Animal Hospital, Inc.
45-1123 Kam Highway
Kan`eohe
(808) 247-3211

Ko`olau Bed & Biscuit
(Dogs only)
Sheryl, Michael and Kelly Chang
47-785 `Ahuimanu Road
Kane'ohe
(808) 239-1214
koolaubedandbiscuit.com

Makai Animal Clinic
Drs. Robert Morris,
Alan Zane, Thomas Chlebecek
420 Uluniu Street
Kailua
(808) 262-9621
makaianimalclinic.com
makaiclinic@earthlink.net

Nalowinds Kennels
41-502 Flamingo
Waimanalo
(808) 259-7349
nalowinds@hawaii.rr.com
All breed boarding; in-home for small
breeds. Includes dog park.

Pet Express Boarding Kennel Inc.
Wayne Takishima
989 Dillingham Boulevard
Honolulu
(808) 847-0058
petexpressboarding.com
In addition to boarding, Pet Express
grooms pets and will pick up and
deliver animals island-wide. Useful
for military families who must be
housed at hotels until their return
flights to the mainland. Pet Express
also ships pets anywhere in the world
and door-to-door in North America.

VCA Kane`ohe Animal Hospital
45-608 Kam Highway
Kane'ohe
(808) 236-2414
Fax: (808) 235-4074

BUSINESSES
related to pets

Aloha Hidden Dog Fencing
Ha`iku, Maui
(808) 575-2275
Electronic fencing, anti-bark collars, remote trainers.

Ceremonial Services for Pets
Rev. Kermit Rydell
(808) 227-0150.
WaikikiCentral.com
Weddings, adoptions, birthdays, breeding, anniversaries, memorials, funerals.

Dino's Doggie Deli and Bakery
26 Ho`olai
Kailua, O`ahu
(808) 263-2255
Restaurant, deli and fun place for pets. Pet owners can celebrate occasions such as birthdays, obedience school graduations or release from quarantine with on-site baked cake, hats, prizes.

Hawai`i Doggie Bakery & Gift Shop
Ward Warehouse
Ala Moana Boulevard
Honolulu
Also King Street
and Pearlridge locations
(808) 521-7297
Taro and healthy ingredients go into specialties like Surfdog Sushi and Fish N' Poi Pup Treats baked on site. Also Hawai'i print clothing and gifts.

Pet Alert of Hawaii
Gabriel Oberman
Kapa`a, Kaua`i
(808) 822-3639
Training with sales and installation of hidden fences.

Purr-fect Paws
417 Ku`ulei Road
Kailua, O`ahu
Boutique. Bakery. Day Care.
(808) 262-4896

The Stool Tool
1920 Ala Moana Blvd. Suite 709
Honolulu, HI 96815
stooltool.com
dahtool@aol.com
(808) 983-2600
Tool captures dog's feces.
(See page 63 of this book.)

Waggin Tail Pet Boutique
Alice and Patrick Mo
1365 Nu`uanu Avenue, Suite 3
Honolulu
(808) 585-8823
waggintailhawaii@yahoo.com

Whiteside Digital Imaging
O`ahu
Pet photography on location.
(808) 382-6072

BREEDERS
Cats

Bengals (Asian Leopard)
Bengal Cattery
Karen Kaberadek
Wailea, Maui
(808) 874-9366
(808) 269-2585

British Shorthair
Scottish Fold
Ali`i Kats
Honey Justman
`Aeia, O`ahu
(808) 486-6657

Exotic and Persian
Pokazot Cattery
Clarice and Yvette Oganeku
Kane`ohe, O`ahu
(808) 235-8142
pokazot@hawaii.rr.com

Maine Coon
David and Jill Burrow
Kihei, Maui
(808) 891-8323
coonsboromauai@hawaii. rr.com

Norwegian Forest
Mea Aloha cattery
Sharon Au
Honolulu
(808) 734-1067

Persian
Pacific Paws
Kailua, O`ahu
Joan Harris
(808) 261-4354
jharris@lava.net

fetch
more information

The American Kennel Club and responsible pet organizations such as the Hawaiian Dog Fanciers Association and Aloha Cat Fanciers urge pet owners to allow several months of recuperation time between litters. Most breeders are careful not to overbreed their animals. For that reason, most of the kennels, catteries and breeders listed here do not always have puppies or kittens available for sale. However, many breeders indicated a willingness, even an eagerness, to answer questions about their animals and to discuss breed characteristics with anyone legitimately interested. Phone numbers are provided here.

Siamese and Himalayan
Sealpoint, Bluepoint and
Flamepoint
Judy Williams
O`ahu
(808) 671-7990

Siamese (all colors)
Charlee Abram
Kaluamoa Farms
Lawa`i, Kaua`i
(808) 332-7900
kksp@juno.com

Somali
Becarine Cattery
Beth Pagel
Kailua, O`ahu
(808) 262-4291

BREEDERS
Dogs

Afghan hound
Richard Brown,
Barbara Benson
Volcano, Big Island
(808) 985-8579
*Qualified referrals
from Australia.*

Australian Shepherd
Aumoehoku Kennel
Lily Bhalang
Wai`anae, O`ahu
(808) 696-8221
*Obedience, herding,
conformation, pet.*

Australian Shepherd
Windstar Kennels
A.J. Tavares
Honolulu
(808) 732-2799

Basenji
No Ka Oi Basenjis
 & Kennels
Kula, Maui
(808) 878-3455

Basset Hound
Penkay Kennels
Gale Yamanaguchi
North Shore, O`ahu
(808) 638-7769

Bichon Frise
Kay Arakawa
Honolulu
(808) 625-6034

Bichon Frise
Jetaime Kennels
Jacquelyn Yasui
Honolulu
(808) 955-6771

Bouvier Des Flandres
Marion Penhallow
Hilo, Big Island
(808) 968-8860
penlani@aloha.net

Boxer
Koawood Kennels
Gail Lindsey
Kane`ohe, O`ahu
(808) 247-3607

Boxer
Halakau Kennels
Janis Goto
`Aina Haina, O`ahu
(808) 377-5762

Brussels Griffon
Marion Penhallow
Hilo, Big Island
(808) 968-8860
penlani@aloha.net

Bulldogs, English
Muttnick
Sandy Reed
Honolulu
(808) 395-5925

Bullmastiffs
Dynasty Bullmastiffs
Linda Fox, Debbie Blunt
(808) 386-1967
dynastybullmastiffs.com
DynstyBullies@aol.com

Cavalier King Charles Spaniel
Ali`ßi Kennels
Bob Shigeta
Mililani, O`ahu
(808) 623-2930

Cavalier King Charles Spaniel
Bastien Kennels
Olinda Amtsberg
Honolulu
(808) 522-5600
(808) 949-2784

Cavalier King Charles Spaniel
Tropicano Kennels
Debbie Cano
Maui
(808) 575-7614
(808) 870-6381

Chinese Crested
Makalea Kennels
Maureen Hillyard
Kailua, O`ahu
(808) 261-6010
Makalea@hawaii.rr.com

Chow Chow
Shin Dou Chow Chows
Lana Pule
`Aeia, O`ahu
(808) 484-9008

Cocker, English
Haroldine Akiona
Hilo, Big Island
(808) 959-9720

Cocker Spaniel
Halakai Cockers
Gerri Cadiz
Kailua, O`ahu
(808) 262-5236
gcadiz@hawaii.rr.com

Cocker Spaniel
Suzanne Pia-Rose
Anahola, Kaua`i
(808) 822-9563

Cocker Spaniels
Prelude Cockers
Bill and Dorothy Ogan
Foster Village, O`ahu
(808) 422-7130
The Ogans no longer sell cockers, but Bill is former president of the island's Cocker Spaniel Club and the Ogans have a long history of working with spaniels. They will answer questions and provide breed information to callers.

BREEDERS
Dogs
Continued

Collie
Rough and smooth collies
Blackpoint Collies
En Chang
East O`ahu
(808) 923-6723
enchang@hotmail.com

Corgi
Penbrooke Welsh Corgis
Kalaniakea Kennel
Winston and Jacquelyn Kupau
`Aiea, O`ahu
(808) 488-3854
www.kalaniakeas.com

Dachshund (miniature)
smooth, longhaired, wire
Char-El Kennel
Elmer and Charlotte Vieira
Hilo, Big Island
(808) 935-2492
cvieira.vol@juno.com

Dachshund
miniature and standards,
long smooth, wire
von Gleishorbach
Kailua, O`ahu
(808) 261-9535
dachsi@gte.net

Dalmation
Rowerdennan Dalmations
Anne Scheffelmaier
Hale`iwa, O`ahu
(808) 638-8672
Fax (808) 638-8672

Doberman Pinscher
Skip Lee
Mililani, O`ahu
majesticdobe@cs.com
(808) 626-0672
A source of information only.

English Cocker Spaniel
Mahealani Kennels
Blue roan, black or red
Paulette Merriles
Waikapu, Maui
(808) 242-4696

German Shepherd
Alpha K-9 Kennels
Ted and Laurel Young
Hilo, Big Island
(808) 963-6000
www.vomyounghaus.com

German Shepherd
Fleetwood Kennels
Fred & Iris Popick
South Kona, Big Island
(808) 328-0622
fleetwoodkennels.com

German Shepherd
Patrick Ayers
Kailua, O'ahu
(808) 254-5400
ayersp001@hawaii.rr.com

Golden Retriever
Penbrooke Welsh Corgi
Kalaniakea Kennel
Winston and Jacquelyn Kupau
`Aiea, O`ahu
(808) 488-3854
www.kalaniakeas.com

Jack Russell Terrier
Kupa`a Kennel
Mary Clarose
Hilo, Big Island
(808) 966-4813
mary@kupaajrt.com

Japanese Chin
Imperial Kennel
Shari Anthony
`Aina Haina, O`ahu
(808) 373-9167

Labrador Retriever
Brasia Labrador Retrievers
Brandi Barretto
Lihu`e, Kaua`i
(808) 645-1616
www.geocities.com/brasialab/

Labrador Retriever
Davaron Labradors
June Sasaki
(808) 988-5052
Honolulu, O`ahu
davaron.com

Mastiffs, English
Pacific Isle Mastiffs
Wayland Lum
Kane`ohe, O`ahu
(808) 235-1959
wlumcon@aol

Miniature Pinscher
Alpha K-9 Kennels
P.O. Box 372
Hakalau, Big Island
(808) 963-6000
www.vomyounghaus.com

Miniature Pinscher
Wailea's Min-Pins
Ted and Laurel Young
Hilo, Big Island
(808) 963-6000
vonyoug-haus.com

Miniature Pinscher
Su Lin Kennels
Amy Wong
Hilo, Big Island
(808) 934-0881
sulin-kennels@hawaii.rr.com

Newfoundland
Alii Shores Newfoundlands
Kane`ohe, O`ahu
(808) 247-5296
YEEW001@Hawaii.rr.com
www.newfs.com

Newfoundland
Barbara Ankersmit
(808) 261-8102
bankersmit@starrtech.com

Norwegian Elk Hound
Anne Sutton
Honolulu
(808) 595-3366

Norwich Terrier
Loxwood Norwich
Susan Miyasato
Honolulu
(808) 533-6552

Papillon
Makalea Kennels
Maureen Hillyard
Kailua, O`ahu
(808) 261-6010
Makalea@hawaii.rr.com

BREEDERS
Dogs
Continued

Papillon
Okekai Kennel
Barbara Ankersmit
Windward O`ahu
(808) 261-8102
bankersmit@starrtech.com

Pekingese
Da Mao Kennels
Cheryl Chang
Windward O`ahu
(808) 239-6693

Pembroke Welsh Corgis
Cinberlin Kennel
Cindy Bryant
Waimea, Kaua`i
(808) 338-1136

Pomeranian, Pug, Shih Tzu
Woodrose Kennels
Clarice and Yvette Oganeku
Kane`ohe, O`ahu
(808) 235-8142
woodrose@hawaii.rr.com

Pomeranian
Sandalwood
Honolulu
(808) 524-3877
sandalwood88@yahoo.com

Poodle: toy and miniature
Bradlene
Brad and Alene Odagiri
Honolulu, O`ahu
(808) 373-3838

Poodle: toy, miniature or standard
Francis M. Kauhane
Honolulu, O`ahu
(808) 841-8426

Poodle, miniature
Pu`ala Kennel
Moanikeala Jellinger
Hale`iwa, O`ahu
(808) 488-4774
Blacks, browns, blues
Miniature only;
no toys or standard

Pug
Windward Kennel
Michael Sim
Kane`ohe, O`ahu
(808) 239-7695
windwardput@hotmail.com

Portuguese Water Dog
Anchor Portuguese Water Dogs
Trudi Gold
Kane`ohe, O`ahu
(808) 235-0314

Retriever, Golden or Labrador
Sand Dollar Kennels
Artie and Susie Saunders
Kula, Maui
(808) 878-2908

Rottweiler
Deborah J. Kent
Kailua-Kona, Big Island
(808) 325-5266

Saluki
Fleetwood Kennels
Fred Popick
Honaunau, Big Island
(South Kona near Captain Cook)
(808) 328-0622
fleetwoodkennels.com

Samoyed
Shiroi Kennel
Amy Sakata
Kalihi, O`ahu
(808) 841-4081

Shar Pei, Chinese
Kauai King Shar Pei
Charlee Abrams
Kaluamoa Farms
Lawa`i, Kaua`i
(808) 332-7900
kksp@juno.com

Sheltie and

Australian Sheepdog
El Solo Kennels
Marjorie Norstrom
Honolulu
(808) 732-2958

Shetland Sheepdog
Cinnabar Kennels
Nola Chock
Honolulu
(808) 487-3116

Shih Tzu, Pomeranian, Pug
Woodrose Kennels
Clarice and Yvette Oganeku
Kane`ohe, O`ahu
(808) 235-8142

Siberian Huskie
Kelly Chang
Windward O`ahu
(808) 239-1214

Siberian Huskie
Nalowinds
Bonnie And Wayne Duarte
Waimanalo, O`ahu (808) 259-7349
Also boarding dogs of all breeds.
Dog park.

Silky Terrier (Australian)
Haroldine Akiona
Hilo, Big Island
(808) 959-9720

Schnauzer, standard and miniature
Lindal Kennel
Linda Caldwell
Waipahu, O`ahu
(808) 671-7855

Yorkshire Terrier
Char-El Kennel
Elmer and Charlotte Vieira
Hilo, Big Island
(808) 935-2492
cvieira.vol@juno.com

CLUBS,
pet organizations

Cat clubs, all islands

Aloha Cat Fanciers Club
Joan Harris
(808) 261-4354
jharris@lava.net

Hawai`i All Breed Cat Club
Charlee Abrams
(808) 332-7900

Sepulveda Cat Club
Cynthia Nakamura
(808) 395-6875

Dog clubs, Kaua`i

Dog Fanciers of Kaua'i
Suzanne Pia-Rose
(808) 246-6889
Training and events.

Dog clubs, Maui

Doggone Dogs 4-H Club
Michelle Mitchell
(808) 879-7006
*Open once a year to new members
ages 9 to 19 with .any breed of dog.
Gathers once a month for meeting,
twice for training. Participates in
fairs and parades.*

Valley Isle Kennel Club
Susie Saunders
(808) 878-2908
All breeds.

Dog clubs, Big Island

Hilo Obedience Training Club
Haroldine Akiona
(808) 959-9780.
*Dog owners voluntarily train canines
in the community.*

Kona Coast Kennel Club
Deborah J. Kent
(808) 325-5266
All breed shows.

Orchid Island Dog Fancier Club
Lei Taft
(808) 967-7303
All-breed shows.

All breed dog clubs O'ahu

Hawaiian Kennel Club, Inc.
Gerri Cadiz
(808) 949-7819
*Member club of the
American Kennel Club.*

**Hawaiian Herding Dog
Association**
Sheila Conant
(808) 988-3960

Hawaiian Hound Association
Margie Rodriques
(808) 235-2462

**Leeward Training Club
of Hawai`i, Inc.**
Ted Ketcham
(808) 674-8792

Tropical Toy Dog Fanciers of Hawai`i
Cheryl Chang
(808) 239-6693

West O`ahu Kennel Club
David Char
(808) 696-8096

Aloha State Sporting Dog Association
Laurella Pang
(808) 732-7451

Non-sporting Dog Club of Hawai`i
Anne Scheffelmaier
(808) 638-8672

Obedience Training Club of Hawai`i
Cathy Suguitan
(808) 456-9565

Breed-specific clubs

Clubs are listed alphabetically by breed rather than by name.

Akita Club of Hawai`i
Winnie Nakatsu
(808) 735-1384

Bassett Hound Club of Hawai`i
Gale Yamaguchi
(808) 638-7769

Boxer Club of Hawai`i
Wanda Nakamura
(808) 239-7310
Lois Kelsey
(808) 677-0548

Aloha Brittany Club
Carla Cavaco
(808) 395-5807

Hawaiian Bulldog Club
Sandy Reid
(808) 395-5925

Bull Terrier Club of Hawai`i
Amy Nishiki
(808) 734-8966

The Chihuahua Club of Hawai`i
Virginia DeCastro
(808) 261-3275

Cocker Spaniel Club of Hawai`i
Susan Miyasato
(808) 833-9921

Collie Club of Hawai`i
Erin Kawata
(808) 456-8491

Dachshund Club of Hawai`i
Carol Agard
(808) 455-3306

Dalmation Club of Hawai`i
Anne Scheffelmaier
(808) 638-8672

Breed-specific clubs
Continued

Doberman Pinscher Club
of Hawai`i
Skip Lee
(808) 626-0672
hilee@majesticdobe.com

Fox Terrier Club of Hawai`i
Linda Caldwell
(808) 671-7855

**German Shepherd Dog
Club of Hawai`i**
Phyllis Call
(808) 261-5847

**German Shorthaired Pointer
Club of Hawai`i**
Cookie Ng
(808) 259-7762

**Golden Retriever Club of
Hawai`i**
Moke Strassberg
(808) 488-1134

Great Dane Club of Hawai`i
Christy Enright
(808) 247-2773

Hawaiian Hound Association
Margie Rodrigues
(808) 235-2461

Hawaiian Irish Setter Club
Nancy Cenal
(808) 623-3008

**Kerry Blue Terrier Club
of Hawai`i**
Susan Govier
(808) 486-9179

**Labrador Retriever Club
of Hawai`i**
Catherine Staege
(808) 674-4478

Papillon Club of Hawai`i
Barbara Ankersmit
(808) 261-8102
bankersmit@starrtech.com

Pomeranian Club of Hawai`i
Josephine Ching
(808) 526-0114

Poodle Club of Hawai`i
Sally Ventura
(808) 235-5863

Aloha State Rottweiler Club
Pearl Ting
(808) 955-8633

**Shetland Sheepdog Club
of Hawai`i, Inc.**
David Hoota
(808) 373-2643
Nola Chock
(808) 487-3116

Siberian Husky Club of Hawai`i
Kelly Chang
(808) 239-1214

Silky Terrier Club of Hawai`i
Elaine Shimokawa
(808) 521-5544

Terriers in Paradise
Dennis Miyasato
(808) 833-9921

**Tropical Toy Dog
Fanciers of Hawai`i**
Cheryl Chang
(808) 239-6693

**Weimaraner Club
of Hawai`i**
Daryle Oliveira
(808) 236-4052

**Yorkshire Terrier Club
of Hawai`i**
Daisy Yamada
(808) 949-6200

GROOMERS

Big Island

Deb's Kona Klips
Kailua-Kona
(808) 331-2211

Paws University
Kailua-Kona
(808) 325-6436
pawsuniversity.com

Roxies Dog Grooming
Kea`au
(808) 966-6873

Royal Hawaiian Dog Grooming
Keauhou
(808) 322-8898

No Fleez Pleez
Hilo
(808) 934-8544

Kona Paws & Klaws
Kona
(808) 324-6410

Su Lin Kennels
Amy Wong
Hilo
(808) 938-0881
sulin-kennels@hawaii.rr.com

GROOMERS
Continued

Kaua`i

Doggie Doos
Wailua Homesteads
Gabriel O'Brien Hinnebusch
(808) 822-323
cellular (808) 651-3754
All breeds, fancy to scuffy.

Paws of Paradise
Lihu`e
Jo King
(808) 821-2486
joking@hawaiian.net
*Mobile pet salon
comes to your home.*

Pet Pals
Kapa`a
Rhonda K. Lizama
(808) 821-0898
Small and medium size dogs only.

Sue the Dog Groomer
Kapa`a
(808) 823-0925

Summer's Poodle Palace
Anahola Summer K Woolsey
(808) 822-1647
(808) 639-0723

Whiskers Resort
Lihu`e
Moksha McClure
(808) 826-0376

Maui

Dorreen`s Pet Grooming
Kihei
(808) 874-4880

Salty Dog
Wailuku
(808) 249-2525

Makawao Boarding Kennels
Makawao
(808) 573-0080

Island Pet Groomers
Makawao
(808) 572-2472

The Pet Groomers
Upcountry Maui
(808) 572-5628

O`ahu, Honolulu

A-Class K-9 Kutters
1254 North King St.
Honolulu
(808) 841-3269

Ardans Grooming Salon Inc.
1340 Young Street
Honolulu
(808) 593-2322

Beautification Station
Honolulu
(808) 596-0538
(808) 848-6888

Dogpatch Academy
2103 Kane`alii Avenue
Honolulu
(808) 533-0335
Also a grooming school.

Fur Styling by Tammy
1126 12th Avenue
Honolulu
(808) 732-5715

Klassic Kanine
Honolulu
(808) 286-4132

Nola Chock
Honolulu
(808) 487-3116
Shetland sheep dogs only.

One Stop Grooming Shop
2885 S. King St., Suite 101
Honolulu
(808) 941-5998
(808) 941-7898 (fax)

Super Groom Pet Grooming
2357 S. Beretania Street
Honolulu
(808) 949-4123

Touche-The Groomery
2545 N. School Street
Honolulu
(808) 841-0790

Central O`ahu

Pet Styles Unlimited
941 Kamehameha Highway
Pearl City
(808) 456-4124

Classy Clipping
Professional Pet Grooming
94-547 Uke`e Street
Waipahu
(808) 671-6883

Clip and Dip
All Dog & Cat Grooming
524 Olive Avenue
Wahiawa
(808) 621-1911

The Hair Apparent
99-927 Iwaena Street #104
Halawa Valley, O`ahu
(808) 488-4774

Kats Dog Grooming
Pearl City
(808) 455-3647

GROOMERS
Continued

Pampered Poodle
Pearl City
(808) 456-9833

Pats Poodle Grooming
94-877 Farrington Highway
 Waipahu
(808) 677-3301

Pearl City Pampered Poodle
Ala`ala`a Loop # 95-266
Mililani
(808) 456-9833

Windward O`ahu

Dog Shop
28 Oneawa Street
Kailua
(808) 262-8804
(808) 885-6222

Doggone Groomers
45-608 Kamehameha Hwy
Kane`ohe
(808) 236-7000

Fox & Hounds
1322 Akiahala Street
Kailua
(808) 262-2287

My Furry Friends
167 Hamakua Drive, Suite 102
Kailua
(808) 263-4891

VCA Kaneohe Animal Hospital
45-608 Kamehameha Highway
Kane`ohe
(808) 236-2414

So much more...

These days, your island humane society does much more than rescue pets.

- Humane societies enforce laws against abuse of animals.
- Humane societies include community outreach programs such as going into schools to teach children how to treat pets.
- Humane society volunteers take pets to hospitals and nursing homes to visit shut-ins. Volunteers also care for the pets of people who are ill or unable to care for their own pets.
- Your island humane society can become the focus of your social life, through activities as varied as monthly hikes (Oahu) and pet walks to fancy-dress fund-raisers.

For complete details, call your humane society or visit its website:
Big Island – hihs.org
Kaua'i – kauaihumanesociety.org
Maui – mauihumane.org
O'ahu – hawaiianhumane.org

HUMANE SOCIETIES

Big Island

Hawai`i Island Humane Society has three locations.
Ronald Jenkins,
executive director
24-hour emergency service:
(808) 329-1175

Kona shelter

74-5225 Queen
Ka`ahumanu Highway
Kailua-Kona, HI 96740
(808) 329-1175
Fax: (808) 329-4618
www.hihs.org
Hours: 9 a.m. to 5:30 p.m.
Monday through Saturday
Closed Sunday

Waimea shelter

Parker Ranch land
67-125 Mamalahoa Highway
Kamuela, HI 96743
(808) 885-4558
Hours: Noon to 3:30 p.m.
Tuesday through Saturday
Closed Sunday and Monday

Kea`au shelter

Dwayne Mendosa, director of operations
P.O. Box 939
Kea`au, HI 96749
Kea`au-Pahoa Road
(808) 966-5458
Fax (808) 966-8161
Hours: 9a.m. to 5:30 p.m.
Monday through Saturday
Closed Sunday

Kaua`i

Kaua`i Humane Society

Rebecca Rhoades,
executive director
3825 Kaumuali`i Highway
P.O. Box 3330
Lihu`e, Hawaii 96766
(808) 632-0610
Fax (808) 632-0727
www.kauaihumanesociety.org
Emergency mobile number:
(808) 639-2149
Hours:
Intake of animals:
Tuesday to Friday, 8 a.m. to 7 p.m.
Saturday 8 a.m. to 5 p.m.
Sunday and Monday 9 a.m.
to 1 p.m.
Adoptions:
Tuesday through Friday
11 a.m. to 7 p.m.
Saturday 9 a.m. to 5 p.m.

Maui

Maui Humane Society

Jocelyn Bouchard
director of development and interim executive director
(The humane society was seeking a director as this was printed.)
P.O. Box 1047
Pu`unene, HI 96784
(808) 877-3680
Fax: (808) 877-5033
humane@maui.net
Hours:
Monday through Saturday:
office: 8 a.m. to 4:30 p.m.;
visiting 10 a.m. to 4 p.m.
Sunday:
office: noon to 4:30 p.m.;
visiting: noon to 4 p.m.

HUMANE SOCIETIES

Continued

Lana`i and Moloka`i

These two small islands are part of Maui County and the Maui Humane Society accepts homeless animals from both islands. There is an animal control officer on each island.

Moloka`i Humane Society

P.O. Box 1258
Kaunakakai, HI 96748
Nancy Gosnell, president
(808) 553-3943
gosnell@aloha.net
For problems and pick up:
Call Richard Makau, animal control officer, at the police station: (808) 553-5355

At this writing, the fledgling Moloka`i Humane Society consists of "ten wire cages with a tin roof and cloth around to keep wind and sun out" behind a gas station in a county yard at Kaunkakai, according to Nancy Gosnell, president. The humane society is hoping to build a shelter on 3.5 acres of donated land on the east side of the island.

O`ahu

Hawaiian Humane Society

Pamela Burns, president/CEO
2700 Wai'alae Avenue
Honolulu, HI 96826
www.hawaiianhumane.org
(808) 946-2187
Fax (808) 955-6034
Hours:
Emergencies and animal intake:
open 24 hours daily
Adoption and retrieval
of lost animals:
Monday through Friday
noon to 8 p.m.
Saturdays, Sundays and holidays
10 a.m. to 4 p.m.
Administrative offices:
Monday through Friday
8 a.m. to 5 p.m.

Walk the walk

Imagine more than 1,000 human walkers plus 583 dogs, eight cats, two mice, one chameleon, two guinea pigs, two angora rabbits and four squawking birds–all marching through a Honolulu park.

That was a recent O`ahu humane society PetWalk. Walkers raised $57,000 for the society through pledges.

All island humane societies have similar strolls. Maui makes the Walk For Orphaned Animals; Kaua`i takes a Furry Scurry Walk. The Big Island holds three Barks in the Park at various locations around the massive island.

PET SITTING

Also see Boarding

Big Island

Micah's Mom Pet Sitting
Kona Coast
(808) 329-7191

**Patty's Quality Pet sitting
and Dog Grooming Service**
Kamuela
(808) 775-7781

Wanny's Pet Sitting Service
Waikoloa
(808) 883-8303
(808) 937-9973

Watch Your Tail
Layne Novak
Hilo
(808) 969-1817
Laupahoehoe to Puna area

Amy Wong
Hilo
(808) 938-0881
sulin-kennels@hawaii.rr.com
Any type of pet in Hilo area only.

Kaua`i

Akamai Pet Services
Kapa'a
(808) 822-3886
Ellen Carscadden
Cell: (808) 639-7832
Pet sitting and transportation.

Critter Sitter
Laura Wiley
Wailua
(808) 639-2137

Diane Celste Ray
(808) 826-1580
Island-wide service

Kaua`i Animal Hotel
Yvonne Corpuz
Lihu`e
(808) 634-5555
*All animals, including farm animals.
In-home or boarding. Pasture
available.*

Pet Pals
Kapa`a
Rhonda K. Lizama
(808) 821-0898
Dog sitting at her home.

Pet Patrol
Tim & Julie Hale
Wailua Homesteads
(808) 823-6031
*Any type of animal including
farm animals.*

Home Alone
Frani & Vince Marcus
Lihu`e
(808) 245-5904
frani713@aol.com
vincemarcus@aol.com

Maui

Auntie's Pet Sitting Service
32 Kula Highway
Kula
(808) 878-3303

Paw Mates
2821 Kalialani Circle
Pukalani
(808) 573-2269

Upcountry Pet Sitters
Kula
(808) 281-9172

Makawao Boarding Kennels
444B Makawao Avenue
Makawao
(808) 573-0080

Aloha Pet Sitters
Kula
(808) 250-5458
(808) 250-7971
All areas but Hana and Lahaina.

Uiko's
Wailuku
Debra Lusher
(808) 268-8456
(808) 891-9205
All areas of Maui except Lahaina.

O`ahu

Pets Are Inn

Mililani
(808) 626-9446
www.petsareinn.com
*Unique boarding service places pets
in private homes while their owners
are away. Transportation also
available.*

Pets Companion Service Hawaii
Kapolei
Vera Higashi
(808) 672-5530

The Pet Pal
Kailua
Jayne Gretz
(808) 262-1104
Dogs, cats, birds, turtles, etc.

Pet Express Boarding Kennel
989 Dillingham Boulevard
Honolulu
(808) 847-0058
www.petsexpressboarding.com
*Pet care plus transportation of pets
for shipping, etc.*

Purrfect Pals Pet Services
(808) 292-1427
Honolulu
www.purrfectpetpals.com
Pet sitting, playing and transporting.

PET STORES, pet food and supplies

Big Island

Paradise Pet & Supply
74-5590 Eho Street, Suite 101
Kona
(808) 326-7521

Stacey's Pets
333 Kilauea Avenue
Hilo
(808) 935-0614

Bar-King Dog Kennnel
Orchid Land Estates
Kea`au
(808) 966-8733

Del's Farm Supply Inc.
430 Kekuanaoa
Hilo
(808) 935-6378

Island Pet Supplies
74-5565 Luhia St., Suite C-3
Kailua-Kona
(808) 329-5127

Miranda Country Store
845A Kanoelehua Ave.
Hilo
(808) 935-4457
(808) 961-4911

Kaua`i

Del's Farm Supply Inc.
1856 Haleukana St.
Lihu`e
(808) 245-9200

Harvey & Sons Feed Store
Port Allen
(808) 335-0230

The Lihue Pet Shop
4303 Rice Street, Suite B4
Lihu`e
(808) 245-1939

Paradise Pets Kaua'i
4-1286 Kuhio Highway
Kapa`a
(808) 823-8484

Westside Pet & Country
`Ele`ele Shopping Center
Hanapepe
(808) 335-0990

Young's Natural Pet Products
Kilauea
(808) 822-33327

Maui

Del's Farm Supply Inc.
65 Ka`ahumanu Avenue, Unit 33
Kahului
(808) 871-7336

Perfect Pets
991 Limahana Place
Lahaina
(808) 661-3739

The Pet Shop
Maui Mall
Kahului
(808) 877-0863

Pet's Discount
270 Dairy Road
Kahului
(808) 893-2419

O'ahu

Aloha Pet Center
98-201 Kamehameha Hwy.
`Aiea
(Across from Pearlridge
Shopping Center)
(808) 488-0114

Crazy Canines
98-027 Hekaha St. #33
`Aiea
(808) 485-9663

PET STORES, pet food and supplies

O'ahu

Continued

Enchanted Lake Pet Center
Enchanted Lake Shopping Center
Windward near Kailua
(808) 262-2219

The Kennel Shop
4420 Lawehana Street
Salt Lake
(808) 423-0799

Marina Pet Supply
377 Keahole
Hawai`i Kai
(808) 395-4267

Mililani Pets
95-221 Kipapa Drive
Mililani
(808) 623-5225

Moanalua Pets, Inc.
Stadium Mall
4510 Salt Lake Boulevard
Honolulu
(808) 488-8843

Modern Pet Center
1331 Makaloa Street
Honolulu
 (808) 949-4916

Paradise Pets
Town Center
Mililani
(808) 623-2225

Petland
Ala Moana Shopping Center
(808) 941-2040
and
4400 Kalaniana`ole Hwy.
(808) 734-7387

Pet's Central
2333 Alahao Place
Honolulu
(808) 848-1688

Pet's Discount Warehouse
Bougainville (808) 422-5763
Waikele (808) 678-8808
1415 Kap`iolani Boulevard
(808) 955-3774
Hawai`i Kai Towne Center
 (808) 395-0448

Pets, Etc.
26 Ho`olai
Kailua
(808) 263-2255

Pets 'n Plants
98-020 Kamehameha Hwy.
`Aiea
(808) 488-9922

Pets Plus
250 Ward Avenue
Honolulu
(808) 593-9788

Pets Unlimited
2295 North King Street
Kalihi Shopping Center
(808) 841-5234

Purr-Fect Paws
46-056 Kamehameha Hwy.
Kailua
(808) 235-4773

VCA Kaneohe Animal Hospital
45-608 Kamehameha Hwy.
Kane`ohe
(808) 236-2414

Other pet food sources

City Feed Inc.
1827 S. Beretania Street
Honolulu
(808) 949-1457

Kane`ohe Farm Supplies
45-1048 Kamehameha Highway
Kane`ohe
(808) 247-2792

Photo courtesy The Boo Boo Zoo

RESCUE PROGRAMS, sanctuaries

Listing here does not constitute endorsement of any organization by the author or publishers. Readers are advised to get more specifics and do additional research before donating funds to any organization or effort.

Big Island

Advocats Inc.
(808) 326-3724
A non-profit organization dedicated to reducing the number of unwanted kittens and cats through a program that includes trapping, neutering and spaying.

Animal Rescue Coalition of Hawaii (ARCHawaii)
(808) 987-ARCH (2724)
archawaii.org
ARCHawaii promotes the welfare of dogs and cats on the island of Hawai`i and works to eliminate unnecessary euthanization through spay and neuter incentives, adoption support, and public education.

RESCUE PROGRAMS

Continued

Pacific Pet Foundation
Kona Coast
Deon Kane, president
(808) 322-7387
Foster care and adoption for homeless pets. This no-kill organization strives to "get good animals into good homes," according to Lyn Brewster, vice president. Future goals: to have a pet sanctuary and to involve youth groups in its program.

Rainbow Friends
Hilo
(808) 982-5110
rainbowfriends.org
Lanny and Mary Rose Sinkin and volunteers care for 80 dogs and 125 cats on 7.5 acres in Kurtistown. About 15,000 animals are euthanized each year on the Big Island and Lanny calls their work "a thimble in the waterfall."

Maui

9th Life-Hawaii
P.O. Box 538
Makawao
(808) 573-7877 (PURR)
This non-profit organization, operating under a no-kill philosophy, offers compassionate cat control. Traps, neuters and returns cats to the wild, offers spay/neuter assistance, and maintains a cat sanctuary for adoptable cats. Works with the Maui Humane Society and other animal welfare groups such as the Feline Foundation.

East Maui Animal Refuge
(also known as The Boo Boo Zoo)
Ha`iku
(808) 572-8308
www.booboozoo.org
Susie and Sylvan Schwab care for all kinds of injured and homeless animals, tame and feral, in a home-like atmosphere on a small compound in Ha`iku.

Feline Foundation of Maui
Pu`unene
mauicats.com
(808) 891-1181
Non-profit organization provides funding for spay/neuter of feral cats. Helps people who are feeding cats by giving them traps and appointment at vets. Advocates trapping, testing for feline AIDS and leukemia, altering and releasing.

Homeward Bound
Lahaina
(808) 669-5701
This program, under the Feline Foundation of Maui, cares for homeless and feral kittens and mother cats. Volunteers foster the feline families until the kittens are old enough to be altered and find homes. Jane Dettwiler and Melody Law are founders.

O`ahu

Animal Care Foundation
Dr. Sabina Wenner, D.V.M.
Kane'ohe
(80) 941-2452
www.animal-care.org
Advocates trap, neuter, return to wild for animals. No kill philosophy.

Hawaii Cat Foundation
Honolulu
(808) 739-2287
www.hicat.org
This all-volunteer group, formed in 1993, is a "trap, neuter, return, manage" non-profit organization. It maintains two feline sanctuaries, in Manoa and Kahulu`u, and plans a learning center.

K-9 Rescue League
Wai`anae
(808) 696-4397
Offers dogs and cats, pupppies and kittens free to good homes. Also gentle dog training.

O`ahu Cat Coalition
Jean Pickering
(808) 396-6096
The goal of this organization is to help all cats, says Jean Pickering, leader. The coalition of "private people who care" encourages and supports neutering of cats, including feral cats, and is against the unwarranted killing of cats.

Sylvester Foundation
Waimanalo
(808) 259-0064
All kinds of animals cared for on a ranch in the dhadow of the Ko`olau Mountains, including 300 cats.

TRAINING

Big Island

Alpha K-9 Kennels
Hilo
(808) 963-6000

Fleetwood Kennels
South Kona
Fred Popick
(808) 328-0622
fleetwoodkennels.com
Handling and confirmation classes.

Hilo Obedience Training Club
(808) 959-9780
Volunteer trainers. Complete range of classes, from "kindergarten to high school, including Good Citizen classes," says Haroldine Akiona, president. The club meets once a week at St. Joseph's School grounds and accepts all dogs. Two trials held each year, December and June.

Paws University
Kailua-Kona
(808) 325-6436
pawsuniversity.com
Tammy Goodreau-Daniels and Allen Daniels offer a variety of services including training, boarding and grooming. Classes from puppy kindergarten to agility.

TRAINING
Continued

Kaua`i

Dog Fanciers of Kaua`i
(808) 246-6889

Pet Alert of Hawaii
Gabriel Oberman
Kapa`a
(808) 822-3639

Maui

Valley Isle Kennel Club of Maui
Pukalani
(808) 573-1192
(808) 572-0257
Inexpensive dog training classes.

Sand Dollar Retrievers
Kula, Maui
(808) 878-2908
Obedience classes.

Dog Sense Unlimited
Kinee Hanson
(808) 283-1715
Dog behaviorist will visit your home to train.

O`ahu

Art's Obedience
Kahalu`u
(808) 239-8138
Puppies and beginners.

Cinnabar Kennels
Honolulu
Nola Chock
(808) 487-3116
Obedience, socialization, tricks, clicker training, behavioral consulting.

Clever Canines
Waimanalo
(808) 259-7363

Conformation Handling Classes
Barbara Ankersmit
(808) 261-8102
bankersmit@starrtech.com
From beginners to experts. Craig Garcia and Fay Yamamoto teach two classes every Sunday at Pohakapu Park, Kailua. Very reasonable, no sign ups, just come to the park.

Doberman Pinscher Club of Hawai`i
Mililani
Skip Lee
(808) 626-0672
hilee@majesticdobe.com

Ho`olaka Canine Specialists
Kailua
(808) 263-6076
hoolakacanine@hawaii.rr.com
Behavioral constultants Carol McPherson and Doug Serrall train family pets of all breeds, solve and prevent behavioral problems.

J n' C Obedience Training
Jeff Wong, trainer
(808) 523-8489
Cell: 226-5549
*Puppies through all levels
of competition.*

Jo's Dog Obedience
Jo Long, trainer
(808) 395-2082
Puppies 2 to 6 months old.

Leeward Training Club
Mililani
Ted Ketcham, president
(808) 674-8792
ltch.org
*Volunteers conduct obedience
training for all breeds and all levels,
including "utility and agility." Very
reasonable cost. Two trials per year.*

**Obedience Training Club
of Hawai`i**
Leurella Pang
(808) 732-7451 or
Cathy Suguitan
(808) 456-9565 or
Winston and Jackie Kupau
(808) 488-3854
*At reasonable rates, volunteers
conduct three sessions per year in
kindergarten puppy training (dogs up
to 6 months of age); basic novice
(dogs over 6 months of age);
tracking; and basic conformation
(dogs over 6 month of age). Four
sites all over O`ahu.*

Sirius Puppy Training
Honolulu
Wendy Mah
(808) 732-0258

VETERINARIANS, hospitals, clinics

Big Island

Ali`i Veterinary Hospital
Ocean View Town Center
Na`alehu
(808) 929-8231
aliivet@aol.com
Dr. Aaron Lorshbough

Ali`i Veterinary Hospital
Keauhou Shopping Center
Keauhou
(808) 322-9133
Emergency: (808) 899-4998
Dr. Maria Jose
Dr. Elizabeth Jose
Dr. Aaron Lorshbough

All Pets Mobile Veterinary Clinic
7 Kukila Street
Hilo
(808) 935-3400
Dr. Skip Pease

Aloha Veterinary Center
202 Holomua Street
Hilo
(808) 935-7387
Dr. Trevor L. Rodrigues
Dr. Lei Imaino-Hata
Dr. Alfred J. Mina

Big Island Pet Care Center
Kea`au
(808) 966-5402
Dr. Sterrett C. Grune

VETERINARIANS, hospitals, clinics

Big Island
Continued

Hawaii Veterinary Clinics
400 Hualani Suite 387
Hilo
(808) 964-2208
Dr. David Almond

Hilo Veterinary Clinic, Inc.
711 Kanoelehua Avenue
Hilo
(808) 961-3486
Dr. Boyd Tastro
Also boarding, by appointment

Kamuela Animal Clinic Limited
67-1161 Mamalahoa Highway
Kamuela
(808) 885-6988
http://www.kaclinic@interpac.net
Dr. Greg Timmel
Dr. Annette Timmel

Keauhou Veterinary Clinic
78-6728 Walua Road
Kailua-Kona
(808) 322-2988
Dr. Steven Poleshuk

Kilauea Veterinary Services
P.O. Box 450
Kea'au
(808) 966-8582
Dr. Seeske Versluys

Kohala Pet Clinic
P.O. Box 267
Kapa`au
(808) 889-6405
Dr. Stanley Lavine

Kona Coast Veterinary Hospital
P.O. Box 730
Keauhou
(808) 322-3469
Dr. Gary Ota

Kona Veterinary Service
73-4730 Mamalahoa Highway
Kailua-Kona
(808) 325-6637
Dr. Betsy Webb

The Pet Hospital Hilo Inc.
667 Kanoelehua Avenue
(808) 961-0638
Dr. Roy Nagakura
Dr. Alan Nagakura

Pet Medical Center
74-5543 Kaiwi Street, #A-125
Kailua Kona
(808) 334-0994
Dr. Kevin Y. Kawamoto

Veterinary Associates Inc.
Kamuela
(808) 885-7941
Dr. Tim Richards
Dr. Jim Gressuard

Kaua`i

All Creatures Great And Small
6001B Kaapuni Road
Kapa`a
(808) 822-4229
Dr. Ihor Basko
drbasko.com
Holistic services

Kapa`a Animal Clinic, Inc.
4-1571 Kuhio Highway
Kapa`a
(808) 822-9791
Dr. Patrick Ahana
Dr. Fran Azeka

Kauai Veterinary Clinic Inc.
1864 Haleukana Street
Lihu`e
(808) 245-4748
Dr. Joanne R.S. Woltmon
Dr. Michael O. Woltman
Dr. Susana K. Pulawa

Lihu`e Veterinary Hospital
3113 Oihana Street
Lihu`e
(808) 245-4961
Dr. David Haas
Dr. Walter Haas

Paradise Animal Clinic
Kalaheo
(808) 332-7315
Dr. Craig Nishimoto

Maui

Animal Care Hospital
4640 Lower Kula Road
Kula
(808) 876-1000
Dr. Dennis B. Brown
Dr. Cindy Krach

Central Maui Animal Clinic LLC
45 Ho`okele Street
Kahului
(808) 893-2380
(808) 893-2579 fax
cmac@maui.net
Dr. Shae T. Martin
Dr. Curtis Willauer

Island Animal Hospital
Haiku Marketplace
810 Hai`ku Road, #317
Hai`ku
(808) 575-2811
Dr. Cynthia Jo Trawick

Kahului Animal Hospital, Inc.
111 Hana Highway
Kahului
(808) 871-7387
Dr. Debbie Dorsey
Dr. Terry Smith

Kihei Veterinary Clinic
1476 South Kihei Road
Kihei
(808) 879-5777
Dr. Roger K. Kehler
Dr. Jenny Li Hellsen

Lahaina Veterinary Clinic
910 Honoapi`ilani Highway
Lahaina
(808) 661-3515
Dr. Leo S. Murakami
After hours, emergency number:
(808) 242-0061

Makawao Veterinary Clinic
444A Makawao Avenue
Makawao
(808) 572-9003
Dr. Kathryn Rice
Dr. Toni Ilgen
Dr. Marc Miller

Maui Veterinary Clinic
1758 Wili Pa Loop
Wailuku
(808) 242-5088
Dr. Wayne Kot

Shepherd Veterinary Clinic
300 Ohukai Road, C108
Kihei (808) 874-9372
Dr. Diane Shepherd

South Shore Veterinary Care. LLC
Azecka 1 Shopping Center
Kihei
Dr. Demian Dressler

Upcountry Veterinary Services
House calls and appointments
P.O. Box 880359
Pukalani
(808) 572-9665
Emergency appointments:
(808) 229-0011
Dr. Ronald Moyer

Wailuku Pet Clinic, Inc.
1728 Ka`ahumanu Avenue
Wailuku
(808) 244-7275
Dr. Winford M. Ideue

O ahu

`Aina Haina Pet Hospital, Inc.
5140 Kalaniana`ole Highway
Honolulu
(808) 373-2111
After hours emergency:
(808) 988-2188
Dr. Al K. Takayama
Dr. Allen K. Takayama

All Pets Clinic Waipahu Inc.
Westgate Center
Waipahu
(808) 671-7424
Dr. Suellen J. Kotake
Dr. Iris Y. Kubo

Aloha Animal Hospital Associates Inc.
4224 Waialae Avenue
Honolulu
(808) 734-2242
Dr. Douglas K.Y. Chang
Dr. John K. Kaya

Animal Clinic, Inc.
3270 Waialae Ave
Honolulu
(808) 734-0255
Dr. Nam Young Chung
Dr. Clifford T. Kumamoto
www.animal-clinic-inc.com
animalcl@gte.net

Animal Clinic Waipahu
94-806 Moloalo Street
Waipahu

(808) 671-1751
Dr. Catherine Kasai
Dr. Thomas Lee
Dr. Tyrus Watanabe
animalclinichawaii.com

**The Animal Hospital
of Hawaii, Inc.**
3111 Castle Street
Honolulu
(808) 732-7387
Dr. Philip Kau
Dr. Sabina DeGiacomo

Blue Cross Animal Hospital
1318 Kapiolani Boulevard
Honolulu
(808) 593-2532
Dr. Jayne W. Alison
Dr. Darrell Allison

Cat Bird Vet Mobile Hospital
94-658 Ialeleiaka Place
Mililani
(808) 623-5466
Dr. Jill Voeks

The Cat Clinic
1131 Kapahulu Avenue, Suite 201
Honolulu
(808) 732-8884
Dr. Suzanne Sylvester-Palumbo
Dr. Nicholas E. Palumbo

Companion Animal Hospital
1090 Keolu Drive, Suite #102
Enchanted Lake, Kailua
(808) 262-8141
After hours emergency:
(808) 524-2575
Dr. Jennifer D. Brundage
Dr. Christopher Dold

East Honolulu Pet Hospital
6650 Hawai`i Kai Drive
Hawai`i Kai
(808) 396-3333
Dr. Demian Dressler

Ewa Beach Animal Hospital
91-919 Fort Weaver Road,
Suite #114
Ewa Beach
(808) 689-1797
Dr. Lisa Karpinski
ewabeachanimalhospital.com

Family Veterinary Clinic
98-1254 Kaahumanu Street
Pearl City
(808) 484-9070
Dr. Rod L. Pearson
Dr. Larry Evans
Dr. Clifton Hashimoto
Dr. Christy Anbe

Feather and Fur Clinic
`Aikahi Park Shopping Center
Kailua
(808) 254-1548
Dr. Mark Caspers
Dr. Elaine Allwine
Dr. Brian Walsh

Gentry-Waipi`o Pet Clinic
94-1040 Waipi`o Uka, Suite 8
Waipahu
(808) 676-2205
Dr. Nadine N. Nanbu

Haiku Veterinary Clinic, Inc.
45-773 Kamehameha Highway
Kane`ohe
(808) 235-6405
Dr. Sharman R. Elison
haikuvet@msn.com

Hawai`i Kai Veterinary Clinic
Koko Marina Shopping Center
Hawai`i Kai
(808) 395-2302
Dr. Kerry K. Yoon

Home Pet Service
Veterinarian visits homes.
(808) 261-6000
Fax (808) 263-2000
Dr. Eric Pearson

The Honolulu Pet Clinic
1115 Young Street
Honolulu
(808) 593-9336
Dr. Roger M. Kondo

Island Veterinary Care
830 Coolidge Street
Honolulu
(808) 944-0003
Dr. Bertram H.S. Lau

Kahala Pet Hospital
Veterinary Center of the Pacific
4819 Kilauea Avenue
Honolulu
(808) 735-4433
Dr. Patrick A. Leadbeater
Dr. Richard Fujie

Kalihi Pet Clinic
Kalihi Shopping Center
2295 N. King Street
Honolulu
(808) 841-6313
Dr. Timothy S. Y. Lau
Dr. Mike Wong

Kailua Animal Clinic
111 Hekili St., Suite 104
(808) 263-8863
Dr. John D. Haddock
Dr. Mike Wong

Kapalama Pet Hospital
551 Dillingham Blvd.
(808) 841-2861
Dr. Gleason K. Hirata
Dr. Pauline Koreyasu

Kilani Pet Clinic Inc.
810 Kilani Avenue
(808) 622-2607
Dr. Carole T. Fujioka

Kokua Pet Clinic
1111 Dillingham Blvd., Suite E5
Honolulu
(808) 843-8382
Dr. William A. Myatt

Ko`olau Animal Hospital Inc.
45-1123 Kamehameha Highway
Kan`eohe
(808) 247-3211
Dr. Sterling S. Iwashita
Dr. Jeffery C. Zane

Leeward Pet Clinic
593 Kamehameha Hwy., Unit A
Pearl City
(808) 456-2121
Dr. Edward D. Gulliver

Makai Animal Clinic
420 Uluniu St.
Kailua
(808) 262-9621
Dr. Robert A. Morris
Dr. Ed Alan Zane
Dr. Thomas Chlebecek
makaianimalclinic.com

Dr. Carolyn McKinnie
1129 Ala Moana Boulevard
Honolulu
(808) 294-0313
Works primarily with dolphins;
does some consulting with dogs
and cats.

Mililani Town Center Pet Clinic
The Town Center of Mililani
(808) 625-6744
Dr. Randal Y. Sakaino
Dr. Karin T. Fujitani
Dr. Dorene Nagamine

Newtown Veterinary Clinic, Inc.
98-1247 Ka`ahumanu, Suite 111
`Aiea
(808) 488-3667
Dr. Francis T. Kamiya
Dr. Elden Uruu

North Shore Veterinary Clinic
67-292 Goodale Ave.
Waialua
(808) 637-6202
Dr. Troy Smith

Ohana Veterinary Hospital, Inc.
Waiakamilo Shopping Center
1414 Dillingham Blvd., Unit 102-3
(808) 845-1762
Dr. Lissa Kam

Pearl City Veterinary Clinic Inc.
941 Kamehameha Hwy
Pearl City
(808) 456-2221
Dr. Peter D. Herman
Dr. Heather E. Honda
Dr. Michelle Hatami

The Pet Clinic
1947 South Beretania
Honolulu
(808) 946-5096
Dr. Craig R. Harada
Dr. Scott T. Harada

The Pet Doctor
4400 Kalaniana`ole Hwy., Suite 6
Honolulu
(808) 733-8828
Dr. Eric Ako

University Pet Clinic, Inc.
2728 Woodlawn Dr.
Honolulu
(808) 988-2111
Dr. Wendy M. Asato
Dr. Russell M. Shoji
Dr. Arleene D.K. Skillman

VCA Kaneohe Animal Hospital
45-608 Kamehameha Highway
Kane`ohe
(808) 236-2414
Fax: (808) 235-4074
Dr. Michael B. Curtis
Dr. Janice J. Lem
Dr. Leianne K. Lee Loy
Dr. James S. McBane
Dr. Renee H. Nagata
Dr. Jennifer A. Parker
Dr. Richard Poll
Dr. Ann M. Sakamoto
Dr. Daniel J. Severson
Cathy P. Todd, hospital manager

Wahiawa Animal Hospital
823A Olive Ave.
Wahiawa
(808) 621-7000
Dr. Richard R. Lawton

Wai`anae Veterinary Clinic
85-816 Farrington Highway
Wai`anae
(808) 696-4161
Dr. Herbert Rebhen
Dr. Cynthia Collier

**Waipahu-Leeward
Veterinary Clinic, Inc.**
Waipahu Professional Center
94-801 Farrington Hwy., Suite #3
(808) 671-4095
Dr. Jamie K. W. Furutani
Dr. James H. Higa
Dr. Darin K. Hisanaga
Dr. Andrea Tiberi
Dr. Dawn Kimata

**Windward Veterinary
Service, Inc.**
45-521A Halekou Road
Kane'ohe
(808) 247-3038

Good Ipo! Come, Hana. Stay, Pua!

Fido? Fluffy? Forget it. Hawai`i pets have creative, distinctive names. Whether you've obtained your pet here or brought it along, you'll want to give your pet a Hawaiian-style name or nickname. You may want to name your pet from the area of island where he was born—as we did our first dog, Kula. Or you could name him after a characteristic or talent. I know a very active Pomeranian who dances around a lot. Her owners call her Hula.

It's a good idea to live with your pet for awhile and learn his or her personality traits before choosing a name. *Ali`i* (chief) the Rottweiler would be embarrassed by the moniker *Pupu* (appetizer) given to his Miniature Pinscher neighbor. And you probably wouldn't want to name your tough Tomcat *Pua* (flower), but you might want to call him *Pilikia* (trouble), especially when he overturns your favorite vase as he struts across a bookshelf.

Of course, you may choose to give your pet an ironic name like the miniature long-haired Chihuahua who visits O`ahu's Bark Park. He's a bantam weight at about six pounds, but that doesn't keep him from running right up and rubbing noses with 90-pound Rottweilers. His owners named him Hercules.

Here are some names from Hawai`i's cultural mixed bag:

`A`a
  rough lava

`Ai
  food or to eat

Aikane
  friend or pal

`Aina
  land or earth

`Aka
  laughter

Aku
  a kind of fish

Akua
  ghost

Ali`i
  chief, boss, ruler

Bento
  Japanese plate lunch

`Ele`ele
  black

Hana
  work

Hanohano
  honored

Haole
  white person

Hapa
  half, as in hapa-Hawaiian

Hapai
  pregnant

Hau`oli
  happy

Haupia
  coconut pudding

Hina
  Goddess Pele's brave sister

Sistah

Bruddah

`Ele`ele (Black)

Ipo (Sweetheart)

Brewster

Hoku
star

Holo
run

Hula
dance

Huli huli
rotate or flip

`Ilio
dog

Imu
oven in which to roast pig

Ipo
sweetheart

Kaha
fat

Kahuna
wise person

Kaipo
loved one

Kaiko
a policeman

Kaka`a
to roll over

Ka la
the sun

Kama
a child

Kame`e
hero

Kamele
melody

Kana
an expression
connoting surprise

Kanani
beauty

Kane
man

Kapu
forbidden

Ka pua
a flower

Kaukau
slang word for food
(This dog is a Chow)

Ke aloha
love

Keiki
offspring, child

Ke koa
warrior

Kiki
quick

Kiko
spot or dot
(Popular for Dalmatians)

Koa
native wood

Kokua
to help, sympathize or share

Kualapa
the top of a ridge

Kuhaku
lordly

Kukui
a nut used for lamps,
torches, lights

Kulu
to drip or leak

Kuma
Japanese for bear

Kumu
teacher

Lani
heaven, sky, high chief

Lehua
kind of tree, a sacrifice

Liholiho
fiery

Li`ili`i
small

Limu
seaweed

Lohi
slow or late

Maile
a fragrant vine, gentle

Mahina
moon

Maka
raw, fresh

Makana
gift

Make
dead—this pitbull was black

Mele
a song or chant

Meli
honey

Menehune
Hawaiian elf

Miki
energetic, active

Miko
tasty, seasoned with salt

Mililani
to praise or thank

Mino
wrinkly

Mochi
candy or sweet

Momi
pearl

Nau
chew

Nene
goose

Noni
superior

Nonohe
beautiful

Nui
large, big, great

`Ohule
bald

`Okole
rump or bottom

Ola
alive

`Ono
delicious

Opihi
shell fish

`Opu
belly or stomach

Paka or **Pakalolo**
marijuana

Pele
a goddess

Pilikia
trouble

Pohu
calm, quiet

Poi
food from taro plant

Poke
a small piece

Pomaikai
blessed

Pono
good, blessed

Po`okela
champion

Popoki
cat

Pua
blossom

Puka
hole or small space

Pumehana
warm, loving

Punahele
friend, favorite

Otis

Kiko (Spot)

Momi (Pearl)

Pupule
crazy, insane

Pupu
a small snack

`Uku
flea

Wahine
woman or girl

Waikiki
spurting water

Wela
having fun; making whoopee

Wihi
to wink

Wiki
hurry

Wohi
favorite of the king

Of course, you could just name your dog `ilio. That's Hawaiian for dog. And here are some Hawaiian place names that are used as pet monikers. You'll have plenty, specific to your area, to add to this list:

Kai
the ocean

Ko`olau
An O`ahu mountain chain

Makai
Toward the ocean

Mauka
toward the mountain

Pali
mountain cliff

Pu`u
hill

That's not to say that English names can't be just as much fun. Here are some favorite *haole* pet names.

Dogs: Brewster, Henry, Whipple (the Whippet), Snores

Cats: Vicious, Precious, Cat-O-Mine, Shine, Dribbles, CleoCATra

And more:

Angus	Bogart	Comedy
Asia	Bravo	Crouton
Baby	Brewster	Cujo
Baxter	Brigadoon	Ditzl
Bon Bon	Brutus	Diva
Buttercup	Bruzer	dot.com
Belvedere	BunBun	Emmet
Bijou	Calliope	Enough
BoBo	Capuccino	Fancy
BooBoo	Cherish	Gato (Spanish for cat)

Gigi

Gogi

Governor

Gremlin

Grumpy

Gumdrop

Gypsy

Hamlet

Hershey

Hooch

Inky

Jimminy

Jurisprudence

Kiska (a Polish sausage)

Kumquat

Linus

Lobo

Mai Tai

Mischief

Mocha

Mongoose

Moon

Mouse

Mr. Clean

Murphy Brown

Muttley

Odie

Pavlov

Papa

Pax (peace)

Pepe

Pepski

Phatsoe

Phoebe

Purr-cy

Pussy Galore

Radish

Raisin

Reason

Robert Redford

Robert Redfur

Romeo

Sachi

Scrunch

Secret

Sergei

Shiloh

Shinola

Slug

Smergio

Snuki

Spooky

Squeaker

Squirrel

Stuart

Success

Sunshine

Sweet Pea

Taco

Target

Tootsie

Torpedo

Tristan

Truffle

Tut

Twinkles

Vanilla

Vegas

Watson

Webster

Winkie

Woofie

Yorick (as in "alas, poor... ")

Zelda

Zeus

Zinfandel (Zinny)

Kolohe (Rascal)

Rockie

Sydney

Index

A

B

C

Photo of Maggie by Scott and Marianne Schultz

The Producers

Toni Polancy is a former newspaper reporter, columnist and managing editor who moved to Hawai`i from Pennsylvania in 1991. Her first book, *So You Want to Live in Hawai`i*, is an islands' bestseller. Toni wrote *The Hawai`i Pet Book*; her cat, Skat, and dogs, Archie, Betty and Winky, served as creative consultants.

Deborah Booker has been a photojournalist since 1978 and a photographer for *The Honolulu Advertiser* since 1993. She has loved animals all her life, nurturing dogs, cats, turtles, fish, and rabbits. She shares her home with her husband, David, and two Golden Retrievers, King Aurum and Gypsy Prince.

Jody van Aalst was one of several people who edited and researched this book. She and her husband, Tom Spaulding, owned *The Island Bookshelf* in Portland, Oregon, for several years and moved to the islands recently. Her cat Ditzl calmly survived 30 days of quarantine.

Ann Rose is a graphic designer, working in the industry since 1994, current resident of New York and former resident of Hawai`i. She designed this book as well as *So You Want to Live in Hawai`i*. Ann brought her feline compadre, Sugar Betty Moss, from Hawai`i to New York in 2001. Both cat and designer miss the warm Maui winters, but not the fleas.

Mahalo...

To Dr. Eric Pearson on Oʻahu, Dr. Shae Martin on Maui, Dr. Maria Jose on the Big Island and Dr. Isaac M. Maeda on Oʻahu for reviewing parts of this book and for generously answering questions. To Dr. Rebecca Rhoades, director of the Kauaʻi Humane Society, for her interviews and comments.

To state veterinarian Dr. James Foppoli for patiently interrupting a busy schedule to answer calls and questions.

To Liz Huppman, research associate at Lyon Arboretum in Honolulu, and Bob Hobdy, district manager of the Maui County division of forestry and wildlife, for their help in identifying plants in the Protecting section.

To Kapulani Antonia, Maui Community College lecturer, for Hawaiian language assistance.

To Christine Flanagan for her editing talent and support. To Blair Thorndike, Jack Polancy and Marty Jean Bender for additional editing. To Mike Sidney for technical support and cover design.

To The Maui Humane Society, the Hawaiian Humane Society on Oʻahu, the Kauaʻi Humane Society and the Hawaiʻi Island Humane Society for advice, sharing and caring in this three-year-long project.

Especially to K.T. Haase of the Hawaiian Humane Society for ideas, help and outstanding editing skills and Jocelyn Bouchard of the Maui Humane Society for her expertise.

To designer Ann Rose for her patience and perseverance in producing this book.

To Kris Kim who made hundreds of phone calls for the Resource section. To the many people who answered those calls and went out of their way to help complete the resource lists.

To pet owners on all islands who shared their stories.